THE WORKAHOLICS ANONYMOUS
BOOK OF RECOVERY

THE WORKAHOLICS ANONYMOUS BOOK OF RECOVERY

Second Edition

**Workaholics Anonymous
World Service Organization**

California
2015

We welcome your comments and suggestions for the revision of this book as well as for future literature:

Workaholics Anonymous World Service Organization
P.O. Box 289
Menlo Park, California 94026-0289
USA

Telephone: (510) 273-9253
Email: wso@workaholics-anonymous.org
Website: www.workaholics-anonymous.org

ISBN 13: 978-1-7325768-2-7

Library of Congress Cataloging Number 2005931980

TABLE OF CONTENTS

FOREWORD AND ACKNOWLEDGMENTS

We have a lot for which to be grateful. The old days of rushing, anxiety, toxic depletion, self-hate, and isolation have been replaced with sanity thanks to recovery from workaholism. Such peace has been made possible by the program outlined in this book, and we hope that you will discover in these pages the hope and guidance we found upon entering into the fellowship of Workaholics Anonymous (W.A.). The materials presented here are drawn from the personal experiences and writings of recovered work addicts. Much has been inspired by *Alcoholics Anonymous, Twelve Steps and Twelve Traditions*, and other writings that were originally developed by our fellows in Alcoholics Anonymous (A.A.) – to whom we are eternally grateful for setting our foundation and granting us permission to adapt their literature. We believe that all Twelve-Step programs add to and deepen our knowledge of addiction and recovery, and we are thankful to each of them for their contributions to our understanding of workaholism as it is presented in this volume. We wish to thank all authors, known and anonymous, who contributed to this book.

Because most of us come to W.A. not completely understanding our attraction to compulsive work and/or activity, we must first identify our compulsive thinking and behavior if we are to ultimately free ourselves of it. As such, this book begins by describing the problem of workaholism in its many manifestations. The sections afterward describe the solution, including our tools for finding recovery, a guide to working the Twelve Steps, and personal stories written by W.A. members that provide further insight and encouragement. You will also find supplemental resources, including information for friends and family as well as a brief history of the fellowship.

INTRODUCTION

W.A. is a fellowship and program of recovery that has successfully addressed the problems of work and activity addiction. We welcome you to join us on the journey to finding sanity and balance in work and life. Many of us came to W.A. skeptical and defeated, yet we credit this program for bringing about a transformation that has enhanced our lives. It has worked for us, and it can work for you.

Read before meetings, the W.A. Preamble describes our fellowship:

> Workaholics Anonymous is a fellowship of individuals who share their experience, strength, and hope with each other that they may solve their common problems and help others to recover from workaholism. The only requirement for membership is the desire to stop working compulsively. There are no dues or fees for W.A. membership; we are self-supporting through our own contributions. W.A. is not allied with any sect, denomination, politics, organization or institution; does not wish to engage in any controversy; neither endorses nor opposes any causes. Our primary purpose is to stop working compulsively and to carry the message of recovery to workaholics who still suffer.

Many of us, when we first heard workaholism characterized as a real problem, thought that it was some kind of joke. We had many reasons for our skepticism – founded mostly in larger cultural belief patterns and industry norms that seemingly encouraged or even mandated our own personal habits. It did not feel within our control to improve the conditions, so we disclaimed responsibility. We would not really have chosen this lifestyle for ourselves, would we? Anyway, we knew people who worked much harder than we did. Some of us had periods when we hardly worked at all or even actively avoided work, so we felt certain that overworking was not an issue at all.

The common thread, in the beginning, was that most of us were ambivalent about recovery. We were in denial about the benefits that initially propelled our addiction – such as prestige, material rewards, and temporary escape from our feelings. We were afraid we would be forced to change, surrender important goals, or give up a nice paycheck. We may have liked the idea of slowing down to have a balanced life in theory, but the lure of rushing to generate intensity and cultivate a sense of self-importance was overpowering.

Workaholism is not strictly about the amount or type of work we do. Instead, our disease impacts the emotional and spiritual relationship we have to work and activity. Such distortion can negatively impact us as well as those around us – often without our knowing it. Our health, happiness, and relationships suffer. Workaholism involves both a substance addiction (to adrenaline and other stress hormones) and a process addiction (compulsive doing or not doing), and its reach extends far beyond our paid work life. We have found that we have also exhibited workaholic tendencies when engaging in everything from household chores and exercise regimens to various hobbies, service/volunteer activities, and codependent attempts at saving the world. Most of these endeavors seemed admirable at first, but – as we lost ourselves to incessant doing – we fell prey to the compulsivity of addiction.

Since this is a progressive disease, we became more driven until we hit bottom. Our unmanageability sometimes came in the form of burnout, a serious illness, or an ultimatum from our partner or employer. At some point, "workaholic" was no longer a label we prized. Because of the many misconceptions about workaholism, recognizing it sometimes took a long time. Slowly, we came to understand the debilitating, progressive grip workaholism can have. We came to believe that, unchecked, it would prove fatal. Many of us lost our families and health before we found recovery.

If you are wondering if you or someone you care about could benefit from this program, the following questions may help to evaluate the situation:

The Twenty Questions

1. Are you more drawn to your work or activity than close relationships, rest, etc.?
2. Are there times when you are motivated and push through tasks when you do not even want to and other times when you procrastinate and avoid them when you would prefer to get things done?
3. Do you take work with you to bed? On weekends? On vacation?
4. Are you more comfortable talking about your work than other topics?
5. Do you pull all-nighters?
6. Do you resent your work or the people at your workplace for imposing so many pressures on you?

7. Do you avoid intimacy with others and/or yourself?
8. Do you resist rest when tired and use stimulants to stay awake longer?
9. Do you take on extra work or volunteer commitments because you are concerned that things will not otherwise get done?
10. Do you regularly underestimate how long something will take and then rush to complete it?
11. Do you immerse yourself in activities to change how you feel or avoid grief, anxiety, and shame?
12. Do you get impatient with people who have other priorities besides work?
13. Are you afraid that if you do not work hard all the time, you will lose your job or be a failure?
14. Do you fear success, failure, criticism, burnout, financial insecurity, or not having enough time?
15. Do you try to multitask to get more done?
16. Do you get irritated when people ask you to stop doing what you are doing in order to do something else?
17. Have your long hours caused injury to your health or relationships?
18. Do you think about work or other tasks while driving, conversing, falling asleep, or sleeping?
19. Do you feel agitated when you are idle and/or hopeless that you will ever find balance?
20. Do you feel like a slave to your email, texts, or other technology?

Three or more positive answers indicate that there may be a problem with workaholism. After carefully considering the above questions, and perhaps even discussing them with family and friends, the issues may become more apparent. Most of us were slow to fully comprehend the extent of the damage of our longtime behaviors. Recovery began when we identified our destructive patterns as part of a powerful addiction beyond our conscious control. Awareness and acceptance open the door to possible solutions.

Characteristics of Workaholics

1. It is very difficult for us to relax. We often, if not always, perceive the need to get just a few more tasks done before we can allow ourselves to feel good and take a break. When we complete our list, however, we just seem to find more to do. These uncontrollable desires often result in frantic multitasking and the accompanying fragmented attention. We operate out of the

mini-crisis mode as an escape from our core issues. Our inability to pace ourselves leads to breakdown and burnout as we rob ourselves of the enjoyment of conclusion and rest.

2.   Many of us grew up in chaotic homes where the stress and intensity of an adrenaline high was normal, so we seek out a similar workplace or create crisis where none exists because it feels familiar and comfortable. With no issues to resolve, we suffer withdrawal – becoming anxious and depressed. Such mood swings destroy our peace of mind.

3.   We have an obsessive desire to make sense of everything in our lives, including our every thought and feeling. We cannot allow ourselves to experience things over which we cannot maintain a sense of control. We have an underlying fear that if we surrender and allow our emotions to surface, we will become raving lunatics for the rest of our lives.

4.   We are so used to doing what is expected of us that we are often unable to know what it is that we really want and need to do for ourselves. We often betray ourselves by giving in to the demands of people whom we perceive as being "in authority."

5.   We often feel that we must complete certain tasks even though we do not want to, but we are too afraid to stop. We feel resentment at perceived external forces as we tell ourselves we would choose to relax or play if we had a choice. At these times we often procrastinate, wallowing in self-pity but also self-condemnation for our lack of discipline. We cannot concentrate and yet refuse to fully surrender for a moment to allow ourselves the space we need.

6.   Our self-esteem is based largely on how others judge our performance at work and in other areas of our lives. Accordingly, our self-concept is highly unstable. We often think of ourselves as either the most intelligent, capable people we know or the most worthless, hopeless people we know. It is hard to see ourselves honestly and accept reality when we are always trying to look through the eyes of others rather than trusting our own perceptions. We often go on intense work binges with the illusion that we need to get the praise of our coworkers and bosses to be safe or happy.

7.   When we do judge ourselves, we generally look only to our tangible accomplishments – believing that we must always be in the process of achieving something worthwhile in order to feel good about ourselves. We find it hard to love and accept ourselves otherwise. Our work has become an identity and a means for justifying our existence.

8. We have the illusion that people will not respect us unless we appear more competent than we actually are in reality. When praised by others, we often tend to discount ourselves as unworthy of such affirmation. We tend to schedule ourselves for more than we can handle – striving to do more and do it faster. We are often dishonest about our past experiences and present capabilities, tending to not mention our failures and exaggerate our successes. We think that looking busy will make people think that we are important and garner their admiration.

9. We are perfectionistic. We do not accept mistakes as part of being human and find it hard to ask for help. Because we believe no one can meet our standards and that we are indispensible, we have difficulty delegating and end up doing more than our share. Our unrealistic expectations often cheat us of contentment. We are not aware of any difference between job-imposed and self-imposed pressure.

10. We tend to be too serious and overly responsible. All activity must be goal-oriented. We feel guilty and restless when not doing something "productive." Because we often work at our play, we rarely experience such as activities as recreational. We neglect our sense of humor, failing to enjoy the healing power of laughter.

11. We use our compulsion to cope with the uncertainties of life. We lie awake worrying. We compulsively plan and organize. By being unwilling to surrender control, we lose the ability to be spontaneous, flexible, and creative. We cannot feel joy.

12. Waiting is hard for us. We are more interested in results than process, focusing on quantity rather than quality. Our impatience often sabotages our work by not allowing for proper timing.

13. We are in denial about aspects of our work and activity. We lie to ourselves and to others about the amount we do. Often subconsciously, we hoard projects to be sure that we are always busy and never bored. We fear free time as breaks and vacations often seem painful rather than refreshing.

14. Even when we are not working, we are thinking of our next task. Most of our activities are work-related. We neglect our spirituality, health, and relationships. We deny ourselves the enjoyment of a balanced and varied life.

15. Instead of a haven, our home is an extension of the workplace. Our families and friends often struggle to arrange themselves around our schedules, vainly hoping that we will finish our tasks and spend more time with them.

THE PROBLEM OF WORKAHOLISM

The Physical Consequences of Workaholism – A Doctor's Opinion

We believe that workaholism is a disease. We believe it to be a physical addiction to adrenaline and other stress hormones as well as a process addiction to compulsive activity. Our experience has shown that it is progressive and potentially fatal. Workaholics experience chronic high stress levels that are known to have major effects on vital body functions, including interference with normal repair mechanisms. In the following account, an M.D. – herself in recovery from addiction – outlines some of the physical consequences of the disease.

One commonly accepted definition of addiction is the continued use of a substance or participation in an activity despite negative consequences. The medical complications of certain addictions are well known; for example, chronic alcoholism can lead to cirrhosis of the liver and damage to the nervous system. Nicotine addiction is associated with the development of heart disease, lung cancer, and emphysema. What results have we come to expect from chronic work addiction?

The physical effects of work addiction are not published in medical literature as such, but we can infer from the extensive literature concerning the effects of stress on the body as well as from our own personal experiences that we are dealing with a serious, life-threatening illness. Reviewing the lists of symptoms for illnesses known to be associated with chronic stress can be helpful. In addition, psychological harm to individuals and families results from the social isolation brought about by the disease. Depression, anxiety disorders, obsessive-compulsive disorders, and chemical dependency are all common. Divorce and estrangement often result.

Some physical ailments that you have experienced may not have seemed related to your attitudes and behaviors toward work but may well be linked. When an alcoholic drinks excessively and has a motor vehicle crash, the incident is tallied as an alcohol-related accident or death. What about the workaholic who, after an 80-hour workweek, falls asleep at the wheel and runs the car off the road? Law enforcement officers would not make a connection between the earlier activity and the accident. Often family members and workaholics themselves do not make the connections between physical symptoms and work behaviors until the disease has progressed significantly or until they get into recovery. Many workaholics suffer serious bodily harm before waking to the fact that we have a life-threatening illness and require help to arrest its progression.

The stereotypical image of the workaholic commonly depicted in popular culture is of a man sitting up in his hospital bed after a heart attack, talking (or yelling) into the phone at an employee with the EKG electrodes still attached to his chest. As such, many people could have predicted the results of the research concerning the association of the so-called Type A personality and heart disease even if it had not been widely publicized. These individuals are described in the medical literature as competitive, aggressive, and impatient – driven by a strong sense of urgency. Of course, not everyone with a Type A personality develops heart disease because factors such as heredity, diet, exercise, and smoking contribute to the etiology of cardiac problems. Recent research on the Type A personality, however, has identified that the characteristic most clearly related to the development of cardiac disease is free-floating hostility.

Not every workaholic has all the characteristics of the Type A personality. Some of us do not come across as hostile or even remotely aggressive. We may exert considerable control over our feelings and appear calm in emergencies. Common sense and medical science agree, however, that if certain feelings – such as anger and fear – are not discharged, they will get stored in the body. These suppressed feelings sometimes find expression in accidents or other types of psychosomatic illness.

Many of the physical consequences of workaholism can be traced back to the body's fight-or-flight response. When an animal perceives a threat to its safety, a protective mechanism gets activated which leads to the release of stress hormones (one of which is adrenaline) and to a series of changes in the nervous system. The reaction prepares the animal to flee or to fight for its life. Once the mechanism is activated, the body responds with an elevation of heart rate and blood pressure, increased blood flow to the muscles, and decreased blood flow to the digestive organs. Adrenaline and other stress hormones produce the "rush" that is associated with this type of response.

Besides the direct ill effects of prolonged exposure to stress hormones, there are comorbidity issues related to the abuse of other substances.

Many of us became multiply addicted. We used other addictive substances to counteract the feelings of depletion and/or anxiety associated with workaholism. Some of us used alcohol to "come down" after work. Many of us used caffeine, sugar, or other stimulants as fuel in order to be able to sustain the level of output required to keep up our work habit without adequate rest. As a result of other addictions, some of us developed other medical problems such as liver dysfunction, obesity, Type 2 diabetes, and lung disease.

Over time, long hours coupled with character traits such as perfectionism and obsessive worry caused serious stress. Many of the body's functions were likely affected by the chronic pressure. The following is a partial list of the symptoms commonly associated with stress, listed by organ system:

1. Cardiovascular: hypertension, heart disease
2. Neurological: migraine and stress headaches
3. Musculoskeletal: injuries, back pain, repetitive stress syndrome, tooth loss (due to grinding teeth)
4. Gastrointestinal: ulcers, colitis
5. Respiratory: shortness of breath, stress-induced asthma
6. Immunological: susceptibility to infection
7. Reproductive: low libido, impotence, menstrual irregularity, premature labor
8. Dermatological: psoriasis

Other diseases and manifestations also occur with a pattern of high anxiety. Notably, research also suggests a connection between suppressing emotional expression and the development of various types of cancer. Identifying as a workaholic does not mean that you will acquire any of these conditions, and we are not ignoring the importance of such variables as heredity, diet, exercise, environmental toxins, and other "lifestyle" factors. We are stating, however, that you may be at increased risk for the development of one or more of these conditions.

In addition to being a contributing factor in the development of certain symptoms and illnesses, workaholism can have a major impact on our willingness to make time for health maintenance. When work is the first priority, we put other things off. In recovery, we are learning to make time for self-care. When is the last time you had a physical checkup, including routine screenings for cancer and other serious illness? Are you current on your immunizations? Do you keep up with dental cleanings? Having a lot of work to do is a common excuse for delaying seeing a healthcare practitioner for a new symptom or complaint. Following up with appropriate medical care and making time for rest, exercise, and other healthy habits can be a way of making "living amends" to ourselves.

Knowing that suppressed feelings can lead to physical problems reminds us of the importance of working the W.A. program. Meetings and contact with other members provide an opportunity to express our underlying emotions. Doing a Fifth Step or listening to one helps us to feel less alone. Doing an inventory pursuant to the Fourth Step or a regular Tenth Step practice allows us to admit (and then release) resentments, thereby providing an effective way of processing some of the anger and hostility that can literally kill us or make us sick. Meditation alone, just one part of Step Eleven, can reverse or prevent some of the serious health consequences of workaholism. It has been shown to improve survival in certain disease states, prolonging life as well as enhancing it with a sense of peace and serenity. Prayer, the other portion of Step Eleven, has proven efficacious in shortening the length of stay for patients in Intensive Care Units. These patients did not know that they were receiving prayers but nevertheless reaped the benefits.

People who do not understand the concept of powerlessness sometimes ask why a person would continue to indulge in an activity that is potentially fatal to themselves and harmful to others – or why a person would simply fail to do things for themselves that are obviously beneficial. Many of us trace the roots of our addiction to childhood. Current psychological theories and physiological evidence strongly support our intuition in this regard. Certain types of childhood trauma threaten not only physical survival but also the very essence of the child's being – the spirit or core identity – with annihilation. Some of us experienced profoundly disturbing events such as these in which ordinary defenses were inadequate to deal with them. Some of us had caretakers who were incapable of helping us learn to cope with strong feelings because they carried their own unhealed traumas inside themselves.

When a child experiences trauma that overwhelms "ordinary" defense mechanisms (like dissociation), they develop extraordinary defenses. Such defenses will protect the spirit of the individual at the expense of everything, up to and including life itself. Strong emotions later in life evoke the trauma defense. Because closeness brings up strong emotions, intimacy itself can feel threatening. A trauma survivor will go to great lengths to avoid intimacy, including acting in ways that jeopardize his or her health. Once trauma defenses are in place, they persist indefinitely unless there is some type of intervention. A lone person is no match for these defensive maneuvers in the same way that we as individuals cannot overcome the disease of addiction. When a person is experiencing a flood of stress hormones, situations that are not actually "life and death" appear to be. We wonder why other people are not as excited about some detail as we are. Everything can feel like an emergency. Ironically, the converse is also true. Actual dangers are sometimes treated as trivial. For self-defeating, protective reasons, we often remain in denial.

Let us take another look at the scene of the man in the hospital bed after his heart attack. We can imagine what feelings he might be trying to avoid. Overwhelming feelings of terror, fear, sadness, rage, and anger ("You mean I really am mortal?!") may arise. Without a recovery program, compulsive work is a tempting option for exerting some control when one's life feels unmanageable. People who cannot tolerate the experience of strong emotions persist in old behaviors until there is enough support available to allow them to change. There is a reason that the A.A. text declares that without help, addiction is "too much for us" (*Alcoholics Anonymous* 59). Illness is frightening. Change of any type can be terrifying. Studies on childhood attachment and emotional development have given rise to theories about why feelings are so scary for many people.

Recovery begins as we each find a regular meeting to attend (a "home group"), get a sponsor, and begin to establish a relationship with a Higher Power of our own understanding. We know we are no longer alone. We are perhaps forming the kinds of attachments that many of us missed out on earlier in life. We are certainly forming the kinds of alliances that will be a match for the pull toward destructive compulsions and other "defects" or defenses. With help, we can develop inner resources and no longer have to avoid life or rely on outmoded behaviors that set us apart from our fellows. Human connection can prevent the progression of physical disease; it allows infants to thrive and keeps elderly people alive longer. With the help of the W.A. program and a Higher Power, we can benefit from all that life has to offer – including real intimacy and connection. We can come down to earth, freely walk among our peers as equals, and experience release from the bondage of fear and the compulsion to do, to work, and to achieve. We can experience happiness and peace. We can just be.

Getting High – Adrenalizing

Adrenalizing means creating pressure, suspense, and chaos. We often do this by over-scheduling and under-preparing, implying a lack of clear priorities and proper pacing. By not allowing time for savoring or proper assimilation, a scattered, cluttered, and racing mind often results. Some examples of such behavior that we can come to identify and release include:

1. Beginning trips and projects without enough preparation or information.
2. Not asking for help when lost or puzzled.
3. Not reading instructions before using something.
4. Worrying incessantly.
5. Regularly engaging with difficult people (individuals who are angry, critical, controlling, unstable, and scattered; people who are constantly rushing or talking too fast), adrenaline junkies, and codependent relationships.
6. Provoking people out of boredom.
7. Isolating socially.
8. Neglecting car maintenance and risking imminent breakdown (i.e. not refilling gas tank until almost empty).
9. Speeding.
10. Ignoring body signals and physical health.
11. Overeating and indulging in junk food (especially sugar).
12. Not getting enough rest, exercise, or play.
13. Debting, overspending, underearning, and living in chronic financial vagueness.
14. Not checking or recording due dates.
15. Maintaining excessive to-do lists and overly tight schedules.
16. Agreeing or trying to adhere to unrealistic deadlines.
17. Time-stuffing (i.e. spontaneously adding to agendas, cramming another action into every spare minute).
18. Multitasking (i.e. simultaneously running water, heating food, and starting the car – requiring one to be perfectly in sync).
19. Leaving a message for someone to call you back on one line and then making a complex call on another line.
20. Taking classes that are too advanced or difficult.
21. Not allowing for the unexpected.
22. Entertaining too many interruptions.
23. Working nonstop without bathroom breaks or meals.
24. Hurrying and being chronically late.

25. Not maintaining an extra set of keys or adequate security for your property.
26. Overloading on data, including world news.
27. Subscribing to too many magazines.
28. Checking out or reserving too many library books or films.
29. Attending too many classes and lectures.
30. Participating in too many organizations or making too many volunteer commitments.
31. Not keeping your clothes and property in good repair.
32. Cluttering which leads to misplacing, breaking, dropping, spilling, and tripping.
33. Being disorganized about time, space, ideas, paper, objects, and people.
34. Practicing other addictions and not maintaining abstinence.

Technology and Work Addiction

The W.A. program suggests simplicity in living. We are reminded to do one thing at a time and to be present for our tasks, other people, and ourselves. We are cautioned against doing too many things at once because it results in our attention becoming fragmented. We are encouraged to allow time for enjoyable activities and play. The W.A. program is invaluable to recovering workaholics because it helps us to set effective boundaries around work, however, it often requires diligence, patience, and willingness. It is therefore important for us to be aware of the hazards we face every day that threaten to rob us of our peace of mind and sabotage our recovery efforts.

We live in a habitat of ever-increasing technological complexity. As we are met with yet another new techno-gizmo we "need" in order to proceed with our lives and jobs, it may feel as though we encounter stress at every turn. In the effort to keep up with the quickening pace of life of our families, friends, and coworkers, some of us made sacrifices for convenience. Those whose work addiction is active tend to live at a rushed pace, thinking the ability to multitask a great virtue. For workaholics in recovery, it is important to be aware of the way we use technology and how it impacts our lives. Technology has evolved to bring more individual choices than ever before. Such gains, although certainly desirable in many respects, bring with them responsibility for deciding when and how to engage them. In years past, some predictions were made that technology had the potential to become so wonderfully powerful that we would be able to cease working, just sitting back and letting machines do the work for us.

The promised "technotopian dream," however, has yet to arrive. Instead of living in a world where technological inventions do all of our work, which admittedly sounds at least a little naive, there have evolved some uncomfortable realities for those of us with this disease. Our society has created a world where we can carry our work with us 24 hours a day, seven days a week. The line between work in the workplace and work we are expected to do after hours has certainly blurred. The smartphone and the laptop computer have made the portable office a reality. As a result, we need never be too far from our work. Some of us are employed by corporations that expect us to work before the official workday begins, through lunch, and at home in the evenings. We may feel that we are always on call. Our technological developments have made excessive work easy and convenient. Those of us with poor boundaries may find ourselves indulging in a greater quantity of interaction. This can, of course, easily translate into a reduction in the quality of individual interactions.

The portable electronic office can easily render the home an extension of the workplace – something that we try to avoid in recovery. Smartphones now allow work-related calls, texts, and emails to intrude at any hour into our personal time. Through such technology, work has been invited into every corner of our lives. The ability to communicate in any location now seems to justify communication in any such location. We often surrender the local coffee shop, restaurant, and grocery store as well as our homes. Without clear boundaries around work, those in our presence may be expected to wait as the technological intrusion of a smartphone or pager preempts an actual live conversation between people. Portable electronics become enablers for workaholics who are already looking for an excuse to work around the clock. We may become as dependent on, and obsessed with, our technological devices as we are to the work itself.

We live in a world where the images on the television screen change at a very rapid rate, and we have to adjust ourselves to a state of constant hyperstimulation. News broadcasts on our screens are now split into several sections – requiring that we parse out our attention even further. Smartphones act as an invisible ball and chain, tethering us to work. They have the power to summon us at any moment and interrupt any activity should we fail to shut them off completely. We can begin the workday the moment we open our eyes or start the engine of our car, conducting "pressing" business from bed or as we drive. After work, playtime becomes tentative, provided no important phone calls interrupt our activities.

How can we mitigate the obstacles which technology poses to our progress in recovery? The solution to this problem may be a very close rereading of W.A. literature as well as an honest assessment of how the misuse of technology may compromise our recovery. If we are powerless over work itself, we may also become powerless over the tools that connect us with our work. We may argue that we have to work, that we have to use technology, and that we therefore cannot avoid the intrusion of either into every corner of our lives. To some extent, it is true that technology is part of today's reality in many areas formerly left untouched by it. Using these facts as excuses for us to keep working compulsively and avoid taking full responsibility for our recovery, however, would be an example of rationalization or disease-based reasoning. If we make unconscious contact with technology, then we run the risk of becoming less human and more like robots. If we hold love above all other priorities, however – connecting with our own creativity and with others – then technology can be directed to enhance and expand our humanness.

Today, the tools of technology can help us to do many amazing things that were not possible at all for people of even recent generations. We can solve incredibly complex engineering and design problems, have doctors in another part of the world operate on us while we stay at the local hospital, or hear the voice and see a live picture of someone from another continent while we sit in our living room. Such events would have seemed, to our grandparents, as impossible as a trip to the Sun and back! Technology used consciously can help us to be more creative in art and science; to record and reflect more accurately; to schedule more effectively; and even to express love to others. It is certainly true that many companies use electronic communication to over-connect, and that electronics will likely never surpass face-to-face connection with others; however, it is the intent of the people involved that determines whether technology use will be indiscriminate or not. Companies, like individuals, are free to use the power of technology to enhance our human condition or require employees to endure subhuman practices. If we find ourselves addicted to constant connectivity, we may indeed need to give up such devices – unplugging at least for a while – to establish a deeper connection with ourselves and a Higher Power. Some of us establish top and bottom lines around checking email, taking or responding to work-related calls and text messages, and putting away smartphones or computers. Others set times of abstinence from all electronics. Some of us may give serious consideration to letting go of employers that use technology to pressure us if reasonable boundaries are not respected.

Refreshingly, the W.A. program does not require the use of the latest technology. It does, however, require time, discernment, patience, and practice. Recovery often requires us to go slower instead of faster – sometimes shutting off our gadgets completely. We are challenged to do one thing at a time and pay attention to a Higher Power, the world in which we live, and the people who care about us. The Twelve Steps offer the way for an honest assessment of just how we have been living. They also offer us a solution that involves trust in something greater than ourselves – greater even than technology. Fortunately, a Higher Power has no monthly service charges for a high-speed connection. It is all here, waiting for us, with no moving parts and no batteries required!

Workaholism and Other Addictions

In recovery, many of us have been truly baffled by the phenomenon of multiple addictions. In search of the elusive promise of serenity, we may have come to W.A. after spending time in other Twelve-Step programs. If we stay long enough, we may discover the very depths from which all of our other addictions spring.

If we are currently experiencing multiple active addictions, it is important that we begin our recovery from the place where we have the most pain and dysfunction. If we are suffering from the torments of alcoholism, for example, it is in A.A. that we need to begin our recovery. Once we get a handle on that addiction and gradually free ourselves from the numbing effects of alcohol, we begin to face life squarely – stone cold sober. Our once frozen feelings emerge, and we often find ourselves ill equipped to handle them. We never learned to deal with them. At this point, if we do not relapse, many of us cross over into other addictions by substituting food, shopping, sex, relationships, or more work and activity. We use anything to bring on the desired numbness that we no longer allow our primary addiction to provide. We end up feeling like Heracles fighting the Hydra: the moment we cut one head from the monster, two grow in its place.

The possibility of multiple addictions is very real for workaholics. The good news is that the Twelve Steps are a viable solution for all of them. If we switched addictions to compulsive work, our new drug of choice became adrenaline. We had no need for amphetamines because, by living crazed lives, we synthesized our own. For a time, work seemed to fill the void in our lives, providing us with a sense of esteem we had never known before. After recovery from the hopelessness and pain of something like alcoholism, it was very easy to be seduced by the false promises of the only addiction that is both socially sanctioned and financially rewarded. Suddenly, we found ourselves being praised for our dedication, loyalty, persistence, and long hours. We became filled with a sense of self-worth and began to identify ourselves with our work. Driven by the harsh taskmaster of perfectionism, we constantly strived to do more and gain the "all important" approval of others. But our esteem was a house of cards. The first hint of criticism by a superior may have sent us into what seemed like an abyss of shame, self-loathing, and despair.

The apparent success of the workaholic is a hollow victory when we realize we have come no closer to filling the horrible void we feel inside ourselves. We found that we could feel good only when being productive. We became as enmeshed with our work as we had been with alcohol and the people who enabled us. Work became the only way we could feel okay about ourselves. The emptiness we felt was still there, robbing us of any hope for recapturing the sense of peace, wholeness, or serenity that we had perhaps temporarily gained when we got sober. The hidden blessing of finding ourselves in a W.A. meeting was that it was a place where the core issue – addiction itself – could be openly discussed. We had finally found a safe place to confront the horrible dread that each of us carried secretly inside: that we were fundamentally flawed, inadequate, and unworthy. We found that we could talk frankly about our utter loneliness, terror of losing control, overwhelming shame, and sense of worthlessness when not doing something productive.

The darkness always comes with a story. It does not arise in the middle of someone's life for no reason. Many of us grew up in dysfunctional families and were adult children of alcoholics, workaholics, or people with other compulsive behaviors. Under these circumstances, we quickly learned that survival was to be our most urgent priority at all times. The joy and enthusiasm for living, the birthright of every child, was squelched. We may have sought safety by trying to be perfect, getting good grades, being overly helpful, always staying busy, and never allowing ourselves to let down our guard or relax. Experiencing only conditional approval from those around us, we became "human doings" instead of human beings, feeling no sense of identity or value except through our accomplishments. This "hole in our soul" drove us to find the soothing anesthetic that addiction promised. Although for a time addictions deadened the pain, it was a solution that never lasted for long. Many of us eventually found that own lives, even in recovery, had become part of the same, ongoing nightmare.

It is important in recovery to be able to talk about these memories and feelings from the past. Before we found W.A., many of us found it difficult to speak about such core issues in other Twelve-Step programs. The opening comments of most A.A. meetings explicitly request that sharing be kept strictly to the topic of alcohol. Even when members do risk sharing other issues important to their recovery, they may come to realize that it is not a safe place to do so. The result may be several years of sobriety without the serenity that true transformation in recovery can bring. Recovery from addiction is much more than stopping destructive behavior. Recovery in W.A. is about exploring the "horrible alone" that lies underneath all of our addictions. It was in W.A. that we could safely begin acknowledging the futility of using work and activity to fill the void inside of us. Then, through working the Twelve Steps and accepting the support of a Higher Power, the hole began to shrink.

Work addiction is an insidious disease that can easily sidetrack even our well-intentioned attempts to "work" such recovery programs. If we believe that we alone are responsible for fixing everything, then we need to exercise great caution. Further, no matter what the reason, we need to be cautious about rushing. Running around to a multitude of Twelve-Step meetings can create more problems in an already packed schedule, becoming counterproductive to the very recovery that we are seeking. It is important to remember that the first three Steps require "being" and not "doing." We have to stop "doing" long enough to give a Higher Power some elbowroom in order to really transform our lives. This may well be the hardest part of recovery in W.A. – the true surrender of really letting go and letting God. A word of warning: W.A. is not a time management program. Some people come to W.A. looking for a more efficient way to manage their schedule and see the Tools as a way of staying in control. This clinging is like the alcoholic who comes to A.A. hoping to learn how to be a social drinker. The end result for both is relapse.

Unrecognized and unchecked, work addiction also virtually ensures that we will always be – as A.A. puts it – in some state of "H.A.L.T." (Hungry, Angry, Lonely, Tired). Thus, we are continually at risk for relapse in our other programs. Many of us have found that, once our workaholism is addressed, the other addictions mysteriously cease to be a problem. It is truly remarkable. We recommend you give it a try!

Work Aversion

Work avoidance, work anorexia, and procrastination are some of the many terms that describe a very similar set of destructive patterns. As with any illness, identifying an inactivity problem is the prerequisite to implementing a solution. The state of apparent paralysis – like many other forms of reduced living such as underearning, anorexia nervosa, or compulsive social isolation – can be quite difficult to see as it can hide in subtleties and vagueness. As with all addictive behavior, it thrives on rationalization.

It has been said that we would rather perfectly avoid life than imperfectly live it. Addicts of many kinds can identify with that approach to living, however, what separates us from other workaholics is a recurring refusal to deliberately act at all. The only counterbalance to this general trend towards apathy seems to be occasionally throwing ourselves headfirst into action towards a certain direction or goal with the fervent hope of an ideal outcome. We usually putter along, spending a lot of our days on non-priority living – often occupying our time with food, television, or the rescue of others. We engage in these diversions from the pain born out of a wholesale avoidance of the true priorities in our lives. Recovery can only begin when we deliberately face our problems, admit our aspirations, and allow others to help and support us in achieving our dreams.

The delay and distract pattern is perhaps best summed up by the observation that work anorexics are overachievers at underachieving. We who suffer from work aversion actually work very hard to avoid having to commit to any specific action or plan. Unlike other workaholics, we can be very aware of our activity but tend to instead go unconscious in the goal-making or planning department. As such, we especially avoid acknowledging and accepting the results of behavior when they miss the ideal mark. Of course, perfect outcomes would suit us perfectly – or so we think. Deep down, however, we somehow know that worshipping such standards will be trouble in the long run. We have avoided adjusting these perfectionist standards because it would require running the risk of realizing our greatest fear – that we are only human and cannot completely protect ourselves by maintaining constant control. Our pasts have already convinced us that pain is sure to result and recur. Sadly, therefore, our game plan has become to prevent as many results from occurring as possible.

We reason that if we take less action and get fewer results, then we will experience less pain – but is it really true that we cannot lose a race we have not entered? There are many desirable experiences in life that are only reached at the expense of at least some losses along the way, but we have become stuck here. Somehow we have become inspired to damage control as our long-term plan for mitigating the uncertainties of life. We have become obsessed with preventing any disappointment, only behaving in ways that we believe will result in perfect outcomes. Because nothing is truly certain, we are setting ourselves up with mistaken beliefs. Furthermore, our lives eventually become so "safe" and uninspiring that we struggle to let in the light of hope for solutions that foster our sense of freedom. Ignoring facts results in a very painful downward spiritual spiral, and we can be blocked from any real progress or forward momentum for years. The frustration of such stagnation drives us into working more and more to commit to less and less as we progressively back away from life's challenges and choices. It has been said, "the greatest risk is not to risk at all," and that is exactly what this disease ultimately mandates – that we go to any lengths to avoid taking chances. We have therefore justified our procrastination with sky-high standards, terrified to release or reconsider them.

As time goes on, some of us desperately want to take action in certain areas of our lives but feel frozen. We may find that the only way to justify the hope that a particular effort will turn out to be worthwhile is to lie to ourselves, promising ourselves a perfect outcome. Then we commit to involvement, sometimes heavily, and the pendulum swings the other way for a time. At some point, however, we come out of fantasy and are forced to recognize the flaws of this new endeavor. At that point, our voices tell us that we are losers once again and that the best way to proceed is to cut our losses – and so we quit. Most work anorexics have trouble finding work and/or holding jobs for any appreciable length of time. If we do have jobs, we may find that we work for or with an active work addict. In such cases, it would be easy to blame this person for our troubles by saying that if they did not wear us out with ever-increasing demands we would not try to slow things down so much. Many of us discover upon examination, however, that we had childhoods that involved a work-addicted parent, guardian, or sibling. Our work avoidance may be a reaction to such family models and the abuse we once received. In fact, we are probably attracted to workaholics in order to heal our old wounds or because it feels familiar and normal. The pain of teaming up with such individuals, however, makes things very confusing to the point where many practicing work anorexics find ways to stop working with others altogether. We become self-employed or are enabled financially by family, friends, or disability payments. At some point, we see that we are rarely – if ever – satisfied with the results of our actions. Such hopelessness is too painful to bear alone. We realize we need to risk allowing others to help us.

In W.A., we find support for taking actions of all kinds and for letting go of results – however imperfect. We even learn to accept unexpected outcomes as part of life. We may also need outside help. A therapist, doctor, or clergy member can help us to better face the physical and emotional challenges involved in recovering from the spiritual abuse and rigid perfectionism that is often behind work aversion. With growth through the W.A. program and the experience of sharing our burden with others, we finally have the courage to take positive actions on our own behalf. Such efforts do not occur in intense bursts followed by quitting; rather, we have committed to make slow and small – yet solid – changes to generate the forward momentum of healing.

At some point, as the very description of our illness implies a pattern of giving up, we may be tempted to distance ourselves from the W.A. fellowship or some aspect of the W.A. program as we have done with other work or activity. If that is the case, we do not worry about someone judging us for leaving; instead, we pray to a Higher Power for the willingness to return. W.A. has no requirement for perfect attendance. The only requirement for membership is a desire to stop working compulsively, and work avoidance is certainly a compulsive way of managing work. Work anorexics in relapse need not feel ashamed to return to the W.A. program. Many in the fellowship have experienced such setbacks.

Recovery is work – as much as or more so than most paying jobs! It is effort, however, that eventually pays us many spiritual dividends not available elsewhere. Therefore, we are encouraged to risk vulnerability by sharing our secret practices of perfection worship with one or more recovering W.A. members. Such alliances, combined with the healing spiritual framework of the Steps, provide essential relief from the painful state of work avoidance. If we are not skillful in choosing safe people with whom to share our recovery journey, we persevere with a new dignity of purpose – remembering that imperfect outcomes are not to be feared. We must only recognize our mistakes and forgive ourselves rather than condemn ourselves for failing again. We know we have reached a new place in our lives when we come to embrace the "paradox of acceptance." Ironically, the way to serenity is found not by achieving perfection as we had always assumed but by the acquired discipline of connecting regularly with a Higher Power to embrace the flaws in any particular person or situation.

Progress Not Perfection

Many of us in W.A. struggle with unrealistic expectations and procrastination. The belief that we require certain conditions and outcomes to generate positive feelings can – somewhat ironically – actually keep us stuck in negativity as we commit more and more energy to it because we are never quite able to sustain ideal circumstances no matter how hard we try. Subconsciously we know we are fighting a losing battle, manifesting a bunch of painful and often conflicting behaviors:

1. We cannot accept imperfections in others or ourselves.
2. We put excessive demands on others and ourselves.
3. We judge things as good or bad rather than as complex and gray. We believe the lies that we hear from an incessant and critical inner voice, fueling our poor self-esteem. We respond with devastation to any corroborating negative feedback. Our drive to high performance is essential to antidote our constant diet of poisonous internal messages.
4. We swing from entertaining an inadequate self-image to overcompensating with attempts at achieving superhuman ideals. We cannot accept being average like everyone else.
5. We suffer from intense shame if we do not have all of the answers or our work is regarded as lacking. We sometimes try to avoid this feeling by blaming others.
6. We can be totally self-absorbed, obsessed with getting everyone's approval and being at the center of all processes. We believe the behavior of others reflects upon us.
7. We struggle to stop a project to take care of ourselves with regular meals, exercise, and sleep.
8. We have trouble shifting gears – getting started can be as difficult as taking breaks or stopping.
9. We lose track of our biggest priorities, getting lost in details.
10. We avoid work entirely to minimize failure, knowing subconsciously that we are unlikely to meet our own rigid standards.
11. We are plagued with the consequences of our dishonest attempts to cover up our mistakes and imperfections.
12. We hurt inside.

OUR SOLUTION TO WORKAHOLISM

Getting Started

Realizing and admitting that we had a problem was the first stage of recovery. Most of us came to W.A. not completely understanding our compulsive attraction to – or avoidance of – work and activity. Regularly reading program literature, attending meetings, and discussing our problems helped us to identify with other workaholics and to free ourselves. Eventually, we took Step One: "We admitted we were powerless over work – that our lives had become unmanageable."

For many of us, Step One initially seemed counterintuitive and even wrong. After all, powerless seems to mean helpless and hopeless. In W.A., however, we learned that only by ourselves were we unable to solve our problems with work. For a long time, we were in denial that we needed help as we assumed that intellect and hard work could fix anything. In practice, we found that our unaided efforts were not sufficient. Over time our workaholism worsened, despite our resolve and good intentions. We came to see how our responses were not working and how our lives were unmanageable. We came to W.A. meetings having made some progress in crossing the mental barrier of pride and denial. We admitted something was wrong and that we had not been successful when relying on our usual individual faculties. It was a relief as we began to identify with our fellow members and enlist their support. W.A. offered us a fellowship and a program of recovery that helped us to do what we had been unable to accomplish alone.

When we first heard about W.A. meetings, many of us wondered how they could help. We were already too busy. We wondered how it could possibly benefit us to network with other people who also had a problem with work and activity. What could they teach us? On the other hand, we were desperate. Perhaps quite apprehensively, we went to our first meetings. Although we did not feel that we completely understood everything that happened there, we discovered to our immense relief that W.A. is not a cult. There is no belief in or adherence to any particular religion or dogma. By attending meetings we discovered that the W.A. fellowship itself could provide a great power of inspiration as we witnessed certain members of the group who had apparently done that we could not manage to accomplish. They had recovered from workaholism.

Although not a religious organization, W.A. and its members had a deeply spiritual nature. People spoke of how a Higher Power was an important part of their lives, sometimes deferring to the wisdom of the wider experience of the W.A. group and other times appealing to a personally relevant conception of God. In either case, such forces are the sources of strength beyond our finite selves upon which we must rely for our recovery. It is important to remind ourselves that our personal egos are not sufficient to overcome our compulsive behavior or we would have solved our problems long ago. Information of how to find a meeting is available in the Supplemental Resources section of this book.

Turning It Over

Taking Step Two, we "came to believe that a Power greater than ourselves could restore us to sanity." This Step speaks of sanity because workaholism is a kind of insanity as we repeat the same behaviors and somehow expect different results. We began to recover by gradually removing our irrational thinking and habits with the help of a Higher Power. A member writes:

> I have had 27 years of setting unrealistic standards for myself, thinking I should be doing more, pushing myself past where I could go, and thinking others wanted me to do things. I know how many painful problems compulsive busyness caused me, but it is hard for me to remember how my attempts to control it failed. I am starting to recognize times in the past that had been opportunities to cram one more thing into my life.

Another member states, "My obsessing could be about many things: working, not working, a coworker, things that I wish someone had or had not done, things that I was afraid would happen, or things that I would rather be doing." For many of us the obsessions were recurrent and progressive. We could perhaps stop for a while, but – by our own unaided efforts – we could not prevent the ultimate return. Dealing successfully required help from something greater than the self.

In Step Three, we "made a decision to turn our will and our life over the care of God *as we understood God*." Faced with this language, many of us balked based on a concern that the W.A. program was going to require a comfort with or acceptance of certain religious concepts. This Step, however, simply involves making a commitment to allow a caring Higher Power to guide us in the areas that our self-generated ideas have failed. One way to turn our will and our life over is to complete the remaining Twelve Steps despite lingering reservations that the W.A. program may not work after all the effort required. Letting a Higher Power run the show might require giving up our own plans of what we think will help, but we are still responsible for taking the inspired actions. This means learning a new way to solve problems. For those of us who pride ourselves on being self-sufficient, we discover a peace that replaces the toxic thinking and chaotic doing when we honestly did not know what to do that might help the situation.

Recovery is like coming home to the original selves that we forgot: hopeful, playful, appreciative, and joyful. Joining the W.A. fellowship and taking the Twelve Steps brings us in touch with our own inner wisdom and spirituality. As we learn to accept ourselves as we are, we experience a new attitude toward work and activity. We enjoy our work more and find ways to work more effectively. When work has its proper place, we find time to have fun and to nurture our health, creativity, and relationships. We welcome you and wish for you the serenity we have found.

How Recovery Happens

We compulsive workers have found that no amount of will power or determination can make us stick to a sensible program of work for any permanent or lasting period of time. We have found that self-reliance, good as far as it goes, failed us because it did not go far enough. Some of us once had self-confidence, but it did not solve our work problem – or any other problem – completely. We have felt a need and have been seeking an answer to our dilemma. We have realized that our work obsession is only the outward manifestation of our inner emotional turmoil and our essential spiritual disconnection.

We who are recovering from the destructive consequences of work addiction understand, as perhaps few others can, the fear, depression, anxiety, and loneliness of being a workaholic. We are learning that the high we get from the praise of others, the sense of security that we get from avoiding or accomplishing certain tasks, and the chaos engendered by our frantic activity are all means we use to cope with the reality that we cannot completely control our life or our experience of it. We are learning that we will never accomplish or accumulate enough to truly feel good about ourselves. Workaholism is a disease not cured by status or money, and – like all other addictive diseases – it is progressive and fatal if not arrested.

We are also learning that recovery is possible. We start by noticing and identifying our personal "bottom line" addictive behaviors. Workaholism does not lend itself to complete abstinence like many substance addictions, but – with the assistance of a Higher Power – we can begin to identify when we are using work in a compulsive fashion. We can then stop and pray or call a fellow W.A. member for support when we feel tempted to default to our old behavior patterns. We have experienced healing in the W.A. program.

Our stories detail what life was like in active addiction, how we found recovery, and what has changed since we began working the W.A. program. We hope that you decide that you want what we have and are willing to take the Steps necessary in order to get it for yourself. We now know that we deal with an obsession that is destined to overwhelm us if we do not ask for help. Half measures availed us nothing, but we recovered when we surrendered completely to something greater than ourselves.

Moving through the Steps with a sponsor may take varying amounts of time and effort. We can create Step meetings to discuss them and Step groups for actively working them together. We may revisit certain Steps and find new meanings in them. Ultimately, we find we practice them best by fully integrating them into our lives.

The Twelve Steps of Workaholics Anonymous

1. We admitted we were powerless over work – that our lives had become unmanageable.
2. Came to believe that a Power greater than ourselves could restore us to sanity.
3. Made a decision to turn our will and our lives over to the care of God *as we understood God.*
4. Made a searching and fearless moral inventory of ourselves.
5. Admitted to God, to ourselves, and to another human being the exact nature of our wrongs.
6. Became entirely ready to have God remove all these defects of character.
7. Humbly asked God to remove our shortcomings.

8. Made a list of all persons we had harmed, and became willing to make amends to them all.
9. Made direct amends to such people wherever possible, except when to do so would injure them or others.
10. Continued to take personal inventory and when we were wrong promptly admitted it.
11. Sought through prayer and meditation to improve our conscious contact with God *as we understood God*, praying only for knowledge of God's will for us and the power to carry that out.
12. Having had a spiritual awakening as the result of these Steps, we tried to carry this message to workaholics, and to practice these principles in all our affairs.

For W.A. members to recover, the groups themselves must also adhere to spiritual principles. Meetings must provide a safe, stable, and supportive environment if they are to attract, assist, and retain members. The Twelve Traditions were adapted to ensure that W.A. groups would thrive just as A.A. groups have done. Similar to the Steps, the Traditions may be studied individually or in Tradition meetings. It is important that W.A. members grasp the importance of balancing their own immediate recovery needs with principles of cooperation and service in order to maintain a fellowship that provides all workaholics with the opportunity to successfully work the Steps.

The Twelve Traditions of Workaholics Anonymous

1. Our common welfare should come first; personal recovery depends upon W.A. unity.
2. For our group purpose there is but one ultimate authority – a loving God as expressed in our group conscience. Our leaders are but trusted servants; they do not govern.
3. The only requirement for W.A. membership is a desire to stop working compulsively.
4. Each group should be autonomous except in matters affecting other groups or W.A. as a whole.
5. Each group has but one primary purpose – to carry its message to the workaholic who still suffers.
6. A W.A. group ought never endorse, finance or lend the W.A. name to any related facility or outside enterprise, lest problems of money, property, and prestige divert us from our primary purpose.

7. Every W.A. group ought to be fully self-supporting, declining outside contributions.
8. W.A. should remain forever nonprofessional, but our service centers may employ special workers.
9. W.A., as such, ought never be organized; but we may create service boards or committees directly responsible to those they serve.
10. W.A. has no opinion on outside issues; hence the W.A. name ought never be drawn into public controversy.
11. Our public relations policy is based on attraction rather than promotion; we need always maintain personal anonymity at the level of press, radio, and films.
12. Anonymity is the spiritual foundation of all our traditions, ever reminding us to place principles before personalities.

Upon recognizing our unmanageability and commencing to practice the Steps and Traditions, we resolved to do whatever it took when we felt triggered to avoid defaulting to workaholic behavior. At first, certain recovery ideas were uncomfortable, but we eventually noticed a welcome change in how we felt and were received by others. We found a number of actions critical to success in the W.A. program, and we did our best to integrate them into our day-to-day lives. We often found ourselves adopting them effortlessly upon asking for help from a Higher Power. From time to time, each of us may fail to reach for one of these healthier coping skills, but we must remember to strive for progress rather than perfection – refusing to use our imperfect recovery as another excuse to act out our disease of self-hatred. Our best is good enough.

The W.A. Tools of Recovery

Meetings
We attend W.A. meetings to learn how the fellowship works, to remind ourselves of how far we have come in recovery, and to share our experience, strength, and hope with other W.A. members.

Telephone and Internet
We reach out to stay in contact with other W.A. members between meetings for mutual support, especially before and after critical recovery tasks.

Sponsors

We find a W.A. member who is committed to abstinence from compulsive working to help us work the Steps, Traditions, and Tools. Sponsors offer guidance through the recovery process on all three levels: physical, emotional, and spiritual. A member may work with more than one sponsor and may change sponsors at will. We become a sponsor as a way of working Step Twelve, carrying the W.A. message and putting the principles of the program into practice. We ask to be sponsored so that we can benefit from the experience of someone who has achieved what we want. W.A. is a program of attraction, so we find a sponsor whose recovery inspires us and follow his or her lead. A co-sponsoring arrangement is sometimes the most practical or desirable approach, many workaholics having found or deepened their recovery in this manner.

Literature

Reading W.A. publications on a daily basis impresses the truth upon us and expands our horizons. Such writings can provide information, insight, inspiration, and hope. They are available at times when other W.A. members are not. Further, they provide a comprehensive chronicle of the knowledge of recovery from a multitude of sources. We also study the literature of A.A. and other Twelve-Step programs to strengthen our understanding of compulsive disease. We can identify with many of the situations described by substituting terms like "compulsive working" in place of the named substances and processes.

Prayer and Meditation

A daily contemplative practice is something we might formally adopt even prior to reaching Step Eleven. Before accepting any new commitments, we ask a Higher Power for guidance. For many of us, being still and sitting quietly are difficult and painful at first. The practice of letting go of the constant chatter in our heads can, however, lead to a gradually evolving peace of mind. This serenity is a soothing, healing contrast to the intensity sought through our compulsive busyness and constant worry. Meditation lets us experience ourselves insulated from the resentments and fears that drive workaholism and work avoidance. Renewed, we are able to move back into our daily lives in a balanced way.

Writing
Journaling is helpful to clarify our thoughts and helps us to get to the root of feelings that lie behind our compulsive working. As with reading and meditating, getting our ideas on paper is an option at times when other W.A. members are not around to listen – with the added benefit that we are able to express ourselves more freely when we need have no regard for the audience. Sometimes just making notes of seemingly important memories or ideas can help quiet the mind as we assure ourselves that they will not be forgotten and can be revisited anytime in the future. Writings can ultimately be shared with others if we so desire.

Top and Bottom Lines
For many workaholics, abstinence means far more than relief from compulsive working and activity on a physical level. It also means an attitude that comes as a result of surrendering to something greater than the self. We do not merely avoid work, mistaking a lack of activity for recovery. We aspire to freedom from compulsive thinking and worrying. Each of us is free to determine our own way of being abstinent according to personal needs and preferences. Top lines represent our goals and visions, and bottom lines define the point where we cross over from abstinence to work addiction. We work with a sponsor to establish such boundaries as well as to seek support around bottom line behavior. For more information on setting top and bottom lines, see the *Abstinence in Workaholics Anonymous: Top Lines & Bottom Lines* pamphlet that is reprinted in the Supplemental Resources section of this book.

Action Plan
We put on paper what we intend to do each day. We are conscious of the way we spend our time to ensure that we are able to properly care for our bodies with healthy food, appropriate exercise, and an adequate amount of sleep. We carve out places in our schedule for recovery, recreation, and relationships in addition to work and other activities. This helps us develop a healthier, more balanced lifestyle so long as we also commit to concentrating on one thing at a time and setting a reasonable pace for ourselves. Our increased awareness will help us to overcome any lingering denial. Sharing our plans with another W.A. member gives us an opportunity to express feelings that are often at the root of our compulsive behavior if we find that we have trouble adhering to our stated intentions. We get feedback as needed to determine which things need to happen first – which may mean doing nothing. We strive to stay flexible to events, reorganizing our priorities as needed. We do not cram new tasks into our

schedules; rather, we substitute by eliminating activities that demand equivalent time and energy. We under-schedule to allow more time than we think we need, providing a comfortable margin to accommodate the unexpected. We view interruptions and accidents as opportunities for growth. We realize that we are where our Higher Power has intended – in the here and now.

Rest and Relaxation
We work at a comfortable pace and rest before we get tired. We check our level of energy before proceeding to our next activity. We do not get "wound up," so we do not have to unwind. We do not yield to pressure from others or attempt to pressure others. We remain alert to the people and situations that trigger stressful feelings. We become aware of our own actions, words, and body sensations. When we feel energy building up, we stop and reconnect with a Higher Power. Setting aside time for breaks and unstructured events without goals, we learn that there is more to life than we had been experiencing as active workaholics. We allow ourselves to have fun and play without making it into a work project. We exercise our sense of humor and laugh at the funny side of our predicament. We allow ourselves to enjoy the present moment rather than driving ourselves for hoped-for fulfillment in some faraway future time.

Service
As part of Step Twelve, we readily extend help to other workaholics, knowing that assistance to others adds to the quality of our own recovery by fostering a sense of gratitude for what we have learned and how far we have already come. While it may be useful to take a brief hiatus from any new or substantial volunteer commitments in early recovery if such activity was part of our compulsion, we find that we can still contribute to W.A. in many ways. For example, we do service by listening undistracted to other W.A. members as they share, volunteering to read or time the shares at W.A. meetings, and offering contributions pursuant to Tradition Seven.

The W.A. Principles of Recovery

We accept the outcomes of our endeavors – whatever the results, whatever the timing. We know that impatience, rushing, and insisting on a perfect result will only slow any progress. We are gentle with our efforts, knowing that our new way of living requires much practice and that our best is good enough for now. We freely admit our weaknesses and mistakes. We realize we do not have to do everything ourselves. We pray and ask for help, delegating when we need to. We forgive ourselves and others for failing to live up to conceptual ideals.

We hold what other W.A. members share with us in confidence. We respect each other's anonymity in order to foster freedom of expression and protection against the negative impact of gossip. We provide a safe place for workaholics to recover. We treat others as we wish to be treated.

If we are completely honest about ourselves, and together we apply the Steps, Traditions, Tools, and Principles in our lives, we will soon begin to receive these gifts of sanity and balance:

The Promises of
Workaholics Anonymous

1. We are not obsessed by work or plagued by work aversion.
2. Adrenaline seeking loses its hold on us. Excessive worry and anxiety become a thing of the past.
3. We have a daily action plan that faces the reality of time as well as priorities such as recovery, recreation, and relationships.
4. Fears that there will not be enough time, money, or love leave us.
5. We learn to play and have fun together.
6. We repair broken relationships and build new ones.
7. Health and self-nurturance return.
8. Self-seeking and ego inflation do not drive our decisions.
9. We lose interest in selfish things. We gain interest in – and compassion for – our partners, families, friends, and coworkers.
10. We experience how well the program helps us to handle problems that used to confuse and defeat us.
11. We ask for help and reach out to help others.
12. We find that a Higher Power helps us in a way that self-reliance never could.

Are these extravagant promises? We think not. They are already happening in the lives of many among us. For those of you who are new to our fellowship, there are no problems that you have experienced that are not common to us. We welcome you with the deepest respect. When we apply this program with honesty and compassion, a place of serenity grows in us one day at a time.

Characteristics of Recovery

1. We are able to speak such statements as: I do not know. I do not understand. I do not remember. I was wrong. I made a mistake. I am sorry. I need help. I am sad. I am lonely. I am afraid. I am uncomfortable with what you said. I am angry. I cannot help. I feel like goofing off. So what? Who cares?

2. We accept that others need not always be happy. We do not fight their feelings with logic or distraction. We respect limits.

3. We believe that many people can do most or all of what we do as well as we can – or better.

4. We do not expect to predict the future or read minds. We know that failures and incomplete projects are part of the learning process. We realize that no matter how fast or efficiently we work, there are only 24 hours in a day.

5. We respect our body instead of fighting it. We realize that feeling tired or ill is part of the human experience. We rely on intuition as well as inner timing and rhythms.

6. We accept that not everyone may like us.

7. We can refuse responsibility or requests. We can say no without feeling guilty. We nurture ourselves and give from our overflow.

8. We delay, delegate, and lower performance standards as needed.

9. We realize that it is acceptable to be inconsistent at times. We find our own mistakes to be a continuing source of humor.

10. While communicating, we notice people's states and respond to them rather than being solely focused on the matter at hand.

11. We value joy over efficiency. We understand the importance of rest and play. We think of work as part of – but not all of –life.

12. We believe everyone has intrinsic value, whether working or not.

13. We realize we are valued by how we treat others – not by what we own, what we produce, or how hard we work. We know that people do not care how much we know until they know how much we care.

14. We realize we cannot force growth. We know we cannot change, control, or rescue anyone. We have reasonable expectations for ourselves and for others.

15. We live in the present without regretting the past or fearing the future.

16. We believe that others who are part of a joint venture share responsibility for both "good" and "bad" outcomes.

17. We accept change, the unexpected, and conflict as parts of life.

18. We trust our developing relationship with our Higher Power, and we embrace our own goodness and growing serenity.

The Gifts of Rest

Most workaholics discount or ignore rest, thinking it wasteful and unproductive. Rest includes getting enough sleep at night, taking appropriate naps and breaks, scheduling silent time alone, or just sitting and being still as needed. Strolling along the beach or reading an engrossing mystery may be relaxing, but they are not necessarily restful. Likewise, lying awake worrying does not count. Rest is the most important "activity" we do. Here are some of the gifts we may receive if we choose to surrender and accept them:

1. Physical and mental renewal.
   No matter how pleasurable the activity, we enjoy it much more when rested. If we are tired, we have to draw on adrenaline for energy. Even if offered the best, we must say no as rest is the best reward.

2. Experiencing our inner being.
   Being alone with ourselves without the distraction of props or activities, we appreciate the pleasure of solitude and learn the art of self-enjoyment.

3. A slower pace.
   We regain a healthy breathing rhythm.

4. Making connections.
   We integrate the cause and effect relationships of our actions and those of others.

5. Quietness with which to hear guidance from a Higher Power.
   We are able to remind ourselves of our essential spiritual nature and to get out of the way of the universal plan for us. We notice when we have shifted from flow to effort, from a Higher Power's will to self-will, and from surrender to attempts at control.

6. Gaining perspective with a temporary withdrawal.
   We unwind from being hyper-focused, seeing where we lost our vision and noting what we are doing that is unnecessary. We remind ourselves to be selective. We are silent to reflect on the deeper meaning of words and events.

7. Space in our day to savor each event.
    We fully digest impressions, freshen our perceptions, and enjoy life.

8. Catching ourselves before we lapse into ego and self-will.
    We can keep our awareness of emotions and other body signals, including energy level. We are able to change our thoughts to healthier ones. We gain patience, flexibility, and humor. We are able to express creativity and wisdom.

9. Health.
    When we are ill, we allow our body to repair itself.

10. Cooperating with cycles.
    We respect the universal rhythm of ebb and flow, winter and summer. We treat time as a friend.

A W.A. STEP STUDY GUIDE

Overview: Recovery from Work Addiction Through the Twelve Steps

The study of the Twelve Steps of Workaholics Anonymous is the core of personal recovery and progress. At first this can seem daunting, but the Steps are not meant to be studied alone. This is the time to ask for the help of a sponsor or to join a Step study group. Many of us have found the reading of related portions of the Big Book of A.A. (Chapter Five, "How it Works," Chapter Six, "Into Action," and Chapter Seven, "Working with Others") helps us to better understand the Steps. We also read from the related Step chapter from Twelve Steps and Twelve Traditions *of A.A., substituting words such as "alcohol" to "work" as needed, as a way to begin working each Step.*

The Problem

Workaholism takes many forms. Among them: deriving our identity and self-esteem from what we do; keeping overly busy; neglecting our health, relationships, and spirituality; seeing everything as work-related; having no desire to do anything (work avoidance or burnout); procrastinating; postponing vacations and rest; doing unnecessary work; worrying; perfectionism; avoiding intimacy; being controlling.

All these are ways we cope with the pain of having lost our sense of being and of not feeling good enough. Over-scheduling our lives with activities is how we run from ourselves. We keep busy to blot out our feelings. We enjoy the adrenaline highs that come from intensity and rushing to meet deadlines. Maybe we are praised and promoted at work for being responsible and hardworking. We may even be employed by a workaholic company that uses praise and promotion to encourage our addiction. Yet we have paid an enormous price for these "rewards." We have traded self-awareness for burying our pain in work and worry. We have endangered our health and destroyed our relationships. We may have often felt, "Is this all there is?"

Because there are many misconceptions about workaholism, recognizing it may take a long time. It is both a substance (adrenaline) and a process (overdoing) addiction and is not limited to our paid work life. We can also be workaholic in hobbies, fitness, housework, volunteering, or in trying to save the world. All of these may appear admirable, but if they mean self-abandonment due to incessant doing, it is work addiction.

Since this is a progressive disease, ultimately we become more driven until we hit bottom. Our bottom may come in the form of a serious health problem or an ultimatum from our partner, employer, or a friend. At some point, "workaholic" is no longer a label we prize. We realize that we have to change.

To help guide us in our recovery, there are the suggested Twelve Steps of Workaholics Anonymous. Because our work addiction is so entrenched in our lives, the process seems overwhelming. How much time will recovery take? We are already too busy! What do we do with our commitments and responsibilities?

The Solution

As our pain intensifies, we begin to gain willingness – willingness to admit that we are addicted to work, that our lives are unmanageable, and that our way has not worked; willingness not to have all our questions answered immediately or to expect a quick fix; willingness to say, "I am sick. I want to recover and I need help." In W.A., this admission of powerlessness is Step One. We have found it helpful to take this Step and those that follow with others in W.A.

From this initial willingness comes more willingness. Step Two tells us that a Power greater than ourselves can restore us to sanity. This Power can be God, Higher Power, the Universe, the W.A. group – whatever is our source of strength.

Step Three involves making a commitment to turn our will and our lives over to God as we understand God. Letting our Higher Power guide us requires giving up control, not being irresponsible. Our will now becomes a tool to turn self-will into willingness. For those of us who pride ourselves on being self-sufficient and strong willed, taking this Step involves a new way of thinking.

In Step Four we make a written inventory of ourselves in relation to our workaholism. We include both our shortcomings and our assets. We ask a W.A. member for help on how to do Step Four. By taking a close look at ourselves, we become acquainted with the lovable person we truly are, the person we have lost in busyness.

Because many of us feel shame about how our work addiction has hurt others, and ourselves, it is healing to do Step Five and talk to an understanding person. This person can be anyone we choose. When we share our secrets, we often find that others have had similar experiences.

Steps Six and Seven ask us to prepare ourselves inwardly to make amends to those we have harmed. In Step Eight we list those people and in Step Nine we make amends prudently. After these Steps are completed, many of us discover that a great burden has been lifted, that we have a sense of freedom and peace.

Recovery from workaholism is not a cure, but a lifelong process. We are granted only a daily reprieve contingent upon our maintaining our abstinence and growing spiritually. In Step Ten, we continue the process begun in Step Four – awareness of our feelings and taking responsibility for our words and actions. Taking Step Eleven strengthens our conscious contact with our Higher Power, begun in Step Two, by having us stay in touch through prayer and meditation.

Step Twelve tells us we can maintain and expand the spiritual awakening we experienced in doing all the preceding Steps. We can do this by carrying the W.A. message of recovery to workaholics and by practicing these principles at work, at home, on vacations – everywhere.

The best way for us to keep from sliding back into old habits is to share about our W.A. recovery with others. "We can't keep it unless we give it away." We carry the message by being an example of a recovering workaholic in our daily activities as well as by giving service in W.A.

Following the Steps brings us in touch with our inner wisdom and our spirituality. As we learn to accept ourselves as we are, we experience a new attitude toward work and activity. We enjoy our work more and find ways to work more effectively. When work has its proper place, we find time to have fun and to nurture our health, relationships, and creativity.

We welcome you to our program and wish for you the recovery, serenity, and self-enjoyment we have found.

Step One

**We admitted we were powerless over work –
that our lives had become unmanageable.**

The ten questions below were designed to be answered in writing, one question a day for ten days, while working with a sponsor. It is also suggested they be written in a Step group. It takes time to face the full consequences of our affliction and the ways that workaholism is manifesting in our lives. For many of us, Step One is challenging. But we have found that if we do not honestly admit how powerless we really are over this affliction, we are doomed to continue our insane lives. For some of us, we are well aware of our condition. In one setting, we are ready to move on to Step Two, where we begin to feel hope and a path to peace of mind. You are free to use these questions to stimulate your thinking about workaholism and how it affects you.

Step One Questions

1. How has work stress and excess work and/or work avoidance affected my health?
2. What is the history of my workaholism, starting with my family history of addictive work and other addictions? What has my family of origin taught me about work? Including my first memories of work or activity, what is the progression of work addiction in my life?
3. What have I tried in the past to control my problems with work: changing jobs, taking classes, attending retreats, taking time off, reading self help books, etc.?
4. Free write about what I am powerless over and my feelings about powerlessness.
5. Using another workaholic's example of taking Step One, how would I quantify my workaholism? (See first Step One Story.)
6. How have my relationships (or lack of them) been affected by my work problems?
7. What seems unmanageable in my life? How has this addiction diminished my life?
8. How would I describe my relationships with money and power?
9. How would I describe the criticism I direct to myself? What is the effect of my negative thinking on my self-esteem? How do these drive my decisions?

10. How do procrastination, perfectionism, and love of power affect my life? How have I been deceptive and tried to cover for how out of control life feels?

Step One Story I: Quantifying My Unmanageability

As part of my Step One writing, my sponsor encouraged me to quantify the impacts of the disease of work addiction on my life. Answering these questions helped me see the depth of my unmanageability and how deeply the disease had affected my life. Over the course of my Step One writing, I estimated each of the following:

1. Number of times I studied late at night.
2. Number of times I sat in a bathroom stall all night (at graduate school) working on a paper.
3. Number of times I worked all night in my current job.
4. Number of times I worked all night.
5. Number of times I worked until late evening.
6. Number of times I worked until early morning.
7. Number of times I made mistakes due to being tired.
8. Number of times I worked all night and all the next day.
9. Number of days I did not see my infant son, because I was working late.
10. Number of times I came home too late to spend time with my kids ("bucking bronco"), but went ahead and spent time with them anyway (contrary to my spouse's wishes).
11. Number of times I said I will be leaving by ____ or I will leave in _____ minutes, but did not (I worked longer).
12. Number of times I got home after dinner had already started (with grandparents present).
13. Number of times I would stay up even later, after getting home late.
14. Number of times I consumed a lot of caffeinated pop.
15. Number of calories consumed eating sweet foods when tired or stressed.
16. Number of hours spent watching TV to escape.
17. Number of years lost in building relationships with my spouse and children.
18. Amount of lost wages due to probation or lack of promotion.
19. Number of times I have given excuses (lies) for being late.
20. Number of hours I have made people late or kept people waiting because I was late.

21. Number of times I procrastinated about doing tasks for one of my "moonlighting" jobs.
22. Number of fatigue related accidents I have experienced.
23. Net profit from "moonlighting" jobs.
24. Cost (interest expense or lost interest income) of not submitting expenses for reimbursement in a timely manner.
25. Cost to send things by express mail.
26. Cost of health problems due to work addiction.
27. Cost of eating in employee cafeteria versus at home.
28. Number of hours of life lost due to overwork, illness, TV watching, errand/shopping during work time, reading the paper (or other publications for personal reasons) at work.
29. Number of times my tax returns have been way overdue.
30. Number of projects that have been late.
31. Number of times I have been late to work.
32. Number of days I have avoided one or more tasks.
33. Number of times I have tried to hide the fact that I was eating in my office.
34. Number of times I have tried to avoid getting caught arriving late to work and hid reading the newspaper on the job.
35. Number of times I have been in a panic or whirlwind.
36. Number of times I have been reprimanded (e.g., for being late, taking too long, not communicating my whereabouts, completing projects late).

Step One Story II: Insanity, Feeling, and Sanity – A Step One Writing Process

It did not dawn on me how unmanageable my life had become until my friend searched out a recovery program for workaholics and gave me the contact information. The turning point came while on a weekend vacation with her in Los Angeles. I had wanted to remain in the passenger seat of her parked car "to prepare my notes for the following week's workload" as she attended an hour-long recovery meeting.

By the time I read the W.A. flyer (answering "yes" to all but three questions), I knew that I had a problem. The memories of my poor choices started to flow. Sponsors are few in my W.A. program, but after attending meetings for a couple of months, our program grew enough to develop seasoned sponsors. My sponsor encouraged me to work the Steps. In Step One, I identified where I was powerless over this deadly disease and how my life had become unmanageable. Below

I have outlined the process I went through while identifying my powerless behavior.

1. With a small notebook in hand, I went about my normal day jotting down moments when/where I found myself powerless over work or activity. My problem was clearest to me when my intention did not match my actions. The most obvious entries were how often I lost track of time and neglected self-care, such as staying at work during late evening hours and eating my lunch in the mid-afternoon instead of at noon.

2. In the evening at home I sorted the list into three columns, answering the following questions:
    a. What was the insane activity?
    b. What were my feelings/emotions during the time of the activity?
    c. By contrast, what would have been a sane action plan?

Below is an example of my list:

Insane Activity	Feeling/ Emotion	Sane Activity
Leaving work at 8 PM	Tired, anxious, hungry	Leave work at 5 PM; begin to wrap up at 4:30 (not 5) PM
Eating Lunch at 2:30 PM	Hurried, under pressure, very hungry, cranky, irritable	Eat lunch at 12 PM; leave work environment to avoid temptation to return to work early
Departing late to an event	Rushed, anxious, angry at conductor/traffic over slow speed	Plan on arriving ½ hour before event begins, leave extra early, commit to meeting friends earlier for event

| Three events on one weekend: Saturday - long bike ride; Sunday - brunch date in morning and Super Bowl party in afternoon | Excited, rushed, exhausted at night, hungry at times. No time to organize, prepare, or wrap-up | Choosing one social event for the weekend. Allowing unscheduled time for unexpected self-care and nourishing activities (such as walk on the beach, café stop, etc.). |

As the weeks progressed, my list began to grow and I was forced to take a hard, honest look at my choices. It was very disheartening to realize my powerlessness.

3.   At this point, it was extremely important to have support. My sponsor was encouraging and compassionate. Through her, I was able not only to see the signs of this disease, but also to be gentle with myself as I took note of my choices. She kindly reminded me that my addiction is a chemical addiction, like alcoholism. I was addicted to the adrenaline rush my body experienced while maintaining the desire to be busy constantly.

4.   Practicing gentleness. The easiest way for me to determine whether an activity was sane is by asking myself what kind of advice I would give a four-year-old child in my care. Ninety percent of the time, I would suggest eating, resting, and taking care of her body, before attending to a task or a planned event. I just never followed this advice before W.A.

A synopsis of my W.A. Step One process would include:

1.   Recording behaviors in a notebook.
2.   Sorting behaviors into three columns: insane activity, feelings/emotion, and sane activity.
3.   Getting support through sponsorship or with other W.A. members.
4.   Being gentle with myself.

Slowly, I began to see my vulnerabilities and realized that battling this disease cannot be done on my will power alone. I needed guidance from someone that could help create sanity in my life. I was ready for Step Two.

Step Two

**Came to believe that a Power greater than ourselves
could restore us to sanity.**

Step Two introduces us to the concept that a Power greater than ourselves alone provides hope for our sanity and balance. For workaholics accustomed to self-sufficiency and pride in self-reliance, this can be difficult to understand. In the beginning, some will think a Power greater than ourselves indicates a religious entity, but it does not. We are free to determine what restores us to sanity. We come to believe in a Deeper Power: a loving guidance that helps us to deal with the addiction of workaholism.

There are almost as many names for Higher Power as there are W.A. members: Universal Wisdom, Higher Power, Deeper Power, The Great Spirit, Great Mystery, God, Goddess, and many more. For some of us, our W.A. group is our Higher Power.

We tried many other solutions: changing jobs, changing schedules, quitting work altogether, hiding from life. Nothing helped for more than a short time. Belief in a Power greater than us is the antidote to our disease. We find ourselves believing in other things: the goodness of our fellow human beings and the positive aspects of life. We find the courage to reach out to others and get the help we need to recover.

For many of us, faith is a foreign concept. It is not necessary to take Step Two all at once. If we are willing to believe in a Power greater than ourselves and allow that belief to grow in us over time, we are surprised at how our world expands.

Many of us come to Step Two with baggage. We are disillusioned with the religion of our childhood. We do not believe in a Higher Power. Or perhaps we believe, in our suffering, that God has abandoned us. W.A. does not tell us we must believe in any particular concept of a Higher Power; however, we have found that we must believe in something beyond our addicted mind that restores us to sanity.

Step Two Questions

1. Using the work I did in Step One, I can draw a line down the center of a piece of paper, labeling one side "sanity" and the other side "insanity." What are examples of how I know when I

am behaving sanely or insanely? What is a list of anything I do or think that is destructive to myself or to others such as: compulsive behavior, obsessive thoughts (resentments, anxiety, worry, depression), or trying to control others?

2. How have I come to believe change is needed? What have I tried before coming to W.A. to control work binges, pressure, or procrastination?

3. How do false pride and shame avoidance influence my asking for help when I am feeling overwhelmed and powerless?

4. Since my willpower has not helped the consequences of my workaholism, am I willing to look for a Power greater than myself to restore me to sanity?

5. How did I initially relate to the concept of a "Higher Power"? How has my attitude changed?

6. If I do not believe in a Higher Power, how can I "act as if" I believe in one?

7. How do the tools, the telephone, meetings, sponsorship, meditation, and service restore me to sanity?

8. How do I experience belief as reliance on a Higher Power, not defiance?

9. What actions am I willing to take that others have told me worked for them?

10. How do I describe the experience of the presence of a Higher Power in my life?

Step Two Story I: Gardening as a Metaphor for a Higher Power

Gardening has been a great teacher for me. Early on, I would buy some packaged garden soil, spade up some ground, mix it, and plop down my seeds. Without too much luck. Only with luck would anything sprout and prosper. Gradually, I figured out that a garden needs to be in harmony with its location (sun or shade), the time of year (how much sun can be expected), the soil temperature (early or late in the year), the condition of the soil (wet, sandy, etc.), and the water (keep the seeds damp but not wet). The plants chosen need to be suited to this year's garden. These are just a few of a multitude of considerations. The best planning will not guarantee a garden, as there is an interworking of all these forces that is complex and miraculous. In fact, failure is the norm, not the exception. As with most things, the more you know, the more you realize there is to know – until, finally, I learned humility and wonder when thinking about a garden. The opposite to being a good gardener is to use will power (I will grow this here, now) and reasoning (if I do this and this, this will result). Will has its uses; it is what gets me down on my knees weeding or sowing. Reasoning can help me avoid the obvious mistakes, like planting sugar cane in a cold climate. But alone, they do not make a garden.

Somewhere, I came on the concept of "feeding the soil, not the plants." This made immediate sense to me, as I had noticed that when the soil feels right to the hand, the plants are happier, too. If we feed only the plants, they become too tall and fall over, are susceptible to disease and insects, and often have many leaves, but not the root, seed, or fruit that we are looking for. Untended, the soil will not absorb or retain water. It will lose the character that small and large plants need. Plants grown this way have greater food value.

I am coming to apply this philosophy to my life, especially the spiritual side. Instead of relying on my willpower and rationality, which were the tools I was taught as a child, I am trying to take an attitude similar to my gardening. It goes like this:

1. I do not assume that wanting something will make it happen.
2. I try to be patient and not immediately analyze each impasse to find a resolution.
3. I try to pay attention and watch for signs that things are going right or wrong.
4. I try to be flexible and not keep doing the same thing over and over, without any result.

My main principle is to feed the soil/soul by providing proper rest, food, play, love, friends, music, mental stimulation, and healthy support – at the very least. Then comes the selection of what to plant, or how to direct my life, which needs to take into account my appetites, strength, and energy. Then there is the pruning of old stuff so that it does not crowd or shade this year's garden. This old growth includes retained anger, past trauma, and old stress. It must not be dug up and discarded, but needs to be brought into something I can work with and around.

Also, there is weeding in order to avoid the competition of addictions, being rushed, and not having time for the continued care of the seedbed/soul or the time to enjoy what is growing in the garden.

This is as close as I can come right now to the concept of a Higher Power. The Power is both outside me in the miracle of life and inside me as a small voice that leads me to question the forces of will and reason. This Power feels mysterious and unknowable. It was either given in my genes or it comes from elsewhere.

Step Two Story II: Steps One and Two and a Higher Power

From the beginning, I was drawn to accept Step One. Even before attending my first meeting, I had known there was something wrong. I was working all the time, even though I wished I could relax and be comfortable with myself and with others. As an excuse, I always said to myself, "That is the way I am." It finally became clear to me that I was unable to change. Each time I "turned over a new leaf," another one was revealed that looked just like the one before. There were plenty of reasons to make changes, both in terms of my peace of mind and my relationships with loved ones, but the pattern of being obsessed by working resisted all my efforts to change. I had reached a place where I expected to experience peace: my children were on their own as young adults, my health was good, and I had reasonable financial security. Yet, the work addiction lost none of its power.

When I first went to a W.A. meeting, I had an immediate recognition; this was something I had been looking for. I am 78 years old. I was young enough in spirit to aspire to a fuller life, despite the years spent in getting set in my ways. One of these long-held patterns was my extreme self-reliance, which showed up as continuous self-employment. Another was a belief that reason and logic were my best tools for solving life's problems. Reliance on logic was part of my early education and a method I had used successfully to hold my family and business together. However, these attitudes were keeping me from seeing any evidence of a Higher Power. Having accepted Step One, that I was unable to achieve sanity on my own, I believed I could move on to Step Two only if I could honestly grasp the concept of a Higher Power. I tried to go around Step Two, thinking, "It will come." But actively seeking a Higher Power left me frustrated. I tried prayer, but it seemed artificial. I was embarrassed that I could not feel what I was saying in prayer. I began to meditate regularly, starting the day off in a more serene way. I felt as though I was moving in the right direction. However, each time I would hear "Higher Power" addressed at meetings, I felt personally lacking, as though something was missing in me.

Recently, I reflected on the progress I have made since coming to W.A.: connecting to family in a stronger way, being more able to listen, not working compulsively, reaching out by volunteering at a local school, and not taking on new projects at home. I was getting positive feedback from family and friends who had noticed these changes. In going over the recent past, I stumbled on a powerful thought: some kind of magic has occurred. Some sort of catalytic event has brought me to W.A. and made me receptive to its message. These were not the result of my old problem-solving ways of perseverance and analytical logic. They seemed to come from another source altogether, and I sensed that this source was a manifestation of what I can call a Higher Power. I had been looking for something showy or dramatic, such as a vision, and had failed to see that what had actually taken place was a remarkable thing. It makes me wonder how many other events in my life went unrecognized that were similarly remarkable. This is another kind of knowledge, one that does not rely on willfulness or reasoning. I am not yet steady enough on my feet to rely on it, use it in prayer, or say a whole lot about it. But it feels like a beginning in the development of my spiritual life. This realization makes me want to be more alert, so that I will not miss similar truths that come my way.

Step Three

Made a decision to turn our will and our lives over to the care of God *as we understood God*.

The key to success in starting Step Three is willingness to turn our lives over to the care of a loving Higher Power. To "Let Go and Let God" can be difficult for workaholics, who are used to our success depending on our self-will alone. We were self-reliant to a fault. A will of steel had gotten us through long workdays and sleepless nights. If we turn our lives over to the care of a Higher Power, we were not sure who we would become.

Yet, we have found through experience that giving up our illusion of control is the sure path to serenity and recovery. When we turn to our Higher Power, we are able to let go of the outcomes of our endeavors and enjoy the process of living.

In moments when difficult feelings arise, we are tempted to turn back to self-reliance. Our fear tells us we need to take charge of the situation and that we cannot trust God. We learn in W.A. that it does not matter how many times we take back our will and our lives, as long as we turn them over again. Eventually, we realize that our Higher Power is always watching over and protecting us, whether or not we are aware of it. We can choose to live in anxiety and fear, or we can open our eyes to the reality that we are cared for and loved at every moment.

It is often recommended that people read through Step Three on pages 60-64 in the Big Book of A.A. and the chapter on Step Three in A.A.'s *Twelve Steps and Twelve Traditions* as preparation for writing on this Step. Below are two quotations:

> When we sincerely took such a position, all sorts of remarkable things followed. We had a new Employer. Being all powerful, He provided what we needed, if we kept close to Him and performed His work well. (*Alcoholics Anonymous* 63)

> God, I offer myself to Thee – to build with me and to do with me as Thou wilt. Relieve me of the bondage of self, that I may better do Thy will. Take away my difficulties, that victory over them may bear witness to those I would help of Thy Power, Thy Love, and Thy Way of life. May I do Thy will always! (*Alcoholics Anonymous* 63)

Step Three Questions

1. Consider the slogan, "Let Go and Let God." This can be difficult for workaholics, who are used to their success depending on self-will alone. In what ways am I willing to adopt new attitudes toward work and activities?
2. What barriers remain that block my relationship with a Higher Power? Anxiety over giving up self-determination? Difficulty trusting? An unworkable definition of a Higher Power? Old habits? No experience with a caring Higher Power? How does surrendering to a Power greater than myself feel to me?
3. Create a balance sheet. On one side, list my reasons for believing in God. On the other side, list my reasons to and my beliefs that keep a Higher Power out of my life.
4. How do I "play God"? What is dependence, and how can dependence on a Higher Power lead to greater independence?
5. How do I describe the God of my understanding? Do I need a more loving, forgiving, available experience of a Higher Power? What would that look like?
6. How do my work and activities create an illusion of power and control?
7. Am I still trying to handle each problem myself, or am I asking for the help of coworkers and my Higher Power for guidance?

8. What are the signs that tell me I am working from ego, willpower, and pressure? What are the signs that tell me when I have turned my will and my life over to the care of God?

9. Do I invite the presence of God by thinking of God as my employer? Do I begin each day with a prayer, listing what I feel grateful for and asking how I can be of service? Do I take time to cultivate a relationship with my Higher Power? How do I use the Serenity Prayer?

10. Do I misuse willpower, bombarding my problems with it instead of attempting to bring it into agreement with God's universal wisdom? Do I pray for what I want, rather than using meditation and other spiritual disciplines to become teachable and open to the support of a caring Higher Power?

Step Three Story: Living in Divine Flow

A Human Doing

At some point, our feelings became submerged in our non-stop activity. We lost touch with our being and became a human doing.

This transition came gradually. As long as we were enmeshed in schedules, goals, and quotas, we did not notice that our sense of self is missing. We cannot even feel our numbness. This is not like the cry of pleasure deprivation – "Is this all?" – after a grueling week. Rather, this is the profound loss of being that comes after years of not connecting with one's self and of turning a deaf ear to the pleas of our family and friends to stop killing ourselves with overdoing.

The pain of this loss may hit us during bed rest, a quiet vacation, or retirement – all of which were probably initiated against our will. Some of us describe it as the emptiness of feeling unreal, as if we were robots with a dead battery. Our reason for existence – our functionality – was gone and we were lost without it. We did not know how to live in a world we cannot control by agendas, deadlines, organizational charts, and machines. We have no idea how to just be.

Recovery

Recovering what we have lost takes time and patience. So does learning new ideas – generally the opposite of what we have believed:

1. We make haste by not being in a hurry.
2. Efficiency is not effectiveness.

3. The more we take it easy, the more we accomplish.
4. The more overwhelmed we are, the more we need to take a break.
5. Worry causes problems, not vice versa.
6. The more we surrender to time, the more we become its master.
7. Freedom lies not in knowing we can do whatever we want, but in knowing we are doing what our heart leads us to do.
8. The highest form of control is surrendering all control.

Surrender

Once we have worked the Steps and surrendered our life and our will to our Higher Power, we begin to live not merely more slowly, but more "flowly." This means acting from love instead of ego, letting things unfold by effortless effort, moving at a comfortable pace, and allowing time to savor experience. When we stop resisting the flow of life and cooperate with it, we experience more energy – not driven energy or an adrenaline rush, but pure energy.

For those of us who are used to forcing, experiencing effortlessness may be the hardest thing we have ever done. We are not used to being receptive, and we want to take back control. Yet, by getting out of our own way, all is accomplished.

Living flowly helps us recognize our direction and, thereby, make correct choices. We no longer suffer from "experience greed" – wanting to do everything – because we are content with what we have. Before, we feared contentment and valued dissatisfaction as a spur to ambition. Now, we realize that, as we move to our next stage, the unnecessary falls away. We no longer try to push growth. For once, we experience an absence of struggle, and we enjoy it.

We eventually understand that it is useless to desire anything but God's will, because nothing else will bring us the feeling of being in the right place at the right time and the feeling that what we are doing is what we are supposed to be doing. We may have achieved what we thought would make us happy. However, without this feeling of rightness, we only feel hollowness. We learn to want what we have rather than be concerned with having what we want.

Harmony

Living flowly is being in rhythm: our mind, heart, and body act in harmony with divine Power. We know when to be active and when to be still; each phase is part of the whole and nourishes the other phase. We carry our stillness into our activity and our aliveness into our repose. We trust our being to guide our doing. We use our will to become willing.

We make a daily appointment with our Higher Power and listen to Its guidance. We schedule our priorities instead of prioritizing our schedule. Our priorities include breathers, time for just sitting, and time to make sure we are still connected with our being. We become the best boss we have ever had.

Living flowly means doing the work we are born to do – work we would do for free or pay to do, if we had to, and work in which we lose track of time because we are filled with joy. It means carrying a surrendered attitude into routine chores. We welcome such tasks because they do not totally absorb us. They create a fertile void from which we receive breakthrough ideas.

This mode of living connects us with nature and divine order. Regaining our lost sense of wholeness makes us comfortable with solitude and silence. Before, there was shallow chatter and busyness; now, there is depth and presence.

Rewards

Living flowly gives us time to:

1. Recognize the messages of our emotions and body sensations.
2. Retain our self-awareness and perspective and not become enmeshed in events.
3. Hear intent as well as content and build empathy.
4. Realize the impact of our decisions, speech, and actions.
5. Act spontaneously and be more flexible in recognizing opportunities.
6. Find meaning in routine events.
7. Delight in surprise and revive our sense of wonder and playfulness.
8. Enjoy small and simple pleasures.
9. Remember our dreams.
10. Celebrate, grieve, and put closure to experiences.
11. Discover heightened relevance in synchronicity.
12. Become a friend to time.
13. Allow significant memories to emerge.
14. Practice masterly inactivity.

Growth

The spiritual awakenings in Step Three may be bittersweet. We see how impoverished we have become, and how much of the richness of everyday living we have denied ourselves. As we realize that regret is a sign of growth, it eases the pain.

We may become impatient and try to hurry the process. As society's pace accelerates, we may fear being left behind. However, we cannot speed up our slowing down. We will eventually sense that our rhythm is perfect.

We look back at those crowded, blurry days as a bad dream. We feel we have been raised from the living dead – and we have. That human doing seems to be a stranger. How could we have been so cruel to ourselves and to those around us? Then, we remember the perceived payoffs: self-importance from being surrounded by piles of work; an adrenaline rush when we worked against deadlines; admiration for our untiring dedication; feelings of indispensability, self-sufficiency, and invincibility; and the illusion that we could ignore time and space. Now these seem to be paltry rewards for the price we paid in self-alienation, broken health, and lost relationships.

We acknowledge the teachings of workaholism. We grieve our lesson years. We celebrate our new way of living: by keeping our conscious contact with our Higher Power. We nurture our mind, heart, and body. We cherish the people in our lives. We stay grateful that we have been given a second chance through W.A.

Step Four

Made a searching and fearless moral inventory of ourselves.

The following questions are meant to be helpful to the recovering workaholic who is ready to work the Fourth Step. It is advisable to have a sponsor or to be working the Steps in a group with others who have worked the Fourth Step. This set of questions is meant to be a guide. It is best to have worked the first three Steps; turning our will and our lives over to a Power greater than ourselves helps enhance the "fearless" part of this inventory.

The inventory begins by listing our present resentments, guilt feelings, and fears. In this Step, as we name our attitudes and write about our patterns, both helpful and unhelpful, we begin to understand ourselves better. As we move through our Fourth, Fifth, and Sixth Steps, and as we practice the other parts of the program – meetings, action plans, meditation, surrender, and getting help – we notice we have become freer of these character defects and more appreciative of our strengths. The promises of true serenity and a healthy, balanced life will be ours.

Many of us begin by using the Step Four guidelines on pages 64-71 of A.A.'s *Alcoholics Anonymous*. We write our answers. The following set of questions can be used as a guide. Further guidance is available in the Step Four chapter of A.A.'s *Twelve Steps and Twelve Traditions*.

Step Four Questions

Resentments

1. We begin by listing our resentments, fears, and shame. The columns described in the Big Book are very helpful. Part of an example follows:

I am resentful at:	The cause, event:	Affects my (Options include self-esteem, ambition, pride, security, personal relations, sex relations)
Sam, my boss	Fired me	Self-esteem, finances (security), pride
My partner	Bugs me about work	Self-esteem, relationships

Additional columns include identifying "My Part" and "Related Character Defects."

2. What were the patterns of resentment and anger in my family of origin? (E.g., silence then rage, retaliation, passive resistance and acting out, and blaming others.)

3. What are common triggers for my anger and patterns of expressing it?

4. What is my definition of healthy expression of anger and resentments? In what ways have I been respectful and assertive with my anger?

5. How have resentments taken up space in my daily thoughts?
6. Can I express anger without blame or criticism?
7. Am I a conflict avoider, pleasing others at any cost?

Fear

1. How do I experience fear? What patterns of fear, worry, immobilization, procrastination, and anxiety do I have?
2. Is there a family history of fear and anxiety?
3. Where has self-reliance failed me?
4. What and whom do I trust? How have the experiences of surrender, prayer, and meditation led to an increase in my serenity?

Sex

1. Reviewing my past experiences, have I been selfish, dishonest, or inconsiderate about my sexual behavior? Have I taken health risks? Have I aroused jealousy?
2. Do I take my considerations about sex to my Higher Power for guidance?
3. Do I use work to avoid sex? Am I too depleted by work to have a healthy sexual relationship? What has been my pattern of work and worry, and how has it affected my sex and love life? Am I jealously possessive?
4. Can I now enjoy sex that is not manipulative?

Shame

1. What gets in the way of accepting myself as a limited human being who makes mistakes?
2. Can I make mistakes and be imperfect, and still be lovable and forgivable?
3. "We are as sick as our secrets." What major secrets do I have?

Other Questions

1. What am I grateful for?
2. How am I a perfectionist? How does perfectionism feed my patterns of procrastination?
3. For what have I begun to forgive myself? What are some of the origins of my behaviors?
4. Whom do I still need to forgive?

5. What percentage of my thoughts are negative – fearful, resentful, self-critical, and judgmental? Am I sensitive to criticism? Make a list of examples of self-hatred and self-abuse.

6. Do I trust others or situations to work out?

7. How has workaholism affected my pride? How has workaholism affected my ego?

8. To live in balance, I need to feel proud of my achievements and contributions. Make a list of them, letting the self-critic rest.

9. What is a list of my positive attributes (generous, caring, recovering, etc.)?

10. How have substances such as caffeine, recreational drugs, nicotine, and/or alcohol been a pattern in my workaholism?

11. How have food, debting, and/or gambling been factors in my workaholism?

12. How do I set limits on the allocation of my time and energy?

13. Am I power hungry? How do I react when I do not get my own way?

14. How do I try to maintain control of situations and people? What is my pattern, and what was the pattern in my family of origin?

15. In what ways have I been honest? In what ways have I been dishonest?

16. Do I let the needs of others take over, while ignoring my own needs?

17. Have I been unavailable to my children or partners?

18. What is my relationship with time? Was I frequently late? Over-scheduled? How did the reality of ignoring time serve me?

19. How have I avoided taking responsibility for my behavior? My denial? My blame? My distraction? My dishonesty? My rationalization? In what ways do I admit mistakes?

20. What is my relationship to money? Am I debting? Am I a money anorexic who is afraid to earn or spend money?

Step Four Story: Gentleness Tools, Coping Skills, and Character Assets

Gentleness Collage

Before I began my Fourth Step writing, my sponsor gave my Higher Power and me an art project: making a Gentleness Collage. The assignment was to gather images, words, ideas, and, yes, activities that were ways I could be nourishing and gentle with myself. I got out crayons and pens, prayed, crafted words on paper, cut out images from magazines, drew, and glued. Some of the things in my gentleness collage included:

1. Sitting in the garden
2. Taking a nap
3. Walking in the nearby park
4. Picking a bouquet of flowers
5. Taking a soothing bath
6. Reading from comforting books
7. The qualities of kindness, compassion, fun, and joy
8. Images for inspiration
9. Images reminding me of my Higher Power

I placed my Gentleness Collage in a prominent place in my room. My sponsor suggested that I be or do something represented in the collage after each time I worked on my Fourth Step. My Gentleness Collage became my companion through my Step writing, reminding me that the Fourth Step is not a litany of how bad I am (as my developmentally arrested inner addict tended to think), but a neutral snapshot of all resentment, anger, lingering feelings, and fear that stand in the way of my conscious contact with my Higher Power. It was a great way of practicing what was to become a living amends to myself: being internally gentle with myself and cultivating a climate of inner compassion – a practice that I continue to deepen today.

Changing My Language To "Negative Coping Skill"

I had a difficult time with the language of "character defect" in Step Four because the English language I use is a cousin to the language of the original A.A. Big Book authors, and because I am a survivor of intense verbal abuse that I had internalized. "Character defect" seemed like character assassination instead of loving compassion. The phrase "character defect" connected me with a sense of rigidity and fixity. My sponsor offered the phrase "negative coping mechanism" or "negative coping skill" as a substitute for "character defect." This alternative language helped me approach my extensive inventory with compassion for myself, along with a sense that these behaviors were understandable coping skills that had helped me survive tough situations, outgrown their usefulness, and come to harm and hinder me from full living.

Character Assets

Additionally, my sponsor suggested I log entries of my assets ("character assets") as well as my defects ("negative coping skills"). The Big Book refers to taking a thorough inventory, as of a commercial business, not only of what is on the shelf, but also in order "to disclose damaged or unsalable goods, to get rid of them promptly and without regret" (*Alcoholics Anonymous* 64). So I added a column of assets (see below for complete list), which my sponsor asked me to use in two ways. If the entry was about an asset or a situation with a positive feeling, I wrote the asset in the last column. If the entry was about a fear or anger, for example, with an underlying negative coping mechanism, I would not only note the negative coping mechanism (e.g., illusion of indispensability), but also the potential character asset that could be involved, were I to have a healthy response or presence in a given situation (e.g., faith). As throughout my Fourth Step work, there were times when I got stumped about what to write in these particular columns, so I asked my sponsor for help and filled them in as I was doing my Fifth Step. In this way, my Fourth and Fifth Steps were a real learning opportunity for me about healthy living and positive possibility!

Extra Columns

I found that, as I did my Fourth Step writing, I sometimes had feelings – and feelings about those feelings – layers thick. So my sponsor and I added some columns. My sponsor asked me to add a column next to "character defect" for "character asset," as described in the section above. All in all, here are the columns I used:

1. Person (can include myself)
2. Feeling (e.g., anger, fear, shame, gratitude)
3. Issue
4. Affects my (select one or more: security, ambition, self-esteem, personal relationships, sex relations)
5. My part
6. Negative coping skill (a.k.a. "character defect")
7. Character asset (potential or realized, also sometimes "positive opportunity")

I am so grateful to my sponsor for helping me learn to work my Fourth Step with compassion and gentleness!

Step Five

Admitted to God, to ourselves, and to another human being the exact nature of our wrongs.

For many of us in W.A., this Step can be a big stumbling block. Being perfectionists, we procrastinate. Many of us suffer from big egos. We use work as a way to distract ourselves from facing the reality of who we are and the pain of our past. To admit "to God, to ourselves, and to another human being the exact nature of our wrongs" can seem impossible. But if we have completed our Fourth Step inventory and have begun to apply the first three Steps to our lives, this Step will bring a sense of inner peace and self-acceptance never known before. We begin to feel truly connected to God and our fellow human beings. We feel forgiven and experience a healing humility. We become more honest and realistic about ourselves.

Some of us have done our Fourth and Fifth Step as part of a W.A. Step group. Others have given a Fifth Step to a sponsor from another program. Some of us have co-sponsored each other. Some have chosen to give away our Fourth Step to a counselor or religious leader. Some of us have worked this Step in other Twelve-Step programs but have yet to do a Fourth and Fifth Step in W.A. We put it off, without realizing we are delaying receiving the benefits that this Step can provide.

For many of us, the relief from this process is immediate and lasting. We find our relationships at work and outside of work improve, as well as our relationship to ourselves. The negative thinking that drove so many of our relentless work and planning decisions is greatly healed by doing this Step.

> The dammed up emotions of years break out of their confinement, and miraculously vanish as soon as they are exposed. As the pain subsides, a healing tranquility takes it place. And when humility and serenity are so combined, something else of a great moment is apt to occur...even those who had faith already often become conscious of God as they never were before. (*Twelve Steps and Twelve Traditions* 62)

Step Five Questions

1. With whom should I share my Step Five? My sponsor? Another trusted friend?
2. In what way can I admit my character defects to my Higher Power?
3. Recognizing that taking Step Five is an important moment in my life, how can I create space around this time in order to reflect, recover, and nurture myself? Do I want to do Step Five in one day, or spread it out over many small meetings with a trusted advisor?
4. After confiding my Step Four writing, what have I learned about the experience and myself?

Step Five Story: Reaching Out for Help

When I first joined W.A., no one at my meeting was available to take me through the Steps. So I asked a friend to help me. This woman had been in another Twelve-Step program for many years, and had helped others with the Steps. We had known each other for about four years.

When I finished my Fourth Step, I asked her if she could hear my Fifth Step. She took a deep breath. She admitted to me that she had overcommitted herself. She was going through a lot right then and did not feel she had the time to help me with the rest of the Steps. She could not hear my Fifth Step. I was not surprised. As I had started to recover in W.A., I saw this problem in her life. In the few months I had been in W.A. up until that point, I had told many of people that I had to back out of a commitment I had made. Instead of feeling angry, I understood her and I told her so. I thanked her for her help and told her I was glad she was taking care of herself.

She was surprised. My response at other times that she had let me down was anger. We could both see my recovery. I was grateful.

As soon as I hung up the phone, I got down on my knees, which I do not do very often, and prayed. I asked my Higher Power to guide me to the right person to hear my Fifth Step and to help me continue my Step work – if that was my Higher Power's will. Oddly, I seemed to be very confident that I would find the right person.

That night, I ran into someone whom I knew casually. I knew she was active in another Twelve-Step program and had helped people through the Steps. I felt she could keep a confidence and she seemed very nonjudgmental. All these things helped me feel she might be the right person. I explained my situation to her – that I was in W.A., that no one at my W.A. meeting was available to help me, and that the person who had helped me up to my Fourth Step was not available to continue. I asked if she had the time to help me. This woman said she was honored, and graciously agreed to hear my Fifth Step. We scheduled a time when we could get together.

Before that date, I sat down with my written Fourth Step. I needed to admit these things to myself and to my Higher Power. I prayed, asking my Higher Power to help me accept these things I had written down. I also asked for help in believing that my Higher Power accepts these things about me. I looked at the first item, and just sat still. I said to myself, "Yes, I have that resentment. Yes, my Higher Power knows I have this resentment. Yes, this person hurt me. Yes, I reacted selfishly." I did this sort of thing with each item in my Fourth Step. At each resentment, I prayed for the person using one of the Big Book prayers: "This is a sick man. How can I be helpful to him? God save me from being angry. Thy will be done" (*Alcoholics Anonymous* 67).

This was painful. I had to go back to Step Two many times, to remember how I came to believe that there was a Power greater than myself that loves me no matter what I have done. After sitting with each item on my Fourth Step, I felt more at peace than I had in a long time. I started to feel like my Higher Power wanted me to abstain from compulsive working every day, no matter what. I started to feel that I had the help I needed to do that. I started feeling more secure in my recovery.

When I got together with the woman I had asked to hear my Fifth Step, I felt nervous. I did not know her that well, and I worried that some of the things I had to say would upset her, or that she would judge me. I decided I would just start, and if there was anything I wanted to skip over, I would do that. I could find someone else I trusted more for those things, if I had to.

We prayed together, asking Higher Power to help us. As I told her about the things on my inventory, she asked a few questions for clarity. In some cases, I had not been able to see my part in something, and she helped me with that. She did not say much, but she did not judge me. After going through everything, she said she felt I had been very thorough, and we discussed some themes that seemed to run through many incidents in my life. We discussed how we would proceed with Steps Six and Seven.

That evening, I took some time to just sit with myself. I thanked my Higher Power for the gift of this woman in my life and for helping me through this. I looked at the first five Steps and asked myself if I had taken them to the best of my ability. Had I been thorough and honest? I felt I had been. Did I truly believe I was powerless? Yes, otherwise I never would have done this Fifth Step. Did I believe there was a Power greater than myself that was restoring me to sanity? By comparing my life before and after I came to W.A., it was clear that some Power was restoring me to more sanity, serenity, and hope. Had I made a decision to turn my will and life over to this Power? Yes, that is why I went ahead with Steps Four and Five, and why I was taking suggestions. Had I made a searching and fearless moral inventory? Yes, and I had also admitted to a Power greater than myself, to myself, and to another human being the exact nature of my wrongs.

I felt relieved. I felt grateful. I felt hopeful. This marked the beginning of sharing my struggles with others every day instead of letting things build up. I could see the benefit of reducing my isolation. I asked my Higher Power for help to continue working the program.

Step Six

Became entirely ready to have God remove all these defects of character.

This Step requires the support of the first five Steps. We admit we are powerless over work and that our lives have become unmanageable. We have come to believe in a Power greater than ourselves who could restore us to sanity. We have made a decision to turn our will and lives over to the care of a Higher Power we have come to understand. We have made a searching and fearless moral inventory of ourselves and we have admitted to ourselves, to God and to another human being the exact nature of our wrongs. There is usually a great relief from shame at this point. We are ready to continue the healing these Steps have generated so far.

This Step asks for our willingness to have God remove all our defects. As workaholics, we are often plagued with perfectionism and self-will. After working the first five Steps, we come to understand ourselves better. We realize that we are neither perfect nor secretly defective. We are human. Our character defects are made up of dysfunctional survival skills. We are hurt by our old patterns of thinking and reacting. At first, we think we would happily remove any defects of personality: the faster the better. However, this Step is not about our removal of the defects, it is about acquiring the willingness to have God remove all our defects of character. It is not about being more perfect, it is about being better able to do God's will, as we come to understand it.

We begin Step Six by making a list of all of our defects of character. We review our Fourth Step. An example of a list might be: I am afraid of rejection, so I frequently isolate; I feel safer hiding my anger, but then I act out in self-destructive ways; I cannot say "no," because I am afraid of disapproval; I do not take care of myself, skipping meals, sleep, and exercise; I lose myself in the rescue of others; I unconsciously seek adrenaline highs; I am intolerant of change; I become controlling when I am fearful; and I compulsively judge others rather than feel my shame or guilt.

We may notice a character defect we are not ready to ask God to remove. Perhaps it is because of fear of change or loss of enjoyment, or we are not sure how we would cope without it. We are reminded that we are being asked to become entirely ready to ask God to remove all of our defects of character. The naming of our defects and our willingness to have them all removed is a process of trusting that God will remove them in God's time. All of us who have done this Step have experienced relief, sometimes quickly and sometimes slowly. We have become better workers and partners. We can admit our mistakes. We cease struggling and defending ourselves. We dedicate our lives to growth and change.

> Even then the best of us will discover to our dismay that there is always a sticking point, a point at which we say, 'No, I can't give this up yet.' And we shall often tread on even more dangerous ground when we cry, 'This I will *never* give up!' Such is the power of our instincts to over-reach themselves. No matter how far we have progressed, desires will always be found which oppose the grace of God.... What we must recognize now is that we exult in some of our defects. We really love them. (*Twelve Steps and Twelve Traditions* 66)

> The moment we say, 'No, never!' our minds close against the grace of God. Delay is dangerous, and rebellion may be fatal. This is the exact point at which we abandon limited objectives, and move toward God's will for us. (*Twelve Steps and Twelve Traditions* 69)

Step Six Questions

1. Scan through the Step Four entries and extract the character defects. For each character defect, answer the following four questions:
    a. What does the defect do for me? (How is it working for me?)
    b. What does the defect do to me? (What is the negative consequence of it?)
    c. What would bottom look like with this defect? (What would happen at its severest point, if I do not allow it to be removed?)
    d. What would serenity look like? (How might my life be different once this defect is removed?)
2. For each character defect, answer questions about your willingness:
    a. How willing am I for each defect to be removed?
    b. Which character defects am I unwilling to release at this time? What benefits am I still getting from these characteristics? What would it take for me to become willing?

Step Six Story: Not All Roses and Miracles

While doing my Fifth Step, certain problems I tended to have in all of my relationships became clear (mostly due to my sponsor pointing out these themes). As I continued to live my life, some of my defects, or unsuccessful ways of dealing with people, became even more obvious to me. I heard myself saying selfish and judgmental things, but I could not stop myself. Although it seemed strange, I was clearly powerless. I could not control what came out of my mouth, and it bothered me.

Furthermore, it became clear to me that no one else was in denial about these character defects. Others around me had seen them in action for years. My selfishness and tendency to judge others were not secrets. Although perhaps I was seeing them for the first time, I could not comfort myself by claiming that no one else was hurt or affected. That was clearly not true.

This realization certainly brought me more willingness. I did not want people to think I was selfish or rude. (I had not yet gotten to the point where I did not want to *be* selfish or rude.) However, it was also pointed out to me that Step Six did not involve me removing any of my defects myself. I was as powerless over my dishonesty, desire to control others, and unwillingness to admit fault as I was over my compulsive working.

Observing myself convinced me that I was quite powerless. But did I believe a Power greater than myself could help me with this problem? Clearly, some Power had helped me with my workaholism because I had abstained from compulsive working for some time. But for certain defects, it was hard to believe my Higher Power would help me. Should I not be able to control these things by myself? What was wrong with me? But that attitude was not helpful.

What helped was asking others in W.A. to share their experiences with Steps Six and Seven with me. Because my W.A. meeting was small, I also asked people in other Twelve-Step fellowships. Some of the stories were truly impressive: defects were removed through no direct action of the person at all, only humbly asking God to remove them. Other stories did not include clear divine intervention, only the taking of suggestions made by a sponsor. But many people had experienced relief, or at least improvement. This was encouraging.

Not all stories were roses and miracles. I heard one person say that God removed his character defects in the order in which it was useful to God and to others. I was not happy about that! Why can God not remove the one that I find the most troublesome at this time?

Like many things I have learned in W.A., it does not have to make sense for it to work. I decided to try asking my Higher Power to remove all my defects of character.

As I struggled with some defects, people in my life made suggestions. For instance, perhaps if I apologized as soon as I realized I was rude, I could stop right then instead of being rude all day. Perhaps if I prayed for the people I resented, I would treat them better. Taking suggestions required a whole new level of willingness. It involved more than just allowing my Higher Power to see that I was not perfect and needed help, and more than just asking for help when I was alone in a room with my Higher Power. It involved taking action in front of other people.

Looking back over my years in recovery, I can see that I tend to go through various degrees of willingness with different character defects. If I stay in close touch with my friends in W.A., they often point out when my unwillingness to take a suggestion is holding back my recovery. I have also found that if I am not willing, I can pray for willingness. In some cases, when I am struggling with a difficult problem, I call several people until I hear a suggestion I am finally willing to take. Often, taking that one suggestion seems to make me more willing to try other suggestions that I had initially rejected.

I have found that the part of Step Six I forget most frequently is the part about allowing a Higher Power to remove the character defect. I do not have to do it myself. All I have to do is pray and take suggestions. The same Power that helps me abstain from workaholism can help me with my other problems. I never have to do it alone.

Step Seven

Humbly asked God to remove our shortcomings.

When we are entirely ready to have God remove all our defects of character through working Step Six, the next Step is to humbly ask the God of our understanding to remove our shortcomings. In Step Six, we workaholics often fight our self-will and pride. In Step Seven, we can experience the value of humility. We are a people preoccupied with power and prestige in our own accomplishments. We believed we were the one shaping our own destiny, demanding recognition, admiration, and control over everyone, risking our health and perhaps the health of others. Our striving was to control time, people's behavior, and the outcome of everything. There was never enough time, money, or love. We were never enough. Our addiction to work or avoiding work shut down our feelings, from joy to frustration.

Workaholics are not usually comfortable with humility. Yet this is the cornerstone to our becoming truly happy. Humility is the key to abstaining from compulsive work and worry. To be truly humble is to get really honest with ourselves and accept who we are. We are recovering workaholics with dysfunctional ways of coping, self-destructive patterns of thinking and doing, and shortcomings that have gotten in the way of our usefulness to the greater good. Humility is a cousin to surrender. We surrender our shortcomings to a loving God of our understanding, knowing they will be removed. We are putting God first, not ourselves. We do this not by wishing or thought but by positive prayer. Some of us even get on our knees and say A.A.'s "Seventh Step prayer":

> My Creator, I am now willing that you should have all of me, good and bad. I pray that you now remove from me every single defect of character which stands in the way of my usefulness to you and my fellows. Grant me strength, as I go out from here, to do your bidding. Amen. (*Alcoholics Anonymous* 76)

Some of us then list these shortcomings slowly and then imagine in prayer what our life freed of these shortcomings could be like. In that time of "conscious contact" we can be greatly helped to experience our essential selves humbly living a new life free of our addiction and free of the characteristics that hurt us and hurt others.

We may pray to be free of resentment:

> If you have a resentment you want to be free of, if you will pray for the person or the thing that you resent, you will be free. If you will ask in prayer for everything you want for yourself to be given to them, you will be free. Ask for their health, their prosperity, their happiness, and you will be free. Even when you don't really want it for them and your prayers are only words and you don't mean it, go ahead and do it anyway. Do it every day for two weeks, and you will find you have come to mean it and to want it for them, and you will realize that where you used to feel bitterness and resentment and hatred, you now feel compassionate understanding and love. (*Alcoholics Anonymous* 552)

Step Seven Questions

1. Looking back over my Step Six list of character defects, are there some defects of character that I have already released? Are there other character defects I am ready today to turn over? What shortcomings am I honestly still attached to?
2. Character defects can sometimes feel like defining characteristics. Reflecting for a moment on who I am at my core, what is important about who I am as a person and the person I will be without holding on to my shortcomings?
3. How is my life enriched by the experience of humility and surrender?
4. How can I truly have the willingness to have God remove all my shortcomings? What are the obstacles to willingness? What simple action can I take to move myself toward willingness?

5. What can my sponsor, my meeting, and other W.A. program members do to support me in this process? How can I reach out for assistance in truly letting go? Can the experiences of others help me walk through this Step?

Step Seven Story: From Contraction to Arms-Wide Embrace

One way my sponsor coached me to approach Step Seven was to consider why Step Six in itself was not sufficient. In Step Six, I become willing to have the Source of all creation remove my negative coping mechanisms from me.

In working Step Six, I had combed through my Fourth Step – which of course, being a workaholic, I summarized in an Excel spreadsheet that had 400+ alphabetical, unique entries by character defect (negative coping mechanism, a.k.a. liability) and character asset. I scanned the entries. I was really ready to release some of the coping mechanisms, having fully understood how they harmed me. I pondered how others still served me and wrote in my journal on that topic. Upon further reflection, I became ready, in Higher Power's time, to become a fundamentally different person than I had been as a practicing addict.

For me, Step Seven went beyond Step Six because part of my spiritual awakening means releasing my negative coping mechanism of "playing God" (which is related to other defects such as "center of the universe," egoism, egotism, self-will run riot, illusion of control, etc.). Just because I had a willingness to have the defects of character removed in Step Six did not mean that they were instantaneously removed. Step Seven was lived out of Step Three, in which I turned my life and will over to the care of the benevolent universe. Part of the motion of Step Seven was a motion of surrender. I approached my connection to the immense fabric of creation "humbly," with an acknowledgment that I could not skillfully run the whole universe, or even remove one defect by my own will alone. I engaged a larger flow of spiritual power, and "asked God to remove (my) shortcomings." Step Seven helped released me from the imprisoning isolation of workaholism's island of self-centered fear and the illusion of control. As I worked Steps One through Six, I learned that the end run of the "playing God" pattern, which is at the core of my disease, is being cut off from the larger flow of life, from intuition, energy, and guidance. This pattern makes my life smaller and smaller and my vision and my body more and more constricted.

Through working the Steps, though, this process of contraction and dis-ease was brought to a stop on a daily basis. The motion of Step Seven was an outward sweep of my arms to embrace a larger spiritual Source with the power to lift the patterns of the illness. Humility for me is not my head bowed, feeling bad and wrong. Humility for me is an outward swinging, arm opening, heart opening welcome of the larger resource of energy, life force, balanced knowing, and deepening that comes from my reconnection with a Power greater than myself. I put down the defects and I became open to receive daily blessings of balance, clarity, groundedness and wholeness. By working Step Seven, I opened up more deeply and wholly to Divine Will, allowing source energy to more fully flow through me. I go beyond the willingness and humility that was enforced by pain, to a heart-centered openness that promises a different daily experience. The practice of surrender, of opening, which is at the heart of my taking of Step Seven has been the healing and balm that has nourished my re-patterning to health. As my sponsor reminds me, that motion toward partnership with Higher Power, condensed in the wisdom of Step Three and Step Seven, can be engaged as a practice of daily renewal, in prayer and in living from assets, one day at a time.

Step Eight

Made a list of all persons we had harmed, and became willing to make amends to them all.

After we have humbly asked God to remove our shortcomings in Step Seven, we turn our attention to our relationships. In our past experiences of long hours, frantic deadlines, stress depletion, and burnout, we had little time to nurture healthy relationships with other people. Even as we begin to work and schedule ourselves more realistically, many of us discover we cannot deal with the pressures of life or the pain of our past. If we are to stay in a healthy relationship to work, activity, and other people, we need to take an action on those patterns that bring harm to others and ourselves.

We begin Step Eight by making a list of all persons we had harmed, including ourselves, because of our addictions and/or character defects. Most of us go back over our Fourth Step inventories and list the names we had written there, including our own.

The next action of Step Eight is to become willing to make amends to all the people on our list. It means being willing to see our part in the problem. It means having compassion for the other person and forgiving them and ourselves. We begin to admit that we are human with character defects and that we make mistakes. We begin to experience the inner calm that comes with forgiveness. Step Eight calls us to become willing to make amends to "all" the people on the list. Most of us have found that real serenity comes when we can finally truly and completely forgive everyone. When we are not yet ready to forgive, we pray for the willingness.

This is a two-part Step: first the list, then the willingness to make amends. Amends can mean we are truly sorry. As we progress through the Steps, we admit our character defects with the help of our relationship with our Higher Power. Most of us define amends to mean a change in our thoughts and behaviors – a change in the way we live, in which we do not harm ourselves or others. Although it is very meaningful for others to hear us say we are sorry, a greater impact occurs when people see the changes we make in our lives, as the character defects and addictions are removed. Step Eight is not about deciding exactly what the amends will be, whether direct, indirect, or living. That is the activity of Step Nine. Step Eight focuses us on our spiritual condition: our willingness to do our part in healing from this fatal affliction.

Step Eight Questions

1. Going back over my Fourth Step, whom have I harmed?
2. What are my patterns of doing harm to others?
3. To whom am I not willing to make amends? How does holding onto that resentment hurt me?
4. Rank each needed amends by level of willingness: Am I completely willing, somewhat willing, or not willing at all?
5. How have I harmed myself? Am I willing to make amends to myself?
6. Have I gotten help from a sponsor with this Step? What are other stories of strength and hope in doing Step Eight?
7. Am I willing to make amends for only my part in the relationship problem?
8. How does progressing through the Twelve Steps in W.A. help maintain spiritual and physical changes?

Step Eight Story: Cultivating Honest Willingness

I was hoping that all my character defects would be removed before I started on Step Eight. But it became clear that I would never get to

Step Eight if I waited until I was perfect. A couple of months after my Fifth Step, I had experienced improvement in some of my character defects. There were instances where I could see that my changed behavior prevented what would have otherwise been an unavoidable problem with someone. I could see how my relationships had improved, and I wanted to mend some of the previous harm I had caused. I discussed this with my sponsor and others in W.A. Most people agreed it made sense to start an Eighth Step list.

I set aside some time one weekend and sat down with my Fourth Step. I started going through it, using it to remind me of the people to whom I might owe amends. I wrote down the names of people and organizations to which I felt I owed amends. I included anyone from whom I had stolen something, people to whom I did not deliver what I had promised (such as a work product), people whom I had clearly hurt, and people with whom I had bad relationships. After each name I wrote a brief sentence as a reminder of what amends I felt I owed. In some cases, I owed one person amends for several separate things. The list looked something like this:

> Marcie, coworker: Did not give her report I promised.
> Eric, coworker: Never followed up with promised information.
> John, coworker: Never followed up with promised information.
> Mark, product vendor: Never followed through with purchase, as promised.
> Peter, husband: Promised to spend time with him and then worked instead; constantly told him what to do.
> Employer: Lied on my timesheet and so was paid for work I did not do.
> Jeff, roommate: Left my stuff all over the house; left the fridge a mess.
> Mary, friend: Promised to make her a clock. Made it, but never gave it to her.
> Teresa, friend: Promised to make her a piece of art. Never made it.
> Pat, friend: Promised to meet for coffee several times and forgot to go.
> Andrea, friend: Promised to buy her something, but when I took her to the mall I made her pay for it.
> Lisa, boss: Gossiped about her behind her back
> Laura, coworker: Gossiped about her behind her back.
> Amy, coworker: Gossiped about her behind her back.

Barbara, coworker: Gossiped about her behind her back.
Caroline, coworker: Gossiped about her behind her back.

After I had finished making the list, I arranged to meet with my sponsor. We went over the list. I told her very briefly about each amends. She had questions about some of them. She asked me for some details that did not seem important to me, such as exactly what I had said to someone or what I had done after I let them down. She asked me about some people on my Fourth Step, as well as other people in my life who she thought might need an amends but were not on my list. This discussion helped me complete the list and determine whether or not I really owed each of these people amends.

Then my sponsor asked me which amend on the list seemed like the easiest: not the one I wanted to do the most or the one that seemed the most urgent, but the easiest. She suggested my friend Mary might be the easiest. I had promised to make her a present (a clock) and I had made it but never given it to her. We were on good terms, so all I had to do was call her and arrange to give it to her. This made sense.

I certainly was not willing to make all my amends right then, but I thought I might be willing to make amends to Mary. My sponsor and I discussed exactly what that amends might involve. There were no hard feelings between Mary and me, and I had not promised to get her the present within any specific amount of time. My sponsor suggested that I discuss this anonymously with a couple of other people who had experience making amends, so that I could get the perspective of others before I decided what I wanted to do. She also suggested that I start praying for Mary every day in preparation.

It seemed ridiculous to call other people and discuss such a little thing with them. It also felt embarrassing. How many people were going to know about my stupid behavior? But I had learned previously that it could prevent a lot of problems to discuss my plans with someone who is outside of a situation. So I prayed for willingness. I eventually thought of a couple of people with whom I could discuss this. I called one of them and explained the situation. I asked if she had ever had to make amends in a similar situation. She had not. But she thought my plan of calling Mary and arranging to give her the present made sense. I called someone else who said the same thing. So I called my sponsor, and discussed my plan with her.

When it came time to make the phone call to arrange to give Mary the present, I was a little scared. I had to get on my knees and ask my

Higher Power for help to make the phone call. Once I did that, I was willing. I picked up the phone and arranged to meet with her.

I became willing to make one amends at a time. After making the amends to Mary, other amends seemed more possible. As I progressed to the more difficult and complicated amends, I spent more time discussing things with my sponsor, seeking out people who had made a similar amends so I could hear their experiences, and contemplating my options. For each one, I first had to become willing to look honestly at what I had done to hurt this person. Then I had to become willing to consider all the different ways I could make amends – even the scarier, more direct ways. Then, I had to become willing to make the amends in the way that was the most generous and effective. For each amend, I had to pray for willingness at each point in the process. I found it helpful to pray for the person I had injured. Then I had to trust that my Higher Power would provide me with the willingness and perspective to make this amends at the right time. Discussing my fears with others also helped develop my willingness.

The last amends I became willing to look at was the one to my employer for lying on my time sheet. While I had worked overtime for all my previous employers, my current employer was the only one that had paid me for hours I claimed to have worked but had not actually worked. It was my first episode of long-term work avoidance.

One person suggested the first task was to sit down with my time sheets and my records and look at how much I had actually overstated my work hours. How could I become willing to make an amends if I did not know how big a financial issue it might be? I had a year's worth of records to go through. About once a week, I set aside an hour to go through my records. Each time, I had to pray for willingness. At the end of the hour, I put things away and asked for help not to think about this until the next hour I had set aside for the task.

Thinking about this amends too much filled me with fear. Each time that fear came up, I told myself that I had set aside one hour a week to work on this and the rest of the time my Higher Power can work on it. All I had to do was my part, and trust that I would receive guidance and willingness at the right time. I did not have to be willing to make amends right now.

I compared my timesheets to my records of computer use, my phone log, and my date book. Some weeks I had worked *more* than I had claimed. I wrote that down. Other weeks I had worked less than I had claimed. I wrote that down, too. I did not try to do it perfectly. In some cases, I had to estimate or guess. I did not worry about that. I did the best I could with the information I had. It took me many months to complete this exercise. When I was done, I added it all up. I had been paid for many hundreds of hours more than I had actually worked. When I multiplied that by my hourly wage, I saw that I potentially owed my employer almost one-fifth of my annual salary.

I was very upset and called a W.A. friend right away. Just hearing an understanding voice on the other end of the line was helpful. My friend reassured me that I was still a good person, and that my Higher Power would show me the best way to make amends. I did not have to figure it out now, nor did I have to figure it out myself. Again, I did not have to be willing right now. I could trust my Higher Power to take care of that.

I contemplated various possibilities for how to make amends. My employer had no idea that I had lied, and it was very tempting to contemplate never telling them. I accepted that the right thing to do might not become clear for a while. I actually spent more than four months discussing this amends with various people in W.A. and other Twelve-Step fellowships, telling them the various ways I thought I could make amends, and listening to their suggestions. The suggestions varied widely, from not saying or doing anything to telling my boss everything and cleaning out my IRA account to pay the debt.

One person asked me a very important question that had not occurred to me: who was actually injured? My firm, a nonprofit, was funded by grants to assist certain people in doing a particular task that would benefit society. Although I had assisted these people to do the task, I could have assisted many more had I actually worked those hours I claimed. Was my firm actually injured? Was the grant maker injured? Were the people I was supposed to help injured? Or was society harmed because it would have benefited from more people doing this task?

Through discussions with others and contemplative prayer, I came to a decision about which parties had been actually injured, and what I could do to change that. I also came to the conclusion that I did not need to live in poverty to make amends. I came up with a reasonable plan that would not negatively affect my financial responsibilities to my family and other obligations. Then I prayed for willingness until I was willing to write that first check.

Step Nine

Made direct amends to such people wherever possible, except when to do so would injure them or others.

When we finish with Step Nine, most of us begin to experience the freedom our Promises had predicted. Freed from the wreckage of the past, we find ourselves free to start a new life of community with our family, friends, and coworkers. Although this Step takes courage, good judgment, and a Higher-Powered sense of timing, the rewards are great. Using our list from Step Eight, we reflect carefully on each person we have hurt. With the help of our Higher Power and our sponsor, we can discern the people to whom we need to make direct amends right away.

We remember that an apology is not an amends. An apology is helpful, but the Step is about how we are changing. We begin our amends by integrating into our lives the principles of the W.A. program. We make amends to our family by maintaining our own recovery, being healthy, and "showing up." We make amends to our coworkers by setting reasonable goals, being honest, maintaining our sanity, respecting time, and so on.

Another caution is that this is not the time to unburden our guilt at another's expense, just to clean our conscience. Nor should it be a veiled effort to let go of any festering resentments by bringing up old hurts. The other person may be more to blame than we are, but we stick to our own errors. Telling a spouse or boss about someone else's misdeeds may compound problems. This is the time for us to explain how our work addiction impacted another and how we are changing our life. We do not want to inflict new wounds while trying to correct past harms.

Although the outcome of working this Step provides a big piece of our serenity, how the other person reacts need not do so. We need to guard against the exhilaration of a surprising forgiveness from someone formerly hostile, just as we need to protect ourselves if the person to whom we make amends is cool and skeptical.

Being workaholics, we might procrastinate on taking Step Nine. We ask our Higher Power for guidance and courage. There may be underlying issues that are especially hard for us, such as false pride covering up vulnerability and shame. We can discuss the underlying causes with our sponsors, and we can pray for an obvious opportunity to come our way. Some of us bookend the call for our appointment with phone calls to program friends. Step Nine encourages us to make the amends in person; the Step does not say "whenever possible," it says "wherever possible." If the opportunity for direct amends is not possible, we can write a letter. We seek an "attitude check" from a sponsor or spiritual advisor before we send a letter.

We make amends to ourselves. We forgive ourselves. We are powerless, we are human, and we can be restored to sanity by our loving Higher Power. We continue to integrate the program of W.A. into our lives. We might find ourselves saying, "I forgive myself for actions that hurt me and others that came from fear, vulnerability, resentment, envy, selfishness, and preoccupation, as my Higher Power forgives me. I am being helped to lead a new life, and I am grateful."

Step Nine Questions

1. How can I take good care of myself during the process of making amends? What extra kindness can I show myself? What is the best way to space out the amends process to keep myself from feeling overwhelmed? Who are some people I can reach out to and share the feelings that come up during this process?
2. To whom on my amends list am I ready to make amends today?
3. How would I categorize each amends in terms of direct, indirect, or living amends?
4. How has my life as a result of coming to W.A. become an amends to myself and to my past?
5. To which people on my amends list might I never be able to make direct amends? In what ways might I make these amends?
6. Will any of my amends harm the person or others? If so, what alternative amends might work in this situation (e.g., writing a letter that is not sent)?
7. What might be a good time and place for each amends? How can I plan what I am going to say to each person to ensure that my apology, not my resentment, comes through?

Step Nine Story: Freeing Amends

Making amends was the most healing Step for me and the Step that made the most difference in my life. Each amends was a practice session in learning how to have right relations with others. Once I learned how to admit my faults, take responsibility for my behavior, and make up for the harm I caused, I no longer had to live in fear of not being perfect. I now know from my own experience that no matter what I do, I can always find a way to make amends. I spend a lot less time paralyzed with fear.

For each amends I needed to make, I started by praying for the person I had injured. Somehow, over time this action lessened any resentment I had towards them and my resistance to admitting my faults. I sought out people who may have had to make a similar amends. I listened to their experience and the results of their amends. In many cases, I could not find someone who had the exact same amends to make. By asking around, I found people who had made a similar amends. It was helpful to talk to people who had been hurt by someone like me. I got to hear what the consequences of my actions might have been, how I might have affected someone, and how I might be able to avoid hurting someone further.

I did not necessarily make amends exactly the same way that others did in similar situations. In most cases, I spoke to several different people who did very different things to make amends for the same type of behavior. I thought some people did not make as full and generous amends as they could have. When I heard others discussing their experience, I thought they had really gone overboard. I wondered if some had not caused more hurt to someone. One of the biggest gifts I got from Step Nine was the ability to understand that what is right for others might not be right for me. This does not mean they did their amends wrong, just that I had to look deep within myself and decide for myself what was required to make up for the hurt I caused and to establish right relations with the person I injured. As useful as it was to talk with others, ultimately my decision was between my Higher Power and me.

In a way, Step Nine was the first time I had to bring my changed attitudes and behavior into the world of relationships with people outside of W.A. I had to admit my faults to someone who was actually affected by me. I had to search inside myself for generosity and let go of the attitude that everyone owed me something.

Particularly important was the consideration that I was not to injure anyone else. Would telling the president of my company that my boss let me get away with egregious behavior harm my boss by getting her fired or disciplined? Or would that be just letting her live with the consequences of her actions? Each situation was different, and for me in this case, it was not clear-cut. I decided that I had to take action using my best judgment right now. I could always go back and make amends again if I later see that I should have done more. After praying for guidance, talking to others in W.A., and waiting a few weeks to contemplate this, I decided not to tell the president of the company about my behavior in order to avoid injuring my boss.

Most amends involved both making up for past behavior and changing my behavior in the future. For some amends I had to go back to Steps Six and Seven. One of my biggest amends was to my husband. I had blown him off many times so that I could work more and more hours. I wanted to apologize and tell him I would change, but I knew it would just hurt him more if I apologized and then went back to my old behavior. Instead, I started by asking if we could spend one hour a week together. He consented, and I went to any lengths to make sure I could show up for that hour, asking my Higher Power and W.A. members for help.

This amends also involved not getting angry with him that he did not want to spend more than one hour a week with me. Someone pointed out that I had basically abandoned him while I worked compulsively. Is it any wonder that he sought out other activities and obligations to fill his time? I cannot expect him to give all that up just because I have decided not to work compulsively any more. By honestly acknowledging to myself and my sponsor how my past behavior may have affected and hurt my husband, and humbly asking my Higher Power to remove the character defects related to my relationship with him, I had more compassion for his struggles. I learned how I may have contributed to them and how to avoid harming him further.

After many months of showing up for him that one hour a week, it seemed as if it was time to acknowledge to him that I knew I hurt him when I was working compulsively, that I was wrong to do that, and that I would do everything I could to avoid doing that in the future. I discussed this with others in W.A. and prayed, asking for guidance. I considered how much it would hurt him if I said this and then went back to compulsive working. In the end, I decided to go ahead and have that talk with him. After I said those things, he said he was grateful to have heard it. He also pointed out to me other ways my compulsive working had hurt him – things I had not even thought about. Fortunately, I had been praying for him and had some practice accepting my faults. Even though I was tempted to argue with him and tell him I did not think I hurt him that much, I listened instead. Our relationship has improved greatly. Without W.A., I doubt we would still be married.

Some amends on my list fell into the category of ones that I could only reasonably make if I ran into the person. These were people whom I had hurt emotionally, but were no longer in my life. Seeking them out would most likely bring up an old hurt and disrupt their life unnecessarily. For these amends, I prepared the same as I would if I were planning to seek them out to make a direct amends. I prayed for them and discussed with other W.A. members what I would say to them if I ran into them. In some cases, I asked a W.A. friend to act out the amends with me so I could practice saying the words, "I was wrong." This helped me feel more confident while going about my daily life. I knew that if I ran into one of these people, I would not have to leave or hide. I could say my piece and accept whatever they said in return.

I have not yet been able to complete some amends. For instance, I owed an old roommate some money. I had not been in touch with her for several years. I sent a check to her last known address. The letter was never returned to me and the check was never cashed. I tried other ways of finding out where she was, but I could not find her. So I must be content with knowing that if I ever come across her, I can pay her then. Whether that happens is up to my Higher Power.

The more amends I made, the more evidence I had that admitting my faults improved my life and relationships. Now, I can usually apologize and make up for my wrong shortly after I do something hurtful or inappropriate. I no longer have a lot of people in my life with whom I have bad relations or whom I have to avoid. The freedom Step Nine has given me is wonderful.

Step Ten

Continued to take personal inventory
and when we were wrong promptly admitted it.

The Tenth Step is a daily maintenance Step, as are the other remaining two Steps. Our experiences have revealed that daily practice of the last three Steps is essential to living a balanced life and experiencing continued growth and renewal. In addition, we use them to help us recover if we slip into workaholism, including toxic work binges. Practicing a daily Tenth Step starts our day and our new way of life from a spiritually and emotionally stable place. We will continue to do things that create problems, and events may happen that can throw our newly abstinent and sane life into turmoil. We are humans, not saints. But we can look back over our day and inventory our fears, false pride, envy, self-pity, and resentments. These are our old patterns of negative thinking. We can inventory attitudes and characteristics that were barriers to joyful, healthy living and reliance on our Higher Power that day. This is how we grow and change into sanity.

Twelve-Step literature describes several kinds of inventories: spot check, daily, and intensive. A spot check inventory is useful throughout the day to clean up any hasty actions or words that have caused harm. The spot check inventory helps us to identify and clear up blunders as soon as the event occurs. Many W.A. members conduct a daily Tenth Step inventory in their evening or morning prayer and meditation time. Some write it down, others review the day with a sponsor or program friend. We notice when our behavior harmed or blessed those around us. A Tenth Step is a miniature taking of Steps Four through Nine. Similar to a Fourth Step, we notice both assets and liabilities in our behavior. The A.A. *Twelve Steps and Twelve Traditions* explains:

> In all these situations we need self-restraint, honest analysis of what is involved, a willingness to admit when the fault is ours, and an equal willingness to forgive when the fault is elsewhere. We need not be discouraged when we fall into the error of our old ways, for these disciplines are not easy. We shall look for progress, not for perfection.
>
> Our first objective will be the development of self-restraint. This carries a top priority rating. When we speak or act hastily or rashly, the ability to be fair-minded and tolerant evaporates on the spot. One unkind tirade or one willful snap judgment can ruin our relation with another person for a whole day, or maybe a whole year. Nothing pays off like restraint of tongue and pen. We must avoid quick-tempered criticism and furious, power-driven argument. The same goes for sulking or silent scorn. These are emotional booby traps baited with pride and vengefulness. Our first job is to sidestep the traps. When we are tempted by the bait, we should train ourselves to step back and think. For we can neither think nor act to good purpose until the habit of self-restraint has become automatic. (91)

We practice this Step in order to live in peace. The intent of this Step is to conduct a daily self-search, but not to experience additional remorse and self-criticism. We review our day to give ourselves appreciation for our progress and credit for things well done. We acknowledge where we need to take an action that is due. We cannot afford to risk our serenity with long-held negative emotions. We ask God to reveal what part we played in our upset. We pray for the willingness to forgive others and ourselves. We promptly make amends. We do not blame others for our negative feelings or actions. With this inventory, we admit and correct our part. In addition to listing our fears and resentments of the day, some of us make a gratitude and appreciation list.

Step Ten Questions

1. Have I been afraid, resentful, or controlling today? Did any of my character defects flare up today?
2. What actions in my day might require correction or amends? How can I make the amends that I need to make in order to maintain my spiritual fitness? How can I show myself forgiveness for my faults and accept my imperfections with self-love?
3. How can I create space and time each day for Step Ten? Where is a good place in my home to practice Step Ten?
4. What prayers or rituals would I like to use?
5. What positive actions can I acknowledge today? What help have I received today? What help have I given to others today?

Step Ten Story: "G" for Generous

I think that taking a daily written inventory has been a key factor in my continued abstinence and the happiness and joy I now have in my life. It has helped me focus on gratitude, and change from judging my day based on how much I got done to evaluating my progress based on how well I have behaved in accordance with my moral principles in every situation.

If I happen to have a day or a few days when I do not set aside the time to take a written inventory, I base my next inventory on the events that have passed since my last one. There is no need to berate myself for not doing it perfectly or every day.

Each thing I write down as part of my inventory involves prayer. The first thing I write down is, "Thank you." I start by thanking my Higher Power for helping me to abstain from compulsive working, to the extent that I was able to do so.

Then I think about the day. I consider my actions. I look for times that stick out because I felt angry, had a bad interaction with someone, worked compulsively, or strayed from my abstinence plan. Then I consider whether or not I acted selfishly by trying to get my own way, or hurting someone because I was focused on my own needs above theirs. Then I write down a short phrase about the incident under "S" for selfish. Was I dishonest? Did I lie? Then I write it down under "D" for dishonest. Did I act out of fear? Did I do something or avoid doing something because I was afraid? I write it down under "F" for fear. For me, every time I work compulsively it is because I am acting out of fear or selfishness, or because I am being dishonest with myself or someone else.

For each incident I write down, I say a prayer of thanks and ask for help. For instance, "Thank you for helping me see where I was selfish and took the last piece of food. Please help me be generous today," or "Thank you for helping me see where I lied to my boss. Please help me to tell him the truth today."

If I need to make amends (for example, by telling my boss the truth), I think about how that will happen and what exactly I will say. Often I need to call another W.A. member for help in deciding what to say and becoming willing to set things straight.

Then I go back over my day again and look for times when I was generous, especially when I wanted to be selfish. Did I give up my seat on the subway? Did I thank my spouse for making dinner? Did I answer the phone when someone called? I write a short phrase under "G" for generous. Then I consider where I was honest. Did I want to lie, but instead told someone the truth? Was I tempted to tell my boss I could get done more than I reasonably could, but instead was honest? I write that under "H" for honest. Then I look for times when I walked through fear to do the right thing. Did I ask for help, even though I did not want to? Did I call a new W.A. member? (That could also be placed under "generous.") Did I try a new thing? These go under "C" for courage.

Again, I say a prayer of thanks for each item. "Thank you for helping me to be generous and answer the phone," or "Thank you for helping me to be honest with my boss."

Instead of berating myself for *feeling* selfish, I thank my Higher Power that I did not act on it. Instead of berating myself for *acting* selfish, I thank my Higher Power for helping me see what I did, and ask for help to make amends and do better today.

I then make a list of all the people I resent. I pray for them, saying, "Please give them everything I need in life, everything I would want for myself." When I start thinking about my resentment during the day, I can say this prayer again and remind myself that I have set aside time each day to think about my resentments (my Tenth Step time), so I do not need to think about it now. Praying for these people seems to reduce my resentment and help me have more compassion for them. Even if I do not want anything good for them, I can agree that if they got everything they needed, they probably would not be behaving in a way that bothered me so much.

My written Tenth Step usually looks something like this:

1/1/05 Thank You

Selfish
- I did not call a member of my W.A. group (also out of fear).
- I would not let my spouse have the TV remote.

Dishonest
- I told my boss I could finish the report by Wednesday (action: tell boss truth today).

Fear
- I did not answer the phone when it rang (also selfish).
- I did not read my email at work.

Generous
- I went to the drug store for my husband.
- I went to bed on time.
- I left work on time (also honest).

Honest
- I called in sick because I was sick (also generous).
- I was honest on my time sheet.
- I told my group I needed help avoiding a bottom-line behavior (also courage).

Courage
- I called a new person in my W.A. group.
- I asked someone at work to show me the new computer program.

Resent
- Mom
- Ted
- Jack
- Lucy

My prayer goes something like this:

> Thank you for helping me abstain from compulsive working to the extent I was able. Thank you for helping me see where I was selfish and acted out of fear, not calling someone in my W.A. group. Please help me to be generous and walk through that fear today. Thank you for helping me be generous and go to the store for my husband. Please give Ted everything he needs in life, everything I would want for myself.

After thanking my Higher Power for each incident where I was generous, honest, or courageous, or where I saw that I was selfish, dishonest, or acted out of fear, and praying for those I resent, I thank my Higher Power for all the gifts in my life, and go on with my day.

I find it helpful to oftentimes discuss my Tenth Step with others. When I first started doing a Tenth Step, I discussed each item with someone over the phone, usually once a week, or sometimes more often. This helped me avoid beating myself up. It helped me see what exactly was going on. For instance, sometimes I had a problematic interaction with someone, but I did not know why. Was I acting selfishly? Out of fear? Or both? Or I would put an incident under "Fear" when it really should have been under "Courage." Usually discussing my Tenth Step inventories with someone in W. A. helps me figure this out and make sure I give credit where it is due.

After years of doing this, I have trained myself to be grateful. Every time I leave work on time, I say, "Thank you." Every time I am polite to someone I do not like, I say, "Thank you." Every time I am rude, I can still be grateful that I noticed it and can make amends. It was not that long ago that I did not even notice that I was rude. Or, if I did, I justified myself, saying that the other person deserved it. My relationships deteriorated, and I did not know why. Now, my relationships are improving and I can see that doing a daily inventory is one of the main reasons why this is so.

Step Eleven

**Sought through prayer and meditation
to improve our conscious contact with God
as we understood God, praying only for knowledge of God's
will for us and the power to carry that out.**

Prayer and meditation are our main sources of conscious contact with our Higher Power, the God of our understanding. How can we turn our will over to a Higher Power without knowing what the guidance will be for us? We workaholics may struggle with Step Eleven. For many of us in the beginning of recovery, if we prayed at all, our prayers were quick, desperate requests for help. We thought there would never be enough time to meditate. We had little patience for sitting still. Our mind, in the silence of meditation, was undisciplined and the to-do list or the self-critic took over. In the beginning, we might have thought that meditation is the skill of mystics. For those of us in recovery who, for whatever reason or belief, had not come to experience a personal relationship with the Loving Spirit of our understanding, this is the next Step toward that experience. The result is the promised spiritual awakening.

Our willingness to practice meditation and prayer began the most healing and soothing experiences of our recovery. With practice and patience, our time of conscious contact has become a relief from our critical, effort-filled minds and our toxic bodies. We incorporate it as a part of our daily Action Plan. We find we need the light and love of our contact with our Higher Power. We discover the nourishment and guidance of that contact. It is good for our minds, bodies, and souls. So how do we start?

We can begin our instruction with these words from A.A. literature:

> The actual experience of meditation and prayer across the centuries is, of course, immense. The world's libraries and places of worship are a treasure trove for all seekers. It is hoped that every [W.A] who has a religious connection which emphasizes meditation will return to the practice of that devotion as never before. But what about the rest of us who, less fortunate, do not even know how to begin?
>
> Well, we might start like this. First let's look at a really good prayer...

'Lord, make me a channel of thy peace – that where there is hatred, I may bring love – that where there is wrong, I may bring the spirit of forgiveness – that where there is discord, I may bring harmony – that where there is error, I may bring truth – that where there is doubt, I may bring faith – that where there is despair, I may bring hope – that where there are shadows, I may bring light – that where there is sadness, I may bring joy. Lord, grant that I may seek rather to comfort than to be comforted – to understand, than to be understood – to love, than to be loved. For it is by self-forgetting that one finds. It is by forgiving that one is forgiven. It is by dying that one awakens to Eternal Life. Amen.'

As beginners in meditation, we might now reread this prayer several times very slowly, savoring every word and trying to take in the deep meaning of each phrase and idea. (*Twelve Steps and Twelve Traditions* 98-99, word substitutions in brackets)

We take these words in with each breath. Our breath is our connection to the sacred and our body temple. It relaxes us and prepares us to be uplifted and held by spiritual energy. It helps to imagine being in a beautiful place in nature. In time, we learn to quiet our mind and relax our body.

We can imagine finding a Divine Presence. We use our breath to bring the Divine close to, or even into, our body. When we begin to feel filled with peace, light, and love, we have made "conscious contact." This is when we can begin our conversation with our Higher Power. We experience spiritual meaning flowing through us. As we find our way to this special state of mind, we can ask to know God's will for us.

Is this just imagination?

There's nothing the matter with *constructive* imagination; all sound achievement rests upon it. After all, no man can build a house until he first envisions a plan for it. Well, meditation is like that, too; it helps to envision our spiritual objective before we try to move toward it. (*Twelve Steps and Twelve Traditions* 100)

This description is a tiny beginning to an amazing life of meditation. We each find our own way. We can seek out classes, groups, and teachers. It can take many forms. In seeking, we find what works for us to improve our conscious contact with Divine love, wisdom, and grace.

A hazard that may face us in meditation is unconsciously projecting our will into the search for God's will. How do we guard against using "well-intentioned unconscious rationalizations" (*Twelve Steps and Twelve Traditions* 103) for behaviors we want to justify? Perhaps the best answer is that we use discernment. We ask ourselves if it lives up to the prayer in the chapter on Step Eleven in the A.A. *Twelve Steps and Twelve Traditions* (99). Before making big decisions, we may use our imagination to reflect on and rehearse the outcome of big decisions in Higher Power's presence. During a time of discernment we check our physical body's reaction, as it is a great truth-teller. We discuss our situation with our sponsor or a spiritual advisor. We grow to trust the wisdom we experience in meditation. We experience the love and forgiveness of this Eleventh Step prayer and align our will with its intention.

Besides all the health benefits of meditation, such as relaxation, reduced blood pressure, renewal after a stressful day, enhanced immune response, and an increased awareness of physical problems that need attention, we may experience another benefit. Regular meditation helps us see the bigger picture of important qualities such as charity, truth, justice, and love. We may find ourselves sensing that we are a chosen and special child of God. We may sense that we belong to something greater than the small world of our work. The hostility of human affairs becomes less important. We find peace of mind.

Step Eleven Questions

1. What am I grateful and thankful for today?
2. When in my daily schedule will I pray and meditate? What time of day works best for me? Where is a good place for me to meditate and pray (space at home or in nature, build an altar)?
3. In what ways have I taken back my will and my life from my Higher Power today?
4. Am I willing to turn it back over?

Step Eleven Story I: Breath and Gratitude

There are days when I do not want to take the time to sit still, pray, meditate, and read W.A. or other spiritual literature. But my experience has shown me that if I am not willing to do this, I will work compulsively. If maintaining and furthering my relationship with my Higher Power is not the most important thing in my day, I will go back to my old ways. Getting things done becomes the most important thing in my day.

I start Step Eleven by asking my Higher Power every morning to help me abstain from compulsive working that day. At the end of the day, I thank my Higher Power for helping me to abstain from compulsive working, to the extent I was able to do so that day. I do not have to have a perfectly abstinent day to thank my Higher Power for helping me do the best I could.

When I came to W.A., I started meditating for 20 minutes every day. I look at meditation as a practice session for sitting still and concentrating. I sit and I attempt to focus on my breath. Whenever I find my thoughts straying from my breath, I see how gently I can bring my thoughts back to my breath. I do not get upset about straying thoughts – they are to be expected. The more I practice this, the better I become at sitting still and concentrating on the task at hand throughout the day. Some days, it is harder to do this than others. That is just the way it is.

My criterion for successful meditation is not how many breaths I was able to focus on. As long as I do my best to sit still, I check that off as a successful meditation. Some days, I only end up focusing on one or two breaths for the entire 20 minutes. Other days, I focus on many more before my thoughts stray. But that does not matter. It is just practice.

Prayer and meditation have been crucial to getting me through some very difficult days. Sometimes something happens that upsets me greatly and I cannot function. I have found that sitting still and focusing on my breath, even if only for one or two breaths, can help me calm down and be more useful during those stressful moments. I meditate while waiting in line, which is one of my least favorite activities. I no longer have to go to a different store or restaurant if there is a line. I can wait, saving myself the effort of finding a store without a line.

Some days I have a great amount of difficulty focusing at work. I do not want to do anything except chat with my coworkers or surf the Internet. I have found that prayer can greatly alter the course of my day on those occasions. First, I pray, asking my Higher Power for help to do the next task. Often, this gives me the ability to do that one task.

I thank my Higher Power for helping me do that task. Then I pray, again asking for help to do the next task. Sometimes I have to break the tasks down into tiny subtasks. Ask for help and get the report out of the file box. Thank my Higher Power. Ask for help and open the report cover. Thank my Higher Power. Ask for help and read the first sentence. Thank my Higher Power. I have gotten through entire workdays doing this for every task, and a day that would have been fraught with dishonesty and procrastination turns into a somewhat productive day at work.

I say prayers every day, thanking my Higher Power for the gift of all the people in my life. I name them individually: Thank you for the gift of P. in my life. Thank you for the gift of A. in my life. I started doing this because I felt so alone, and it has really helped. I now remember that I have people in my life who care about me.

Another type of prayer that has helped me tremendously is praying for people I resent. I am the kind of person who tends to hold a lot of resentments towards people. For example, they do not say hello the right way or do exactly what I want, and I resent them. So I routinely pray for almost everyone in my life every day. I say "Thank you for watching over J. Thank you for being with her in her hour of need. Thank you for showering love and light upon her." I have found that, over time, praying in this way for people who bother me results in me not being so bothered. It does not always lift the resentment completely, especially if it is a particularly big resentment, but it usually helps move things to the point where I can have positive interactions with the person and not spend a lot of time plotting my revenge. In addition, it seems that the more I do this practice, the fewer people I get resentments against in the first place.

Sometimes I get frustrated with Step Eleven. I ask my Higher Power for knowledge of Her will for me, but I do not get an email telling me what to do. Instead, I must use my best judgment and consider whether a planned action is selfish or dishonest, or if I am planning to act out of fear or resentment. I can ask myself how I can be most useful right now, rather than how I can get my way or get what I want. I can discuss possibilities with others. Often my Higher Power seems to speak through others, but I still do not ever receive direct guidance from my Higher Power.

However, over the years, I have found that I am making better and better decisions. I still slip up, but I am making more decisions that are in accordance with my moral principles. I have an idea of what my moral principles are. I am making fewer decisions that place me in a position to be hurt. And I am spending less time obsessing about my past actions and more time considering how I can be useful to my Higher Power.

Step Eleven Story II: Message from My Deeper Power – "M. Therapy"

In the beginning of my recovery, I was trying to cope with the toxic depletion I felt after a week of work. During a meditation, this wisdom popped up. It has served me well over the years. The results are a wonder to me, even now. I seem to need to plan three "M."s in a day to recover from burnout. Your "M."s might be different. The secret is to list things that are transformative to my mind and body. The goal is to come back to my recovery spirit-self that desires healthy food, has a balanced life, feels sane, and sleeps well.

My list of "M."s is: meditation, measured meals, moments in nature, movement (like yoga or aerobic), making love, mass (or spiritual service), meetings (Twelve Step), music, and massage.

Step Twelve

Having had a spiritual awakening as the result of these steps, we tried to carry this message to workaholics, and to practice these principles in all our affairs.

What is a spiritual awakening in W.A.? We find an answer in the chapter on Step Twelve in *Twelve Steps and Twelve Traditions*, where we believe we are now "able to do, feel, and believe that which [we] could not do before on [our] unaided strength and resources alone" (106-107). Looking back, as a result of practicing these Steps, we have become transformed. It seemed to happen without effort. We have a new energy, we are at peace, and we are sane about our compulsive work and activity. Our life has been restored. The presence and guidance of a loving God awakens us to our higher selves and to our body, mind, and spirit. We have the help of a fellowship of people with whom we can share the truth, and they love us all the more. We have received a sense of grace, and it now seems like a free gift. Life does throw us off track every once in a while, but we can face those bumps with our newfound program tools and our W.A. fellowship.

Naturally, we want to give back some of what we found in W.A. We all, newcomer and long-timer alike, feel something special when helping someone find recovery in W.A. It helps us when we watch the lives of other sufferers move from despair to hope and from insanity to sanity. Who can help someone find recovery from work and activity addiction better than we can? We know what it was like and what life is like now.

How do we carry the message of W.A.? There are many ways. Changing our lives is the best message of all. Going to meetings or starting a meeting, making phone calls, and providing sponsorship are as helpful to us as they are to others. We reach out to tell our story to a fellow sufferer.

Accepting a service position for our group, our World Service Organization, or another path of service, is an opportunity that can be challenging to a workaholic. Many of us in early recovery are eager to simplify our lives. Yet we have found participating with other work addicts and volunteering to help the fellowship has strengthened our program of recovery. We are more likely to practice a program of surrender and sanity when we take a service commitment among fellow recovering workaholics. This helps us put into practice the last part of Step Twelve, "to practice these principles in all our affairs." We begin to live and breathe the W.A. program of recovery. We practice our Tools and maintenance Steps in order to continue our spiritual awakening and be of better service to our family, friends, and coworkers.

Workaholics cannot abstain completely from work; we are at risk for slips and relapses. Even in retirement we may over-schedule ourselves. If we find ourselves slipping, we need to work the last three Steps and increase our use of the W.A. Tools, especially meetings, meditation, and phone calls, to help get us back to sanity. It is an ironic truth in recovery: the service we give services us.

> But today, in well-matured [W.A.'s], these distorted drives have been restored to something like their true purpose and direction. We no longer strive to dominate or rule those about us in order to gain self-importance. We no longer seek fame and honor in order to be praised. When by devoted service to family, friends, business, or community we attract widespread affection and are sometimes singled out for posts of greater responsibility

and trust, we try to be humbly grateful and exert ourselves the more in a spirit of love and service....

Service, gladly rendered, obligations squarely met, troubles well accepted or solved with God's help, the knowledge that at home or in the world outside we are partners in a common effort, the well-understood fact that in God's sight all human beings are important, the proof that love freely given surely brings a full return, the certainty that we are no longer isolated and alone in self-constructed prisons, the surety that we need no longer be square pegs in round holes but can fit and belong in God's scheme of things – these are the permanent and legitimate satisfactions of right living for which no amount of pomp and circumstance, no heap of material possessions, could possibly be substitutes. True ambition is not what we thought it was. True ambition is the deep desire to live usefully and walk humbly under the grace of God. (*Twelve Steps and Twelve Traditions* 124-125, word substitutions in brackets)

Step Twelve Questions

1. What benefits do I get when I offer service to others? How does service enhance my recovery?
2. How can I offer service to my meeting or other workaholics?
3. Where does service fit into my abstinence plan? Am I in danger of being compulsive in helping others? Am I compulsively avoiding service?
4. Can I offer assistance to others without ego, seeking nothing in return? How does the act of serving with humility further my own recovery?

Step Twelve Story: The Miracle of Abstinent Service

"Having Had a Spiritual Awakening as the Result of These Steps..."

I believe I have had a spiritual awakening as a result of working the previous eleven Steps. For me, this spiritual awakening consists of two connected parts: changed behavior and changed beliefs.

My behavior changes include:

1. I am now honest with my employer about the hours I work. (Previously, I lied on many occasions, either claiming to work more than I had worked to hide my work avoidance, or claiming fewer hours than I had worked to hide my compulsive working.)
2. I am much more honest with myself and others about how much I could expect to get done in a given amount of time. (Previously, I would tell myself and others I could get a project done when, in reality, that was impossible.)
3. I pray every day. (Previously, I prayed less frequently.)
4. I meditate almost every day. (Previously, I had never meditated every day for more than a few months at a time.)
5. I perform a written moral inventory of my behavior almost every day. (Previously, I had done this only once a month or less.)
6. I enjoy life more. (Previously, life felt like a struggle every day, which I tolerated so that I could achieve "retirement.")

My belief changes include:

1. I believe that my purpose in life is to serve a Power greater than myself that has restored me to sanity. I believe that any action I am considering can be weighed in light of that purpose. (Previously, I thought my purpose was to achieve things and change the world.)
2. I believe every human being deserves to enjoy life every moment of every day. (Previously, I believed everyone deserved to continually suffer because I suffered so much.)
3. I believe I am responsible for earning my own living. (Previously, I felt my parents, family, and employer owed me a living.)
4. I believe, based on my experience, that prayer helps me. (Previously, I did not think it could.)
5. I believe, based on my experience, that spiritual growth can help prevent and mitigate many of my current problems. (Previously, I believed that pushing for my own way was the only way through my problems, and controlling others was the only way to prevent my problems.)
6. I believe that everyone deserves to rest as much as they need. (Previously, I believed everyone should work constantly.)
7. I believe everyone is equal in the eyes of my Higher Power. (Previously, I believed that some people were more worthy than others of love, recovery, attention, or a livelihood.)
8. I believe I am extremely fortunate to have everything I have today. (Previously, I had very little gratitude and generally felt that I deserved more of everything, except rest.)

There were no shortcuts for me to a spiritual awakening. I had to take all the Steps as suggested. I could not force it. The Steps took time, and they took longer than I thought they "should." I did not take the Steps to get a spiritual awakening. I took the Steps so I would not die of workaholism. But, looking back, I can see that by taking all the Steps with the help and advice of others, I have had a spiritual awakening that has contributed to my recovery and my happiness.

"...We Tried to Carry This Message to Workaholics"

Shortly after I came into W.A., I saw workaholism everywhere. I thought almost everyone I worked with was a workaholic, as were my friends and spouse. My relationships with others became strained when I tried to explain to them how their behavior was "workaholic" and I had the solution. I had forgotten Tradition Eleven: this is a program of "attraction rather than promotion." Once I stopped judging and focused on my own recovery, my relationships with others became better. No one around me had to stop working compulsively or recognize his or her own workaholism in order for me to recover. I simply stuck to my abstinence plan and remained willing to go to any lengths to abstain from compulsive working. Some coworkers and friends noticed some changes in me. Some even asked how I am able to leave work on time. I simply told them how I did that. In many cases, I did not even tell them I was in W.A. I just explained how certain things I did helped me leave on time, such as meditation, prioritizing, and substituting. Some people expressed how difficult they found it to do such things without support, and I told them about the support I receive in W.A. Only a few of those people actually came to a W.A. meeting. But that is an important reminder that carrying the message is successful if I remain abstinent. My success is not judged on whether others start recovering from workaholism.

I have to keep my own abstinence a priority when working with others, especially people I sponsor. I need to use the tool of substitution every time I commit to Twelfth Step work. If I say I will be available to talk to someone on the phone or meet with them to discuss a Step, I think about where that time will come from. What will I give up? Even if I am giving up watching TV, I need to be clear with myself about what will come out of my schedule to accommodate any new commitment. I try to be very clear with those I sponsor about how much time I have for them. I do not have as much time as I would like to give them. But I do not believe it helps them if I over-schedule or over commit in order to give them more of my time.

A big part of carrying the message involves being an example. Others, like I, need to see that it is possible to help someone and still maintain abstinence and serenity. This means I may not return phone calls for a day or two or hear a Fifth Step right away. Others have a Higher Power (and it is not me), as well as other resources besides me, such as literature, other members of the fellowship, and all the tools. When I remember that, I can avoid the ego trip that often results when I start believing that other people in W.A. need me right now, and no one else can help them right now. That is simply not true.

Sometimes I have put time into working with someone and they do not take any suggestions, complain that nothing works for them, continue to work compulsively, or frustrate me in other ways. It is easy to get angry with them, but I have not found that to be helpful. Instead, I try to focus on being grateful that I am able to take suggestions. Why am I more willing to take suggestions than they are? That cannot be explained. I can just be grateful and remember that my job does not include making them do anything. All I have to do is listen and tell them what worked for me. That is all I have to offer. I cannot promise them that what worked for me will work for them.

My relationship with most people is better if I limit myself to sharing my experience, avoid giving advice, and do not try to get them to do something. When particularly troubled by someone who continues to work compulsively, I remember the story about Bill W., the cofounder of A.A. He stayed sober in New York for a period of time by working with other struggling alcoholics – none of whom got sober. But working with those alcoholics who never got sober helped *him* stay sober long enough to find Dr. Bob, who cofounded A.A. with him. I am reminded that the people I sponsor do not have to do anything in particular for the interaction to be helpful to me. If the only thing I receive is gratitude that I am not where they are, that is enough to help me abstain from compulsive working for one more day.

I can ask others in the fellowship for help, even though I may sponsor them, they ask me for help, they have less time in recovery than I do, or anything else. Not asking for help is very dangerous for my recovery. Everyone in my local group has less abstinence time than I do. If I had not continued to ask all of them for help, I would not be abstinent today. Every time I have a slip, I am tempted to avoid telling those I sponsor. I wonder if they will think the program does not work if I tell them I have a slip. But it helps to remember that it has helped me tremendously to hear other people talk about their experience of having a slip and then getting back on the wagon. My relationship with those I help in recovery is one of equals. Over time, all of the newcomers I have helped have helped me, and our relationships are mutually supportive.

"...And To Practice these Principles in All Our Affairs"

What are "these principles" to which Step Twelve refers? I think it may be quite fortunate that these principles are not listed in Step Twelve. Each of us is free to look at our own experience with the Steps to determine what principles we see and which principles are important to us.

By looking over my experience, I can see what principles are important to me, what has worked for me, and what has not. The principles that are embodied in my experience with the Twelve Steps include:

Honesty, particularly honesty with myself about everything, including my limitations and others' limitations. This does not mean unnecessarily telling someone something that will hurt them.

Not doing it alone. It is very tempting for me to stop checking in with others about my Step work, decisions, motives, and struggles. But I have found that refraining from asking for help results in lying to myself, hurting others, making bad decisions, and working compulsively.

Generosity. This includes generosity to others and myself. If I am generous in taking care of myself, I find I am better able to be generous with others. For me, generosity is the opposite of selfish behavior. Answering the phone when I have time, going to bed when I need to, and just saying "thank you" are all generous acts.

Compassion. For me, compassion is the opposite of resentment. Resentment often fuels my workaholism. Thus, my recovery seems to depend upon having compassion for the struggles of people who hurt me. This does not mean I continue to put myself in a position to be hurt. It means that an adequate response to injury can consist of taking measures to protect myself and others. It does not need to include revenge. The most effective way for me to acquire compassion is to pray for the person I resent.

Taking responsibility for my own actions. This involves checking out my actions and decisions with others ahead of time. I make full and generous amends when I am wrong or when I have injured someone. This also involves being honest about priorities. When I neglect doing something, it is not because I did not have time, but because I prioritized something else.

So what does it mean to practice these principles in all my affairs? Like most addicts, I find it easier to be honest, generous, and compassionate in some situations than in others. For example, I can be compassionate towards someone I sponsor who has just lied to their spouse, but it is much more difficult to be compassionate when my spouse lies to me. And I have no trouble checking in with other W.A. members regarding my Step work, but I may want to keep it to myself if I am inching towards working compulsively.

Practicing these principles in all my affairs means that I continue, every day, to attempt to make progress in practicing these principles. I am not perfect, and I do not have to be perfect. There are times when I fail miserably. If I am being selfish and dishonest, I can ask for help to stop, and things do not get so out of hand. Every day I have the choice to clean up my past and ask for help to do better that day. The more I do that, the better I sleep, the better my life is, the happier I am, and the easier it is to stay abstinent.

Artistic Responses to the Twelve Steps

Step One

Build an altar to your unmanageability. Select and add an item to represent every major aspect of your unmanageability. Light a candle on your altar and spend ten minutes for seven days in a row in silent contemplation of your Step One Altar. Sit lovingly with yourself and gaze at the aspects of your disease with acknowledgment. Journaling can be a useful activity after the silent meditation.

Step Two

While not displacing your Step One altar, build a different altar, this time an altar about your Higher Power. Select and display tangible items that represent aspects, qualities, and traits of your Higher Power. Are there symbols of your belief that you can add to the altar? Select some more items, particularly those that represent the best, biggest, most powerful, and most loving aspects of Higher Power you could wish for. In order to do this, you might want to write a "help wanted" ad for your Higher Power, or visualize going to the Higher Power boutique and trying on some new Higher Powers. Light a candle and spend ten minutes a day for a week with your altar. Feel free to add items to the altar as your inspiration guides you. Journaling can be a useful activity after the silent meditation.

Step Three

After completing Steps One and Two, conduct a ten-minute meditation with your Step One and Step Two altars. Then take each item, one at a time, from your Step One altar and place it on your Step Two altar. Imagine you have angels, guides, guardians, and/or helpers assisting you in carrying each item to your Higher Power. Place each item beside an object on your Step Two altar that has the power to take care of the Step One item. When you have completely cleared your Step One altar, and given your life, your will, and all aspects of your disease over to your Higher Power, spend ten minutes a day for a week contemplating in deep, restful peace and serenity the nourishing feelings of support and letting go that result from not having to worship at the altar of unmanageability any more. You may find it helpful to place on the Higher Power altar a symbol of putting your whole life and will in the loving care of your Higher Power.

Alternatively, build and collage, decorate, or decoupage a coffee canister or similar container to make a "God Can," expressly for use in turning things over. Decorate both the inside and outside of the can with your favorite images of transformation. Create beautifully decorated notepaper that will then be all ready for writing things down to turn them over. Stickers. Stamps. Go to town!

Remember that "We can only clear the ground a bit" (*Alcoholics Anonymous* 55), unless we continue with Steps Four through Nine to have ongoing spiritual relief.

Step Four

In order to take a fearless and thorough moral inventory, it is often great to start with developing a gentleness tool. You can use this artwork to describe a resource for gentleness with self. These sheets can be bound by hand with dental floss or string into a wonderful Gentleness Book. Step Four entries themselves can be done with crayon or colored pencils on paper using one of the suggested formats. Ask your sponsor to give you fun stickers for each completed entry. Draw smiley faces and give yourself A plusses. Another way to augment the Step Four experience is to make a collage of your best self, highlighting all your assets. Select pictures and words that represent your best assets and glue them on poster board to represent your vision map.

Step Five

Light a candle and make an altar when you meet with your sponsor. Dress as an altar. Wear beautiful clothing, all the colors of the rainbow, or floral and festive prints to your Fifth Step appointment. You are the living miracle. Celebrate it! Another idea: burn your Fourth Step entries as you share them in Step Five (although this can make the defect synopsis in Step Six more difficult).

Step Six

Write each key defect on a piece of origami paper with these four questions answered:

1. What does this do for me? (How has this defect served me?)
2. What does this do to me? (Describe negative impacts.)
3. What would my low point with this look like?
4. What will emotional, spiritual, and mental serenity look like as this defect is removed?

Add the words from Step Six that are assets or positives to the collage mentioned in Step Four.

Step Seven

Fold the origami papers into little boats and let them float away on a river or pond as you become willing to let your Higher Power remove them and ask your Higher Power to remove them.

Step Eight

Draw a picture on a three-by-five card of each person, place, thing, institution, or incident to which you have caused harm. Use pens and colored pencils. Outline each card with a color that represents your willingness level. For example, yellow could mean you are not willing, blue could mean you are somewhat willing, and green could mean you are very willing, because green is for "go." As you pray and become more willing, update the edging colors to update the color codes. Any amends with a green edge means you are ready to work Step Nine.

Step Nine

Stack the cards from Step Eight in priority order of amount of harm caused. (Usually, your "self" card will be at the top of the list.) In your daily prayer and meditation for two weeks, take each three-by-five card and pray for the person on each card (including yourself) to receive every good thing you can think of that you would like for yourself. As you pray this prayer, draw golden light or a halo around each card's figure. By the end of two weeks, the cards will fairly glow.

Step Ten

One possible artistic tool to use for a daily Tenth Step is a sketch of your day. Draw yourself and your Higher Power and list how you collaborated today. What were the healthy choices represented today? Write a "recycle" list of everything you would like recycled or scrubbed away from the day, and highlight in orange any actions you need to take as a way of making amends.

Step Eleven

Create a prayer and meditation space for yourself. Perhaps it is a sweet corner of your living room or den that has a quiet space, or a hand-knitted warm prayer shawl, a beautiful cloth, live plants, etc. Decorate your prayer and meditation space so you can enjoy spending time there. Customize it so that it is just right for you. Do a collage of what conscious contact looks like to you, and post it in the space. Spend time in your special place daily.

Step Twelve

Draw a gratitude list in which each service opportunity or life modeling of your recovery is a starburst firework. Write rays of all the positive things you learn, contribute, receive, and/or get to enjoy through each firework of "carrying the message" and "practicing the principles in all our affairs." Altogether, this is the firework show of your spiritual awakening.

OUR STORIES

A Workaholic's Story

I have been a workaholic since I was 13 year old. My childhood was the meat of a dysfunctional family sandwich. I was pressed on one side by a tyrannical, workaholic father, whom I could rarely please. On the other was an apprehensive and distant mother, who was always within arm's reach of potent prescription drugs. In the middle, aggressively competing with me for our parents' unfulfilled promises of conditional love, was my sister: seven years older, braver, stronger, and smarter than I.

My father was a clergyman, civic leader, and a force in state politics. While I was around him, I was always fearful I would be (and I often was) scolded or punished for some awkward, selfish, or mean-spirited thing I had not intended to do. My mother spoke four languages and digested books on all subjects like some people eat candy. While I was around her, I experienced constant anxiety and rejection, concluding I simply was not worthy of love. Confusion and conflict dominated all family communication. Exuberance was criticized. Sadness was ridiculed. Tenderness was wrapped in mock gestures and delivered with sarcasm.

Ironically, my parents, houseguests, and teachers told me how fortunate I was to be raised in a model, loving home. What did I do with thoughts and feelings to the contrary? Like most kids in dysfunctional families, I denied them, stuffed them, or considered them proof of my selfishness and ingratitude. Indeed, I could not trust any positive emotions as real; I could only trust guilt, shame, fear, hurt, and betrayal. In short, to survive my childhood, I accepted perpetual conflict and repressed my emotions, believing that was normal and benign.

Around spontaneous, self-assured kids I felt puny, ugly, and unpopular. I felt safest – most in control – when playing alone. I could then pretend I was one of my favorite fictional heroes: a strong, respected champion of justice, battling on behalf of the unloved and powerless. Thus, childhood nurtured lethal seeds that later bloomed into workaholism: self-denial, self-control, and idealized self-images.

Then I hit puberty. Emotions swirled in a flood of hormones, forcing my mind to resort to more effective means to channel the raging waves. As my body grew stronger, I selected small arenas to play out hero fantasies. Pitching myself wholeheartedly into school and extracurricular projects let me funnel my energies into creating respected self-images. The only price I had to pay was to spend every waking hour struggling towards some socially accepted goal.

By the time I was 18, I had become a professional musician, seeded tennis player, boxing champion, state champion track athlete, straight-A student, and National Merit Scholar. I was president of the statewide youth fellowship, and my high school's selection for Boys State. For two years I went steady with the school's most popular cheerleader, and a month before graduation was awarded a scholarship to Harvard.

Each day, I stuffed into my hip pocket a worn, week-at-a-glance notebook. It was Bible and scorecard, directing every hour of devotion to my disease, insuring I would not forget a commitment in my frenzied pace. Its margins were crammed with lists of tasks to accomplish between meetings and before going to sleep. As long as I was working, thinking about work, or lining up work in my notebook, I felt in control, important, and powerful. When I recalled it – which was not often – the fearful, shameful, guilty self of my childhood seemed like someone from another planet.

Yet, my parents' attitude toward me did not change. No accomplishment was enough to draw my father's praise or win my mother's warmth. My response? Already up to my knees in disease, I dug deeper, tried harder, and sought more accolades. I looked elsewhere for strokes of respect and approval: to teachers, coaches, teammates, and friends.

Workaholism totally engulfed my life. The proof? Awards, publicity, and self-images replaced love, affection, and self-acceptance. Even when I was out of the limelight, the relentless pace of work numbed my mind to the feelings I had not faced that haunted me: lovelessness, powerlessness, resentment, and shame.

College devastated me. My sense of self-worth was completely dependent on high school triumphs. I viewed existence as a perpetual conflict where only superior people survived and were worthy. At Harvard, however, it seemed that every student was a better musician, scholar, or athlete than I. What is more, they all seemed to know exactly who they were and what they wanted to do with their lives – whereas, I did not have a clue. For me, workaholism had been so consuming that I had been too busy (and, of course, too afraid) to discover who I really was or what career might actualize my true self.

For three undergraduate years I battled suicidal depression, interspersed with belligerent bouts of drunkenness and savage play on rugby fields. My college threatened to expel me for riotous behavior. Molding frustration and fear into macho fury made it easy to win the school's middleweight boxing title.

I now realize that those three years I majored in English literature were a desperate attempt to retreat once more to the realm of fictional heroes. At the end of my junior year, foundering in warring emotions and seeing no other way out, I switched my major to psychology. Perhaps there I could safely discover who I was and why life had lost its direction and meaning.

I also became a Zen Buddhist and chose a career in criminal law. In Zen I could probe reality's core. In court I could wield the power I had fantasized about all my life. I could harness disparate skills and energies, and wage real struggles to make justice more than a concept in books.

After a stint in the Air Force, I finished law school, along the way becoming the only law student to argue and win a client's case before my state's supreme court. The latter won me fellowships for further legal studies. I relished the logic and rationality of the law. I was also in love with the most intelligent, talented, and beautiful woman I had ever encountered: my wife.

For five years I litigated criminal cases for and against the government in Washington, D.C., got an advanced law degree, and mentored law students in court for five city law schools. Proud of not taking a vacation during that entire time, I pitched myself day and night into preparing for and conducting trials.

Relentless activity muffled latent self-doubt, while the stakes involved provided adrenalized, grandiose illusions that my work was a matter of life or death. I resumed playing rugby on weekends, despite numerous concussions and broken bones.

Near the end of this litigation time, my six-year honeymoon jarred to a halt. My wife and I had fallen in love with each other's self-images and now found it difficult to sustain these fraying fictions. Yet, we still feared letting each other see who we really were, displaying true emotions, or revealing how insecure we felt most of the time.

One month I was offered a book contract by a publishing firm and a teaching contract by a California school. Nearing burnout in the courtroom, I jumped at the chance to take what I later learned was a "geographic cure." My disease, of course, came with me and soon had me hurling myself into teaching, writing, and expanding the school's law student clinic.

I toiled long hours in the classroom and office, updating my law book until it became the nation's authority. Evenings and weekends (after long distance runs and pumping iron), I would occasionally swoop up my infant sons into a carrier and trudge off on mountain hikes. In my warped mind, paternal bonding could take place only through strenuous activity. Workaholism's lethal blend of anesthesia and adrenaline let seven priceless years of fatherhood slip by in a flash.

One day by sheer accident – or karmic design – I agreed to participate in a friend's addiction recovery program. While I attended numerous meetings and workshops, it gradually dawned on me that the portrayals of addicts' lives, thoughts, and feelings also described my life. If I substituted "addictive activity" for "addictive drinking or using drugs," I was as much an addict as any I had read of or met.

On August 20, 1983 (the day I consider the start of my recovery), I drafted a long letter to my friend's clinic describing my symptoms and asking if there were any treatment programs for workaholics. Weeks later, a response arrived from a therapist who was not certain my request had been serious. He offered what is now too familiar a phrase: "What, workaholism, a disease?!" This spokesman for a cutting edge clinic for recovering addicts knew of no program for people like me.

For the next seven years, I observed my mental habits in light of what was known of the addictive process. I shared experiences with dozens of alcoholics, addicts, and others who worked from compulsive mindsets. To a few workaholic friends I sent a booklet of my findings, urging recognition of workaholism as a disease and detailing discoveries of my own addictive thoughts and acts. Nearly all were supportive; some said I must have been running for years in their shoes.

During this period, I attended sundry meetings of Alcoholic Anonymous. But when I introduced myself as a "workaholic" or a "political alcoholic," I got little sympathy. As the former, I was just another of those willpower people who had been bashing alcoholics for centuries; as the latter, I was a weirdo in search of a social disease. Still, A.A.'s Twelve-Step program seemed relevant and immensely beneficial. On the gut level of shame, fear, escapism, and low self-esteem, the stories I heard in A.A. were mine.

One perceptive recovering addict suggested I attend an Anonymous program for overeaters. Although not overweight, for me the experience was a major breakthrough. It was true – the exigencies of earning a living kept me from completely abstaining from work (as recovering alcoholics abstain from alcohol). But could I learn to face work without being compulsive, as recovering overeaters must daily face food? Trying to synthesize wisdom from these two other programs, I wrote a year's worth of daily meditations for recovering workaholics.

In 1990, I finally did find other recovering workaholics in the form of a W.A. meeting that had recently started in San Francisco. After contacting them, I decided I could no longer recover alone and started another city's first W.A. group. In two years, over 100 people attended. I volunteered for W.A.'s first World Service Organization. Getting to know scores of other recovering workaholics awakened me to the power and immensity of this insidious disease: its deep roots, its destruction of families and health, its religious and economic rationalizations, and its encouragement by cultures around the globe.

I continue unearthing facets of workaholism in my life: how strong emotions spark tendencies to turn from feelings and engage in distracting projects instead; how feeling powerless beckons me to physically control (or mentally understand) whatever stands between me and my desires; how doubts of self-worth urge me to build and believe in self-images; how inaction prompts me to fidget and make plans; and how silence tempts me to fill my mind with music, movies, or news.

I am resigned to the likelihood that these mental propensities will never cease wailing their siren songs. But from all honest beings I encounter (including dogs, horses, and other non-human beings), I learn how to meet what is real.

Though my parents are dead, I have accepted their steadfast refusal to see what their parenting caused. This includes their refusal to acknowledge who their son actually was and that their lives were ravaged by unrecognized fears. In a volatile marriage of 30-plus years, my wife and I now discover, accept, and nurture each other's true selves, and freely share them instead of dancing or sparring with ghosts and self-images.

My fictional life is finally over. I am more real, more honest, and more me. Most days, I feel wonder and joy from just waking without yellow chalk silhouetting my form. On some days, fierce emotional weather blows in from far poles. But I welcome all genuine feelings, those of others and my own, and refuse to deny, distort, or flee from them.

As a practicing workaholic, I never imagined that serenity dwelt in my core. Now I can feel it merely by reaching through layers of what is not me: titles, accomplishments, and this story of past events. It seems like a daily miracle to me how serenity can prevail through battering by chaos and freefalls, and through mineshafts of "I-don't-knows." And, as sublime paradox and cosmic joke, I am getting much more work done!

Living Flowly

It was January 1988. I awoke one morning totally exhausted, the start of what I was later to learn was Chronic Fatigue Syndrome. (The name CFIDS had not been invented yet.) The doctor said it was the flu, and that it would vanish within a month.

It did not. My normal rushed pace slowed to a crawl. For the first time in my life, I, a perpetual motion machine, learned to rest. Grudgingly, I cut back on my hectic round of activities, one by one. It was humbling and unreliable to say, "I can't," to surrender indispensability, and to have to ask for help even in tiny things. As I lay in bed, my normally racing mind moved glacially.

Despite my frustration at not being able to fulfill my schedule, I felt a deeper peace of mind than I had ever known. I wanted to cling to this serenity forever. I also wanted my vitality to return – but I feared that if it did, I would plunge back into my nonstop pace. What I really wanted was energy without frenzy.

While resting, I recalled parental voices. "Hurry up!" "Can't you ever do anything right?" "Grab it before someone else does." No matter what I did growing up, it was not OK; it was either wrong or not enough. I absorbed my parents' attitudes of shame, guilt, and fear and beat myself up mentally on a daily basis.

The internal flogging made me driven and insatiable. The more I excelled, the higher I set my unreasonable standards. My mind pushed my body to achieve the impossible as I tried to become the family heroine who would heal my mentally challenged brother and psychotic sister, reconcile my battling, divorced parents, and rescue us all from poverty. I became a robot, out of touch with my body and being. I crawled out of bed when I awoke, no matter how little or badly I had slept, galvanized by the blaring, overloaded to-do list that ruled my existence. Then I raced to beat the clock by overdoing. Adrenaline and caffeine kept me hyper until I collapsed each night. Added to this feeling of being driven was my own racing, insatiably curious mind. I wanted to know and experience everything *right now*!

Years in Twelve-Step programs had begun healing my addictions to achievement, worry, hurry, perfectionism, codependency, lack of focus, imbalance, and impatience. But I still had far to go. Because my family members had died before I could rescue them, I felt that I now had to live five lives – that of myself, my parents, and my two siblings.

Even on Recovery Road, speeding is dangerous when powered by adrenaline and when racing without brakes. I thought my life was balanced because I had variety, but it was nonstop variety. I thought I worked sanely because I delegated, prioritized, set limits and rarely worked overtime. I thought I had made a lot of progress because my activities and relationships were healthy. Unfortunately, the emphasis was on "a lot," not on "progress."

I thought I had healed the "rush-aholic" by slowing from 150 mph to 90; the "care-aholic" by no longer needing to be needed; the "drudge" by learning to do things just for pleasure; the "self-hater" by experiencing feelings instead of medicating myself with food and work; and the "compulsive" by collapsing from nonstop activity binges. I now took breaks, working little and often, except that the little periods of time occurred too often. My mechanical methods worked only superficially because I had transferred my addictive behavior to recovery. I did too much service, had too many hobbies, and went to too many meetings.

From being a self-debtor who did not nurture myself, I switched to beating myself up with, "You deserve this. And that. And that." My choices were good, but too much is still too much. Recovery opened endless opportunities, thus encouraging my "experience greed." No program taught me to be selective.

After I had driven myself mercilessly for 55 years, my body finally massively rebelled. Before this, my body had tried migraine, burnout, and breakdown to get through to me, but never this prolonged exhaustion, even after ten hours of sleep! I knew this was the final wakeup call; if I ever were to recoup my strength, I would surely overdo and then collapse with a fatal heart attack. I was terrified and stuck.

What a dilemma! I needed a program to teach me how to do less, yet adding it meant doing more. Wasn't that crazy? But fire is used to fight fire. Maybe the meeting could be used homeopathically the same way.

I did not know whether a fellowship for workaholics even existed. Would it mean I would have to start a whole new organization? Fortunately, a few months later I found W.A., but none of its meetings were near me. Having started Twelve-Step meetings before, I knew how much time and energy they took, even in established programs.

I had always worked alone. There was no way I could do that now. I decided I would start W.A. in the area, if my Higher Power were to send help. While waiting, I wrote a meeting format, acting "as if," and feeling this was right. Then I received literature from W.A. and the feeling intensified. I also got a "click," remembering I had dreamt this sequence.

One day, at the Twelve-Step office where I worked, a woman came in to buy literature. Noting that she seemed anxious, I asked her whether she was all right. She asked whether I knew of a program for workaholics and said her husband needed help.

Finally! "I have been waiting for someone to start a W.A. meeting with me," I said.

"I will tell my husband about you," she replied.

I waited several months for his call. Waiting is hard for me, but I knew that over-eagerness would distort the rhythm of the process.

When he phoned, we arranged to get together in my office to set up the recovery meeting. In September 1988, the Thursday after Labor Day, we began the local W.A. meeting in a living room in a location that was on my way home from work. During some of these early meetings, I would be so tired, I would just lie on the couch. To save my energy, my husband would drive me there.

For several months, it was just one other person and myself, despite our best efforts to find others. That is when I learned to wait. My style had been to plunge into projects and they would take off. Not this time. It took a year of sporadic visitors until our meeting cohered into a committed group.

A month after our meeting began, my energy slowly began to return. It was not the driven kind of energy. It was natural energy. I had not experienced that type of energy since I was a child, so it felt unnatural. Evidently Higher Power understood that, because my natural energy was doled out slowly.

As my energy gradually increased, I stayed attuned to my body. I began to appreciate rest. Until then, I had resented rest as wasted time. Instead, I saw it as part of the cycle of activity. I regained my natural pace and rhythm, just as I regained my natural hunger and appetite in another Twelve-Step program.

My new awareness made my life a film running in slow motion. By catching myself in "do-aholic," adrenalized lapses, I watched with horror, sadness, and compassion as I followed a killing pace set by fear, guilt, greed, pride, low self-esteem, and habit.

I became aware of how I lost track of many of my thoughts, acted hurriedly and needlessly in order to swell my self-importance, set overly high standards, did busy work, filled pauses by inserting activities, read standing up because sitting took too long, and perched myself on the edge of a chair with my heels up, ready to sprint.

I became aware of how I created work stashes, filled calendar spaces without allowing time for transitions, juggled three tasks at once, underestimated the time it took to do tasks (sometimes aware my guesses were fantasy), made mistakes because of rushing or not being prepared, sat in recovery meetings while filling in schedules to ensure that I would always be busy, repeatedly sacrificed my own needs while enabling other people, raced to end a project so that I could plunge into yet another, and let the telephone be a tyrant, my conversations being completely task oriented.

Then the film sped up to "normal" and my life blurred by. As an observer, I tasted the adrenaline dancing in my blood and felt repelled, not exhilarated.

The moments of clarity lengthened. The to-do list and the clock loosened their grip. Impatience, impulsiveness, and living in "when I get caught up" were transformed into being deliberate, thorough, selective, and staying in the now. Some milestones:

1. Learning the difference between driven and motivated.
2. Being content without feeling stagnant.
3. Being able to postpone.
4. Saying "no" without feeling deprived or guilty.
5. Giving only from my extra reserves of energy.
6. Enjoying emptiness.
7. Quieting the S.H.A.M.E. voice (Should Have Already Mastered Everything).
8. Delaying the return of phone calls and the answering of mail.
9. Stopping before I ran out of enthusiasm by saying, "I have enjoyed as much of this as I can stand."
10. Valuing a comfortable pace.
11. Making friends with time, rest, and sleep, knowing that I do not have time not to have time, and that, without sleep and rest, all is worthless.
12. Enjoying being with myself without distractions.

My early instincts for order, balance, timing, rhythm, gracefulness, and flexibility returned. Life became seamless instead of segmented into doing/being, work/play, and leisure/sleep/rest.

No longer racing from one achievement to another, I now acknowledge and celebrate my completions. Enjoyment, ease, and effortlessness have replaced quantity, speed, and struggle. Events happen through me, not to me. I call this way "living flowly," living without resistance, and flowing with God's plan.

A good day used to involve surpassing my to-do list by being Robot, Superwoman, and World Mother. Now a good day is living timelessly, moving at a rhythm that allows me to stay available to Higher Power, being fully present, registering and integrating impressions, noticing small and simple pleasures such as shadows, hearing and heeding my body, speaking from my heart, spotting patterns of ideas, objects, and events, harvesting the messages from dreams and unusual experiences, being mindful of my attention, energy, actions, and growth, and nurturing my new self-friendship.

When I live at the right pace, I fully experience a feeling. I pick up subtle messages from short-term memory. I see what is not there. I hear what goes unsaid. I consider the impact of my words and decisions. I incorporate change and surprise easily. Playfulness, joy, and humor bubble up.

In these years of recovery, society sped up while I moved into the slow lane. As our W.A. meeting grew, I helped form World Service and wrote literature. I had almost the energy level I had before, but without the push of adrenaline. It was a challenge to keep my sane pace and not use service to justify overdoing.

I owe my recovery from Chronic Fatigue Syndrome (CFS) to W.A., to willingness to change, and to my Higher Power. During the illness, if I tried to overexert, I got a firm thought that I must rest and that I knew I had about five minutes' grace to stop, probably because Higher Power realized that years of overriding body signals had dulled my instincts. Those warnings gradually became more faint – similar to the volume of my sense of thirst. I thought I was imagining this, but later I heard others with CFS talk about sharing the same experience. They also said that their biggest problem was to resist impulses to "seize the time" and overdo during energy surges. Because of W.A., I was able to avoid these impulses.

My journey has been an example of divine order: locating W.A. and a partner in recovery to help me start a meeting at the right time; regaining my energy shortly after our meeting began; committed members arriving after we had some recovery; and regaining my harmony with divine plan. I now act by timing, not time.

Joy is the energy of acceptance. When I stop using my will to force life to meet my desires and simply flow with life, the result is joy. By moving at God's pace, I am flowing with life. Join me.

Time Prosperity is My Goal:
Recovering from Work Anorexia

I am the adult child of a work addict. I was born in the early 1960s. My father was intensely work-addicted (as well as afflicted with alcoholism and other addictions) and my mother, as a chief enabler to my father, was quite disengaged from herself. As my parents were in their forties by the time of my birth, their childhoods and early adult lives were profoundly affected by both the Great Depression and World War II. From an already poor family, my father had worked from the age of five years old, only to see all his family's precious savings lost as banks worldwide failed in 1929, when he was just eleven. After this historic and unusual event, my father decided that the ability to perform hard work without stopping was the only hope onto which he could hold in uncertain or unstable times. Once he started running in a race with himself and the world, he never stopped, even many decades later. My mother's Victorian, moneyed, and fatherless upbringing had left her so emotionally shut down that when her husband to be, my father, first appeared in her life, I am sure his intensity and addiction to constant action seemed to her like a wonderful, alive breath of fresh air to her.

I was born the youngest of five children and the third boy. I watched my parents and my siblings work hard, long hours simultaneously at many different self-employment styled businesses. All of my siblings and I worked in these ventures for as long a period as my parents could pressure us into, usually well into our twenties or even thirties. My father was the entrepreneur, breadwinner, and director of all action. My mother was the housewife, eventually becoming his secretary and bookkeeper. Despite all of my family's efforts, we repeatedly sold businesses at a loss. Only recently did I find a great description of this energy in the phrase "professional promiscuity." My father would start a relationship with a business, then withdraw his attention away from that one and start courting another business idea without continuing or finishing the first effort.

Years later, my siblings and I discovered that many of the financial and business gains to which my parents had always credited hard work had actually come from money inherited by my mother. In fact, with all the financial losses we incurred, if my parents had just not gone into about half of the businesses at which we toiled, we would have been far wealthier financially! But I came to learn that financial prosperity, while officially always the stated goal, was actually "the enemy," so to speak. That is to say, if we were to have gotten ahead financially, then there would have been a lot less justification for constant activity. So the money my mother inherited made it seem as though our work addict pace was getting us ahead. In actuality, it just hid the financial loss that I now believe always eventually accompanies the spiritual bankruptcy of work addiction.

From an early age, my siblings and I were pressured by our father to engage in never-ending mental activity. We were told that this was the only way to maintain enough hyper-vigilance to be safe from a dangerous world. "Always be on guard, lest we be unguarded." "Do not take a break because that is when you will fall behind." To stop thinking in order to acknowledge feelings (in other words, having any kind of internal spiritual experience) was considered weak and irresponsible. My father used to refer to people he did not like, for instance those who were not constantly doing something (or men who had long hair!) as "lazy bums." The word "lazy" in my house was considered a terrible slight, and my father used it frequently to shout at the television when he saw certain people appear on the screen. If I was not constantly moving and "thinking ahead" as he put it, he would accuse me of laziness, judging my effort to be a total waste and me to be incompetent. My father was happy to tell me just exactly what a worthwhile effort was and what was not.

But just how I should determine that on my own, without him to do it for me, was never clearly defined. Even though he did encourage me to take the lead at times, when I did take charge, no matter what I did related to work, he or my mother either criticized my effort as being wasteful and foolish, or, less often, they might go in the other direction completely and tell me my work was totally the best they had ever seen! It was all or nothing with little, ever, falling in between. What I learned from this treatment was that I was not capable of telling what was real in the world; was I stupid and lazy or was I a star genius? I did not really feel qualified to be successful on my own without an "action critic" nearby. In many instances, I can remember throwing myself into some kind of activity because I was afraid my parents would be arriving soon, and I had better "get something done" (in other words, get anything, therefore ultimately nothing, done). For all of my father's talk of discipline, he actually was constantly in a "self-will run riot" of ever-changing activity. He would talk about the need for consistent effort at school, business, or life, but then he would display the exact opposite himself. By virtue of her silence about such insanity in my father, my mother's denial made it appear that she sanctioned his view of himself as an effective leader. In fact, it was my mother's and my older siblings' consistent work that kept things functioning, not my father's recurring work binges or erratic directives.

About the time I was 12 or 13 years old, I started noticing other kids at school, as well as adults, who did not work as hard at their life as my parents had assured me I needed to in order to succeed. My fellow students seemed unconcerned if they did not constantly try to learn everything they could, every second. They played and took breaks without guilt and worry. And when the teacher assigned certain sections of a chapter to read, they would study pretty much those pages only. My father had taught me that if I studied all of the pages of all my schoolbooks, I would get ahead. I tried to do that, but there were so many extra pages to read that I would get confused by all the additional information and do poorly on tests because I had tried to learn too much.

Between school and my parents, it was as though life were a sandcastle and there was always an approaching tide that kept washing away all of my efforts. So I did not know what to think. Was life just a big work binge? Was the only way to prevent failure to make everything simultaneously a number one priority, staying vigilant and hurrying so I could keep all the sand in the castle? I began to question the dedication to "eternal work vigilance" that my father had never stopped preaching. I think this was when I became disillusioned with work and goal setting of any kind, believing action to be never-ending as well as never truly fruitful. I saw other people succeed by taking action, but I just felt frozen.

Finally, the intense shame I felt over what I perceived as my total inferiority to "real" goal pursuers caused the pendulum to swing the other way. My only solution became to try to work harder and harder at not committing to seeking to achieve anything. To commit to or become excited by a goal just felt as though it was either creating false hope or signing up for self-condemnation if I could not deliver by the deadline. I came to distrust any ongoing effort from which the results were not immediately evident. Unlike the work addict who does and does and does, just for the mood altering or approval that indiscriminate or repeated action brings, I became obsessed with only taking actions that I could convince myself would pay off big and right away, so as to prevent any delay, disappointment, waste, or regret. I was the quintessential perfectionist. Eventually, all living became about just getting through each day. I avoided all thoughts of any plans beyond the current moment. I had lost any trust in my own desires or my own vision for myself, so what reason was there to create goals or endure sacrifices on the way to anything else? I believe it was in this giving up of my personal visions that I became a work anorexic.

After high school, I had a go at college. My experience of higher education was that these institutions felt entitled to ask a lot of work from me as it suited them. I did not have the benefit of knowing my own desires or goals that could have inspired me to face these challenges. So I quit college and drifted about, alternating many times between what I called "dead end blue collar jobs" and returning to work for my parents. In my personal time, I turned to distracting myself from the intense pain of this "giving up on life" with endless television, fantasizing about women, and eventually compulsive eating. I was always pretending I was a successful action taker like some of the people I saw being interviewed on talk shows. Even setting goals felt too painful to risk. But without deciding on actions and then taking them, I forfeited almost all of life's pleasures, since such pleasures are only achieved or secured by repeated and conscious effort over a period of time longer than a drive thru meal order or a TV sitcom. When the pain of going nowhere in my life was unbearable, I relied on the fantasy that I would be rescued from that hell by someone or something else. But I did not know what. I lived in a day-to-day random pattern, acting as though I were in a waiting room and someday a happy life, complete with achievements, would be delivered. But I had better not move around too much in the meantime, because I might miss the delivery person when they arrived at my door.

Finally, at the age of 26, I emotionally crashed. Hard. I could not work at all. I went to live (where else?) back with my parents. I was facing other addictions and seeing a therapist, and that was a good start. I did hold to a strict line of not working for my father who, of course, would have hired me in two seconds or less for his latest business. Instead, I did odd jobs around the house for my mother, which was bearable. Sadly, my mother died very suddenly one day from an aneurysm, after almost two years of my home-based recovery effort. I knew if I stayed living alone with my dad I would explode. I moved out and went back to the entry level blue collar world I hated. But I had the support of my early Twelve-Step fellowships. I had not heard of W.A. yet, but when I did, I thought to myself, "Well, I am certainly not a workaholic!" However, in early 1993, when a friend put the W.A. general pamphlet into my hand, I was impressed with the ideas inside. Just reading the tools started my healing. They can still give me a serenity break today. That W.A. pamphlet gave me hope about work that I had never before felt. The idea that some things are better left undone was completely revolutionary when compared to the way I was taught to think. My anorexic fear that all goal-setting will turn into a runaway train of action began to melt away with my first reading of the literature. But I still did not go to the one W.A. group I had heard was recently started in town, because I knew I could not be a work addict. After all, I hated my jobs and would have loved nothing more than to quit them right away.

On July first of that year, I got a speeding ticket for doing 51 mph in a 35 mph zone on my way to a haircut appointment across town. It was my day off, and I had plenty of time to leave early enough. But I never could seem to leave early enough for anything. I would always deny how long it actually took me to get anywhere. Then, as the time window to act came and went, I would suddenly come alive in an adrenalized frenzy to be on time. However, this time, like so many times in the past, my "rolling under the gate before it shut" took the form of speeding in my car. Police tend to frown on this. Or smile. The ticket cost me about $115, I think, but in an unusual move, I paid it the same day I received it. I took it as a message from God to get myself to W.A., and so I did.

Since initially attending W.A., my recovery has been in fits and starts and I still have a ways to go. I can say that I am now definitely better able to survive, without so much reaction, unexpected changes in events or someone failing my expectations. I have struggled with getting and keeping a sponsor (or a therapist, for that matter) in any of the several programs for which I qualify. W.A. meetings have been very small and scarce where I live in the Southeastern United States, although now I use the telephone to connect with W.A. members from other areas.

Other areas of unmanageability have pulled me in many directions, and those of us who are "multiple winners" can appreciate how multiple addiction recovery makes simply getting out of bed on some days an act of over-scheduling! Part of being stuck has been that all of my employers, without exception, were active work addicts. Working for and with active work addicts almost every day for many years, coupled with under earning (meaning there is never enough money to take much or any time off), can make the work of recovery seem like...well, just more dang work!

Towards that end, God sent me a wonderful doctor of homeopathy, but being distrustful of his help, I pushed the idea away for over two years. I lowered my standards and raised my behavior. "Try to remember that though God has wrought miracles among us, we should never belittle a good doctor or psychiatrist. Their services are often indispensable in treating a newcomer and in following his case afterward" (*Alcoholics Anonymous* 133). While at a meeting I read this paragraph and I realized I had been fending off a prompting to go to this doctor who, in his case, is really a holistic version of a psychiatrist. I have been his patient for several years, now, and it has helped my recovery tremendously. Things are not perfect, but they are so much better than they would have been without his help. Of course, my goal is to work with a W.A. sponsor and formally go through all of the Steps. But I wanted to acknowledge that, "Bad breath is better than no breath!" Until relatively recently, this doctor was as close of a thing to a sponsor as I could accept without quitting the relationship. I have never felt pressured by him to achieve anything – except, perhaps, patience with my own process!

Defining the powerlessness of work anorexia has been a slow process, and sometimes I feel like I am still working to define it today. I have called myself a "quit-aholic" or a "dishonest prioritizer"! But a surrender to personal or professional long-term plans or dreams is usually absent in the life of an anorexic. Using a "prioritizing prayer" to ask for help seems to really work to help me get off the dime if I am frozen. But by getting as clear as I can about what I really want for my life, even when fear has me stuck, I feel inspired enough to take action. As an anorexic, I was always clear on what I did *not* want in my life! So I make what I want known by writing it out, at a minimum. I also speak about it with friends and sponsors on an ongoing basis.

I used to think admitting what I really wanted was the same as demanding that God make my dreams come true, and that when I admitted it, I would turn into a runaway work addict like my father. But I do not pray for God to give me what I want. If God is my employer, I need only pray for God's will for me and the power to carry that out. I do believe desire is a God-given energy. For me, admitting what my desires are is a form of humility and clarity of self that is necessary to guide my goal setting. I use a definition of happiness I recently found. The anonymous quote is, "Happiness is overcoming obstacles on the way to a goal of your own choosing." Before I attended W.A., my disease would not allow me to risk any effort towards personal goals. But now, with the passing of a few seasons in fellowship, I see that God gave me willingness to begin such efforts some time ago.

My parents are gone now, and although my habit of earning from work-addicted employers is less problematic, my Work-Anon issues are indeed worth revisiting from time to time. The pattern of getting stuck in avoidance or perfection-seeking and losing sight of goals until I grind down to a halt can create a vacuum that draws a work-addicted person of some kind into my life. Yet, it really is my own work anorexia that paves the way for that pattern. Today, I am careful to be aware of my part in any relationships with active work addicts.

In summary, here is a list of benefits to me, so far, from the fellowship of W.A.:

1. I am better at facing the music in many of life's arenas without the near constant pattern of self-sabotage that once plagued me.
2. My relationship with the work I do for earning is much better.
3. I have some money from an investment that I am using to start my own business.
4. I would like to get married (I probably should date first!), and I believe in taking my life one day at a time.
5. I can have fun now during my workday, and if I cannot, I get out of that space or relationship.
6. I used to be in denial about priorities. I knew about them, but I used to push them away as though my awareness of them was optional.
7. Prayer and meditation, which I call daily quiet time, is now a reality for me after years of being totally uncomfortable being alone with just my own thoughts and feelings with no distractions allowed.
8. While there is much healing I would have liked to have achieved for myself by now, I can come to accept that I am OK just as I am in this moment, whatever that may look like.
9. I try to remember to include playful attitudes, so that if my day feels too serious, I sometimes step back from it all. I know that "enlightenment means lightening up!"
10. When my recovery efforts have gotten sporadic, service to others has helped me return to W.A., time and again. Staying connected to other W.A. members makes it easier for me to remember that work is not an end in itself, but my means to God's ends.

I still have days where I leave too little time for errands, or I over-schedule travel time to an appointment and arrive late. My goal is to consistently leave early enough so I will not be tempted to hurry. That way, I have some waiting time when I arrive at my destination, an outcome I used to think of as a "total waste." If I do indulge in over-scheduling, or refuse to reprioritize when circumstances warrant, I can count on feeling "time poor," driven, and desperate. In contrast, when I make "time prosperity" my goal, I surrender (with the help of ongoing Step work) all that my Higher Power indicates I need not do today. Then serenity is mine, and I feel time prosperous, relaxed, and much saner with what I do choose to do today.

For these things and more, I have W.A. to thank. So thank you W.A. Thank you!

Choices: Hitting a Bottom and Connecting to the Queen of Everything

How It Was

I grew up in a small, multi-addicted family in countries of extreme poverty. I was the adult child and I grew up fast. Legally emancipated at age 14, I was accustomed to using work to achieve self-reliance and freedom. After moving to an English-speaking country and learning English, I was lucky to encounter some kind people from whom I asked for help with a couple of things, including my addictions. When Twelve-Step programs were suggested to me at 17 years of age, I joined enthusiastically and immediately worked the program.

I have been fortunate to not relapse. I have 22 years of clean, sober, and abstinent living. The first five years were a journey of self-discovery. Some random examples include discoveries that I had interests and talents in dancing and sports, I loved animals, I enjoyed travel, I was a lesbian, and I was a night owl. In terms of W.A.-related matters, I learned the extent my parents' personal values had affected their professional lives, and that I had adopted their values about education, freedom, and social equality. (Both teachers, they had immense passion about their careers and embodied their values fully at home and at work, despite their addictions.)

I learned that there was a career combination in which I could fulfill my own dreams of helping people in their personal and professional lives. In order to achieve this goal, I worked full-time to fund my studies, completed a dual Ph.D., and set up two businesses (a practice of clinical psychotherapy and a human resources consultancy). I enjoyed the work itself. I also liked my clients in both businesses, and we were able to accomplish their goals together. I enjoyed the fruits of my labor; I could afford nice vacations and a nice home, and I shared my wealth with friends and gave to charities. I had rewarding relationships, danced, and exercised regularly. I worked and played hard. I was passionate about life, and I had a good time at and outside of work. This was the case for years.

What Happened

Then, somehow, the balance tipped. Passion turned to compulsion. Perhaps the guilt of being an immigrant caught up with me during the 2002 U.S. recession; perhaps I hit a level of seniority in my work where gender differences increased and competing was harder; perhaps memories of extreme poverty in Africa resurfaced; and perhaps a dormant disease of workaholism awakened. The way I worked changed markedly within months. Sprinkled in with my usual enjoyment were episodes of worry and compulsion, both at work and on weekends. I took on a sense of seriousness and pressure with projects – even household ones! I started to obsess about work in my free time. Soon enough, I could not leave projects until they were finished, which meant I sometimes went to bed at dawn. This new compulsion/addiction impacted the amount and quality of time with my loved ones and my interests (such as art, dancing, running, foster parenting kittens, etc.). I did not stop any of these hobbies entirely, but they sure slowed down. My hours spent working might have increased a little, but the way I worked was what really changed.

I have a great network of friends, and I asked some of them if they noticed anything different over a period of months. Most said no, but a close friend agreed that going to a W.A. meeting would be a good idea. I must say that, as a high bottom, I did not lose what many others did, such as health, relationships, time, or jobs. Instead, I am a workaholic who jumped off a fast descending elevator, and I am very grateful I took notice and action quickly. I had already lost my work-life balance, peace of mind, perspective, and conscious contact with Higher Power.

How It Is Now

I am new to W.A. I attacked the W.A. program with some perfectionism and compulsion for the first month, but I have settled into a healthy pace now. I balance my work and personal time by asking my Higher Power to remove my money worries and work obsessions. You would think this would come naturally to me, since I have been turning my life and my will over to The Queen of Everything ("Q of E," my Higher Power) for so many years, but it is a daily, conscious effort. Practically speaking, I have also set boundaries on maximum hours worked a week, weekends, lunch breaks, etc. Additionally, I find that carving out gaps in my work and personal schedules for spontaneity yields nice surprises. How can little miracles and fun things happen to me if I am always rushing around?

Another thing that works for me is to make amends immediately to folks around me at work when I get compulsive or impatient, as per the Tenth Step. I have let a couple of close corporate colleagues know about my involvement in W.A., and they support me when I fall off the turnip truck. Sometimes, they laughingly ask me to read my daily meditations, and I cannot help but notice how closely they listen to the meditations when I read them out loud.

I believe that it is Q of E's will for me to continue my lines of work and maintain my work-life balance. I believe that, just like my parents and grandparents, I was destined to be of service in the world. I believe many of us are, particularly we addicts. I find that, just like my other addictions, my journey of recovery from workaholism enriches my existence and increases my ability to serve others. God knows the planet needs more socially responsible world citizens who give back as much, or more, than they take.

I might be suffering from a huge case of projection, but it does seem to me that workaholism is a common, under-diagnosed, socially reinforced disease.

The Myth of a Workaholic Geographic Cure

While I know, intellectually, that this is wrong, I have had a workaholic equivalent of the "geographic cure" in the back of my head for years. I am self-employed and have worked excessively trying to make my business successful. The story I tell myself is that, if my workaholism ever gets so bad I cannot take it anymore, I can give up my self-employment dream and get a "real" job, and my troubles will go away. If I had an office job working for someone else, the story goes, I would be able to leave work at the office and lead a normal life, as long as I pick a low stress occupation. I recently proved to myself what I already knew: that my workaholism goes with me wherever I go. I had been working a part-time temporary assignment as a secretary. I have done this work off and on for years. It is work I consider fairly low stress and not challenging. On top of this, I was a temporary employee, not even a real employee. And yet, during a busy week, I found myself awake at 3 AM, going over in my head a list of things I had to do at the office the next day and strategizing about how I could get everything done. This experience shook me, because it proved once and for all that I would never be able to escape my disease by changing jobs. The truth is, I am an adrenaline addict and I will find my drug wherever I go. My self-employment has given me an opportunity to work unchecked and to work myself into high states of stress. But I know that, even if I worked doing something completely mindless, I would bring my perfectionism, my need for approval, my desire to be the best, and my physical need for adrenaline with me. While some work situations lend themselves to stress more than others, I have to face the reality that I can find stress anywhere. Now that my mental escape hatch is closed, I am more committed than ever to working my program. A change of scenery will not help me; only the spiritual solution I can find through W.A. will save me from my addiction.

Cutting Loose from the Workplace

"So, what are you going to do with all of your free time?" This is the most common question I encountered after announcing my retirement plans.

My initial reaction was to respond by listing all of the activities I planned to do in my typical workaholic mode. However, after reflecting on it, my response evolved into: "What am I going to do? Anything I want to."

After 41 years of government service, I am looking forward to having the flexibility of being able to choose what I would like to do each day, whether it be playing with my three-year-old grandson, taking long walks with my wife, visiting my daughter and son-in-law, working out at the gym, or enrolling in classes.

My retirement on December 31, 2002, has come after a long journey. I was eligible eight years ago, but I was too wrapped up in my job to let it go. I loved the work and the people. I still do, but I have come to realize that too much of my time revolved around the workplace. I spent those eight years plunging into new, exciting projects promoting energy efficiency in the construction of homes and the selection of lighting products. It was rewarding, but it consumed valuable time from my family.

I am 63 years old. Although I have been blessed with good health, I do not want to jeopardize future good times with my wife and family that could come with declining health.

A few months ago, I was visiting my daughter and grandson, who (I am lucky) live in the same city. My grandson asked if I was going to stay after lunch so we could play. I had to tell him "no" because I had to get back to work. As I left, I asked myself how I could give up these priceless moments with him.

Trips to the Pacific Coast with my wife used to be cut short because of work obligations. Now, we are looking forward to extended visits to the seashore.

I really do not know what I am going to do in retirement. My highest priority is spending more time with my family and retaining and improving my mental and physical health. W.A. introduced me to many healthy attitudes toward loved ones and work, so that I was finally able to make the decision to retire in November 2002.

Although I had some trepidation before turning in my retirement papers, I experienced terrific relief right afterwards. Now, each day as I clean out my office, I feel more and more relaxed. Even the photos, letters, and articles that I am removing are not a sad experience; they are relocations of wonderful past experiences. However, I realize that it is time to look up from the treadmill I have been on and experience the rest of the world besides work.

I was hiking one morning recently with my wife when she volunteered to carry my knapsack for a while. It did not feel heavy, so I continued to carry it for two more miles. Then I asked her to carry it. Although it had not felt heavy on my back, as soon as I took it off, I experienced great relief.

I think that I am going to feel the same way after leaving my job. Retirees have already told me that I will not believe the relief of pressure until after I leave. In fact, some have advised me to do nothing for three months to decompress from the work environment.

One final admonition that I am taking from my W.A. advisors is to realize that I will have to remain vigilant to my workaholic tendencies, even in retirement. In other words, leaving the workplace does not mean that I have left my workaholic characteristics behind.

I am looking forward to this interesting transition in my life.

My Friend the Clock

Growing up in a home with two workaholics, I was patterned early on to ignore my biological needs, in enslavement to the anesthesia of compulsive doing and worrying. My father worked 16 to 20 hours a day as a research chemist. What little time he was home was spent raging, silent, or compulsively reading or watching TV. My mother sheathed herself in a world of compulsive writing and reading day and night, and secretly suffered from an eating disorder. The 20 cups of coffee and four packs of cigarettes consumed by each parent every day augmented their fixations. Verbal abuse was shared for anything less than perfect behavior. The only planned meal was dinner, and my parents were incapable of sleeping regular hours. They did not teach us consistent self-care, including regular food, exercise, or sleep. Our home was a temple to the impulsive doing of the moment. Long hours playing in the yard offered some salve to the afflictions within the house. Public school was my island of interactivity and normality into which I threw myself with the fervor of a true young workaholic.

I was a young perfectionist and mostly received perfect marks. My fifth grade teacher marked me a "two" (on a scale of one to five, one being best) for self-control. I would fly in to a crying fit whenever things did not go my way or kids called me names. She noticed that there was a connection between how much sleep I had gotten the night before and my emotional state. She began to check in with me each morning to see how much sleep I had gotten. What she and I never consciously discovered then was that sleep deprivation was a great way to start adrenaline cycling.

By high school, my disease had perfected an intersection of eating disorder, sleep and time debting, and work addiction to maximize adrenaline cycling. I would get two to three hours of sleep, begin school with a 6:30 AM "zero period" academic competition class, then grind through seven more classes (while also leading a 50-person service club and a 300-person academic performance group). In retrospect, I see how sleep deprivation would set me up for a day of being off balance and predisposed to emotional drama, or highly charged emotional releases that gave me a "fix" of adrenaline from my body's own pharmacy. By lunchtime, I would be feeling particularly angry or sad, eat only a sugary cookie for lunch, and then travel the peaks and valleys of that sugar high through the afternoon. Food withholding forced my body into an adrenaline reaction because of the need to maintain at least a minimal blood sugar; skipping meals is an emergency because the body desires homeostasis. Sugar bingeing also generated that "buzz." I used both to maintain the adrenaline. My first meal of the day was usually a fast food burrito at around 5 or 6 PM. I would then stay up until 2 AM, avoiding or plunging into my homework. One of the tricks of maintaining an adrenaline high is to rightly time the balance of food withholding, sugar bingeing, sleep deprivation, and emotional stress. Of course, this was all unconscious for me at the time.

Being late was an adrenaline feast for my disease. Because I was "high," I lived behind and out of my body a lot of the time. I had crammed too much into my schedule. Because of the tunnel of perception within which I was living, the character defect of perfectionism, and the emotional roller coaster caused by adrenaline cycling, I perceived being late as a crisis. I would swear, curse, and speed. I would have internal or external emotional dramas. I had a million stories of victimization and justification for each incident. Of course, all along, being late was really a way to get more adrenaline. To say I was out of control and my life was unmanageable was an understatement. I was like "Pig-Pen" in the comic strip *Peanuts* by Charles M. Schulz. In a dust cloud of drama, self-abuse, and internal "speed," I was mainlining my own body as a drug source.

The process fed on itself. I was so out of control, I was late for everything. Every time I was late, my perfectionism, self-involved anxiety, sugar addiction, and sleep deprivation kept me fully stocked. My body could not sustain the ravages of the adrenaline cycling. By age 16, this resulted in my desperate suicide attempt from intense feelings of self-hatred and isolation. My parents forced me to see a psychotherapist. This kind, well intentioned professional was uneducated about the disease of workaholism and tried to work with me to reduce my commitments, but with an approach that was cognitive, "pull yourself up by your bootstraps" through self-will, and of no long-term help. By age 16, I was getting sick a lot. I missed a third of the days of school due to illness and because my parents would let me stay home to get caught up on my schoolwork. This only caused me to get further behind by missing classes. By age 18, from adrenaline racing, I had caused a car wreck and been run over on my way (late) to a scholarship interview. This is not to mention my other five car accidents while in high school. I also went to school every summer. By graduation, I had received over 30 awards, including several national awards and scholarships.

I moved to a different state for a rigorous college education. Although I had completely left my family (addiction of origin) context by then, the addiction had successfully mastered me and I was faithful to its practices. While taking college classes, I was the editor of the school paper, director of the educational winter term, and ran over 20 student organizations while helping develop new college programs and doing intensive political organizing. I was adrenaline cycling constantly. By this point, I was having not only the emotional and mental effects (daily suicidal ideation, alienating others with my intense drama, perfectionism, and black and white thinking), but also the physical deterioration from the disease. I was frequently sick. I took a year off to take it easy and to try to feel better, only to enroll in classes and teach 12 courses in my sister's town. This was demonstrative of an increasing trend of binge/avoid work addiction, where I would work full tilt and then have a physical or emotional collapse. I also had the pattern of the "three p's": perfectionism, paralysis, and procrastination. I understood this pattern well enough to give a presentation on it to the advanced study skills class I was teaching at a university when I was 18. At the time, I advised my students to break at least the first project down into hour-long tasks and get started. Self-will eventually failed me in this regard. I could get adrenaline from overworking and from avoiding work, a cycle of intense mental self-abuse and recrimination leading to explosive emotional drama. Anything for an adrenaline fix!

My workaholism was fueled by a strange twist; the better I did at school or in life, the more intense the verbal and emotional abuse from my family:

1. Response to a report card with six A's and A-plus' and one A-minus: "What is this A-minus doing here?"
2. Response to my graduating Phi Beta Kappa from a top college: a 20-minute yelling scene, including how I was "worthless," "did not believe in anything," and "had wasted years of my parents' lives that I could never give back to them."

But negative attention was better than no attention at all. I continued my march to stuff the gaping hole in my spiritual life, internal wellbeing, and self-esteem, with work.

By the time I graduated from college, I knew I needed healing. I began a body-centered therapy process, and the disease continued. I was beginning to understand myself better, but I was having no relief from the progressive nature of the disease.

As a graduate, I innovated curricula for gifted kids until the hundreds of books from the research libraries and long nights of preparation for what was only 15 hours of paid work per week grew out of control. I stopped teaching and started working in a health food restaurant. Then I worked learning databases and publishing and moved out to a rural community where I could live at my workplace – it was a great comfort for a workaholic to have a work stash always ready at hand. Then I moved back to the city, changed to working with nonprofits, then to working in construction, then to publishing again, then to house cleaning, county government, and software development, often having two or three jobs at once. As if that were not enough, I would unconsciously increase the chaos (and adrenaline) by moving frequently. I kept living in the illusion that if I could just find the right job, the right home, the right relationship, etc., I would be happier.

Medical science has confirmed that adrenaline eats at the digestive system, cardiac tissue, immune system, and soft tissues and joints. Adrenaline and stress turn off the body's usual self-nurturing, tissue building, and assimilation and repair modes in favor of mobilizing for fight-or-flight. It is an evolutionary response that was never designed for constant use. Constantly used, the adrenaline response and its effects destroy the body and lead to death.

By the time I was hitting my 30th birthday, I was confronted with progressive deterioration and chronic pain in my tissues and joints. I got a medical test and my body had aged to that of a 45-year-old. My digestive system no longer functioned correctly. I had to close my construction business because I could not walk without pain. (Not to mention that my business partners left me because I would take on enormous projects on impossible timelines without enough funding or staffing to complete them. They had had enough. They were increasingly uncomfortable with my emotional dramas.) Adrenal exhaustion and chronic pain afflicted me. I was once again very close to killing myself. I knew that therapy, naturopathy, and self-help books on burnout and perfectionism alone were not bringing me relief.

I hit bottom, swallowed my pride (I did not like the "God" talk), and became willing to work the Twelve Steps to save my life. I went to open A.A. meetings and eventually discovered that W.A. existed. Higher Power gave me a nudge and I asked someone to sponsor me who, it turned out, had also used the Twelve Steps to find relief from converting a hobby into a business and overworking, as well as being a decade-plus twelve-step program member. This sponsor helped me tremendously, including guiding me to develop a recovery plan, including bottom lines, guidelines, and top lines. She helped me learn that, for a recovering perfectionist, I had to keep things simple and focus on gentleness. With the help of my Higher Power, we developed a definition of abstinence that was "not working more than an average of 45 hours per week." Guidelines include: not working more than nine hours per day, having two days in a row off per week, and getting off the computer by midnight. My office is no longer in my bedroom or living room. Soon, it will not even be in my house! In order to avoid adrenaline cycling, it is vital for me to allow Higher Power to restore me to sanity on a daily basis through regular nourishment.

I recently celebrated Higher Power's gift of five years of abstinence from sugar and sweetener, with guidelines of three solid meals per day, regular sleep and rest, exercise, time for fun and creativity, and time for relationships. Guidelines for me include focusing on self-care. For example, my top line was "sleeping at least six hours a night." Now, I have guidelines of "keeping a daily time log on sleep and work," "sleeping at least seven hours a night," and a top line of "sleeping at least eight hours a night." I also attend an average of four to five Twelve-Step meetings per week, do Step work on a regular basis, call my sponsor Monday through Friday, make and receive program calls, and enjoy a daily prayer and meditation practice. My sponsor has given me assignments to enjoy "purposeless fun," and I currently enjoy several hobbies that I have permission to "be bad at." Higher Power's awakening vision for me has changed my life from obligation, fear, and the illusion of control to a life of spaciousness, joy, and faith. Slowly, after decades of diseased contraction, I am beginning to step into the freedom to explore and learn about what I enjoy. I am learning from the process and my deep internal experience instead of forcing solutions by constructing my life to look a certain way on the outside, while being miserable on the inside.

I have to stay off adrenaline in order to maintain conscious contact with my Higher Power. And Higher Power helps me stay away from adrenaline cycling. Putting spirituality time first in my day is most important for keeping me sane and alive. This time helps me have "a daily reprieve contingent on the maintenance of [my] spiritual condition" (*Alcoholics Anonymous* 85).

Step work has helped me tremendously to "clear away the wreckage" (*Alcoholics Anonymous* 164) and learn in Steps Four, Five, Six, and Seven about the character assets underneath many of my negative coping mechanisms (a.k.a., character defects). For example, caring and self-love are underneath the guarded negative coping mechanisms of the illusion of control and playing God, both of which are motivated by fear. Fear is love that is in a container that is too small. Enthusiasm and delight are available beneath obsessive interest. W.A. is helping to unknot my spirit's natural impulse toward health. I was a guilt-ridden workaholic who was sure I had years of groveling and apologizing ahead of me in Steps Eight and Nine, because life is mandatory suffering and I am the center of the universe's defects. However, I was surprised to discover that I was at the top of my Eighth Step amends list, because positive self-care is pleasurable, and I am a beloved part of the universe's assets. I discovered that the "punishments" of recovery were such things as taking trips to the beach, getting to go slowly with developing interests, enjoying massages and great medical care, savoring the sunset, receiving help from others, eating wonderful fresh food, deeply resting through full nights of sleep, gently exercising my body, and leaning into the deep truth that I am OK whatever I do for a living. Living the W.A. program of recovery, one day at a time, has been my Ninth Step living amends to myself.

Step Eleven has helped me deepen my spiritual conscious contact. I am grateful to other W.A. members who have helped me find other words for "God," such as Higher Power, Deeper Power, Great Spirit, Spirit of Creation, Breath of Life, Spirit of Life, Entire Universe, Deep Self, Inner Knowing, Inner Wisdom, Great Blessing, and my current favorite: Divine Love.

Step Twelve has brought me the blessing of learning to live in balance while showing up for healthy service work. I have been deeply nourished and my recovery greatly deepened by sponsoring and doing service work at all levels. In some cases, I have prayed for clear divine guidance about a service opportunity for over two years before saying "yes." I am stepping into learning about living from inner spaciousness and divine delight, and from feeling into each day's rhythm. Conscious contact leads me to a deeper synchronicity that is more satisfying and grounded than racing to beat the clock. Deepening in Step Twelve and balanced service brings me out of obligation into clarity, and out of compulsion into joy and grace.

Recovering All of Me

My name is M., and I am a workaholic. I started working a W.A. recovery program in September 1988 when the first W.A. meeting started in my area. Over the years, I have learned that my addiction to compulsive working and activity happens for two basic reasons: to get a high, and to avoid something in my life. My Higher Power, whom I call God, and the W.A. program have given me recovery in both areas. For this great gift I am grateful. This is my story.

I remember awakening from a nap sometime between three and four years of age and realizing that my growing up just did not feel right. All the "boyish" things I was being taught (i.e., how to think, feel, act, and do) left out the very strong feminine side of my self-identity. So, I began to slowly express my "girlish" side and quickly learned that that was not OK. If fact, not only was I laughed at, I was led to believe that "boys just do not act that way" and that it was shameful to feel that way. I took all this in, and along the way concluded that even though I was somehow flawed, I could nevertheless redeem myself by exceptional performance.

I have now come to understand that this way of proving myself to be worthy set in motion a life-long pattern of compulsively using work and activity to avoid any and all difficult and painful feelings. In particular, I have engaged in this addiction to avoid the pain and fear associated with being "different" and embracing all of who I am: a transgender person. But more about this part of my recovery later.

Throughout my school years, I learned to practice my addiction very well. I always strived to finish my schoolwork before anyone else, so I could just feel inside that I was as good as the other kids in my class. In high school, I completed three majors (math, science and foreign language). But even that was not enough to satisfy my inner needs to gain acceptance and to be considered as one of the "in group." I completed college in three and a half years. After finishing a master's degree in one year, I did not even go to my own graduation, as I already had a job and was working extra hours. This intense focus on accomplishment gave me the illusion of power and control, even while I still had this nagging feeling inside that whatever I did and however well I did it, it would never be enough.

I married a wonderful woman while finishing college and beginning to work on my master's degree. Early in the marriage relationship, I discovered that I was not very good at intimacy: sharing what I was thinking and feeling, who I was, etc. You see, I was terrified that my wife would find out about that feminine part of me that I was trying desperately to hide and leave behind. So, over time, my work addiction progressed to the point that I had great difficulty "turning it off" at night when I needed to sleep. I even took my addiction into the night's sleep by thinking that I needed to "sleep fast" so that I could get up early in the morning to get to work. As I approached my bottom, I would awaken at two or three in the morning and just go into work. I had rashes all over my body from stress. My wife and children were afraid of me and would hide out in another part of the house when I finally did come home. This was because I wanted everything to be perfect at home because I was not able to attain perfection at work that day, and I would be hyper-critical of everyone at home and the condition of the household. Even the dog would hide out. My marriage was on the verge of breakup from my serious lack of loving attention.

I hit bottom when my wife started attending her own Twelve-Step program. She slowly stopped enabling me, such as not bringing the kids and dinner down to my office, and not making excuses when I did not show up for important events because I was working. I started to feel like I was playing a left-handed tennis player. The ball was not spinning right for me anymore. Conflict between us increased substantially. Eventually, she suggested that I look into meeting with another person who was interested in starting W.A. in the area. It took me six months to call this other person. In September 1988, she and I met for the first time, and recovery started for me.

I can see now that over years of recovery – years of working the Steps several times – I became increasingly focused on understanding just how powerless I was over working compulsively. By attending meetings, working the Steps, and sharing what I was discovering with a sponsor, I slowly began to see that I was unable to stop my addictive behaviors on my own power, as well as how much damage I had done to myself and everyone around me because my behaviors. I saw that the depth and extent of my destructive behaviors and the resultant damage was clearly beyond my ability to repair. Out of that carnage, I was able to catch my first glimmer of a Higher Power that could restore me to sanity and serenity. Each time I completed Step Two, my understanding of my Higher Power sharpened. Eventually, I prepared a collage of my Higher Power. I hung up the collage in our home, where I could see it every day. The more I looked at it, the more I learned about my Higher Power. The process of my surrender to my Higher Power began and then deepened each time I completed Step Three.

As I completed several iterations of Steps Four and Five, I was learning how to take contrary action when I observed that I was moving into a workaholic state. I learned to stop and breathe deeply and allow my body to relax. I learned to get up from my desk and walk around for a few minutes. I learned to go into the men's room and say the Serenity Prayer several times. I learned to call another W.A. member. At first, I was able to take these contrary actions only after having acted out my addiction. Later, I was able to take the necessary contrary action while I was acting out. Eventually, I was able to shift to more functional behavior when I saw that my actions and thoughts were about to lead me into a workaholic state. One day, I realized for the first time that these contrary actions were a more desirable alternative to the "high" I got from compulsive working and activity. The moment that insight happened was truly an "Aha!" moment – purely a gift from my Higher Power, and I was deeply grateful.

Several cycles of completing Steps Six through Nine took me through a process of slowly peeling back, layer by layer, the defenses I had built up over a lifetime to that part of myself that I did not want to face. During this period, I also began working another Anonymous program to extend my understanding of how my family of origin contributed to my addiction, and how I relied upon the feelings of others to determine how I was to feel from moment to moment. The descent into that place of fear and shame that surrounded what I did not want to face and that I had so long avoided was very difficult. I got outside professional help and I turned to my Higher Power in my quest for understanding, acceptance, and eventual liberation.

One night, in the front room of my home when everyone was asleep, I got on my knees and asked God to either take my life or to show me a way out of that dark place. Over the next several months, I somehow found doorways to connect with the local transgender community. Then, on my natal birthday, September 11, 1999, I walked into the world for the first time as my feminine self at a transgender support group meeting. On that date, I experienced a rebirth of sorts. On that date, I began the process of embracing all of me without shame and fear, and expressing in an open and honest way to the world what I had avoided almost all of my life.

During this period of liberation, working Steps Ten through Twelve increasingly became a celebration of living a more balanced life: a life increasingly filled with love, honesty, compassion, calmness, and peace; and a life of increasing connection to those I loved. The desire to work compulsively has not gone away, but its power has moderated considerably. From time to time, I still fall into the old patterns, but I am quick to recognize them and quick to realize that I no longer need to act them out. There is no longer a need for me to hide my feminine side. The path of recovery has indeed become sweet.

I have been truly blessed by my Higher Power, the W.A. program of recovery, the W.A. members who have been part of my life over the years, sponsors, and loving friends and family members who are growing to love me in all my imperfection. I do not have to run and hide anymore. Today I am learning what it means to stop my avoidance behaviors and to live in the moment. I am becoming more complete every day, as my relationship with my Higher Power grows deeper. Yes, my name is M., and I am a grateful and blessed workaholic.

Keep Coming Back – It Happens

I was fortunate to grow up in a loving family. I was well cared for, but there were also big expectations in terms of my values, lifestyle, and the type of person I would become. My parents had a certain career choice and status level in mind for me. While it was not what I desired, the overall idea of being "successful" was something that seemed mandatory. On some level, I always wanted their approval – as most children do.

All through high school, college and beyond, I coped with this ongoing conflict between what my parents wanted and who I really was with drugs and alcohol. Although I have been abstinent for many years, I now understand that I coped with workaholism as well; for example, I would get high during school, but also study hard.

When I was 19, my workaholic father died suddenly of a heart attack at age 46. We had been arguing at the time, and this trauma crystallized my inner conflict. For many years I carried around the feeling that if I just worked harder and was an even better person, perhaps nothing else terrible would happen, like losing my other parent. At the time, I had just moved into my first apartment. I was literally at the doorstep of my independence and separation from home. When my dad died, rather than spend the summer grieving, I went to summer school and got straight A's.

Jumping ahead a few years, I established a career in the health care field. I worked in various settings until 11 years ago when I began my own business around an innovative program I had pioneered. I wrote a book; I was invited to speak across the United States and in other countries; and I went to conferences as an expert. I was "famous." I enjoyed the adrenaline rush, the ego boost, and the thrill of it all, but I was constantly pushing myself way beyond my limits. I struggled often with deep depression. Periodically, I would become suicidal. I would tell my family I might not be around much longer. They would beg me to modify my workload and work style so I was not isolated, working at home. I clearly remember looking them in the eye and saying, "No, the work is the most important thing," and actually believing that it was more important than my family or my own health! I did give some thought to how I could change things. But I was not willing to give up being on the cutting edge of my field by staying on top of who was doing what, trying to keep others from entering my niche, traveling extensively to show up at all the events of national and international health care organizations, and, since I was self-employed, doing everything myself, from my own marketing to buying the paper clips.

I did everything not only with great zeal and zest, but also obsessively and with perfectionism. Nothing was ever quite good enough, and I kept trying harder. To deal with the depression, I went into therapy and took antidepressants for many years. These medications did not work well for me. I would have to go on and off of them and try different ones. They would cause uncomfortable side effects and would also lose their effectiveness. My therapist tried to get me to cut down or change my work by recognizing and accepting my limitations, but I would continue to repeat the same pattern. I really did not know how to say no or let go. Looking back, I am not sure whether I did not see the relationship between workaholism and the chronic depletion and depression, or if I just did not make it a priority to do something about it.

About five years ago, I found out about W.A. The tools sounded good but impossible. I kept at it, and eventually worked with a sponsor for a time, which was helpful. I continued in therapy, exploring my family dynamics. Close to three years ago, my therapist recommended that I take a sabbatical for six months to rest and seek a new perspective. It took me about six months to plan it, and such a long time to give myself permission, while fussing around getting ready for it, that I ended up with about a month and a half off. But it was a major breakthrough to go from all I had been doing to doing nothing for any time at all.

At first, the silence and stillness were so disorienting. I was racked with anxiety. Who was I without my professional identity and activities? What was I supposed to be doing with my time?? I was at a total loss. Then somebody told me about a local Buddhist meditation center, and I began to listen, learn, and practice. This was the perfect thing at the time. Meditation taught me to observe the habits of the mind and to be kind to myself. I saw how my thoughts were filled with self-judgment and criticism, and I eventually supplanted those with permission and self-acceptance. I discovered that one did not have to be busy and productive to be a worthy person; one could "simply be." I learned that slowing down and rebuilding my life with recreational activities and social relationships apart from work was an even more important accomplishment than what I had strived for in my career, and that I could approach it with just as much passion and determination.

At this time, I also began exploring yoga. I literally felt detoxification happen on a cellular level as I breathed and stretched. The meditation continued to be emotionally healing, intellectually fascinating, and spiritually new for me. All of this overlapped nicely with W.A., which also emphasized staying present, listening to oneself, and finding a spiritual path.

After the sabbatical, I went back to work. It took a while to find the right amount and mix of projects and trips, and to integrate work with the new activities I had developed in the rest of my life. While the negative side of self-employment was the lack of built in boundaries against overdoing, the positive side was the flexibility and the autonomy to do something about overdoing, once I got a handle on it.

For the past three years, I have worked part-time and monitored myself pretty closely. I have experienced a slow but steady and significant transformation from being irritable and depleted to having prolonged peace, calm, and well-being. I think it has been a synergistic combination of reducing work stress, doing meditation and yoga, working through life issues in therapy (which I ended close to a year ago now), taking fish oil capsules (which seem to impact my mood more than medication ever did), and attending W.A. meetings – all of which have given me new ways to take care of myself. The wisdom, consistency, and support of my peers in W.A. have helped me to incorporate under-scheduling, prioritizing, substituting, balancing, and nurturing into my life. I work less, take fewer trips, and do fewer projects at one time. I allow time to recuperate between tasks and trips, while spacing them apart more consciously. I no longer try to be everywhere in my field, and I no longer have quite as much of an emotional investment in being at the forefront of it. It took me a long time to come to terms with other people getting into my niche, but once I finally surrendered to that, I have been surprised to find that new opportunities have opened up to me.

In these past three years, I have not experienced depression or been on any medication, and I have a confident sense that I never will again. I have built a new lifestyle with new coping skills and habits. I feel so much healthier and happier. I have now surpassed the age at which my father died, and I am so grateful to have "turned my own ship around" before heading for a similar fate.

I have always been fortunate to have a good marriage, but now it is even better. I am about to celebrate my twelfth anniversary. Instead of my husband spending so much of his time picking me up from the puddles of my depression, we both have more time and energy for a high-quality relationship. I am a better partner, and I hold up my end of the responsibilities. I no longer put my husband's needs behind my work demands; I am there for him, as he has, incredibly, been there for me time and again.

Looking back, it almost seems too good to be true. But this is how it all happened. Now there is a new chapter. As I have continued to feel so good, I have more energy, interest and enthusiasm for my work again. So I have to be careful that the pendulum does not swing back the other way. I am working more than I was and feeling excited about new challenges in my field. Now I see what people mean when they say that recovery is a continuous process. It does not end. I will have an ongoing need for W.A. and have to stay vigilant. But now I recognize my old habits when they kick up, and I am not willing to become so fatigued and miserable again. I believe I have begun to establish new patterns that form a mental, physical, and emotional road map inside of me. If I pay attention, I know when to stop and what direction will keep me healthy.

In conclusion, as we say at the end of our W.A. meeting: "Keep coming back – it happens!" (We do not say, "It works!") There is hope. Keep at it, and supplement W.A. with whatever else you discover works for you. Thank you for listening and for your own contribution to this organization that has truly changed my life.

Before, During, and After

I was not born a workaholic. I do not believe there is a genetic predisposition toward workaholism. I was born into a middle class family where my father worked and my mother stayed home to care for me. There was enough time, enough money, and enough emotional stability to bring up a normal child.

When I was six months old, my family uprooted itself and moved across the country to my mother's home. My father took up a new career and my mother stayed home to care for me and do volunteer political work. Life must have been a little unsettled, especially for my father, but they had a community of friends to support them and my mother's family for help. All in all, life must have seemed positive to them.

However, by the early 50s, things were falling apart. The government was cracking down on communists and my mother was on the verge of going underground without my father or me. The FBI was harassing them and their friends and coworkers. People were being arrested, imprisoned, and deported. People were being blacklisted, and some were leaving the country to find work. At home, people were losing their jobs after the FBI pressured their employers. In my opinion, my parents must have been under a lot of pressure and feeling quite frightened. As I remember, none of this pressure and fear was communicated to me directly. I do not remember being told what was going on. All I remember was witnessing my parents being frightened and instructing me in the procedures necessary to protect them and me from exposure and persecution.

I lived with this unexplained and unacknowledged fear in my house for many years. I was expected to understand the situation and act appropriately without ever having specifically discussed it. For example, when my parents were in their seventies many years later, they expected me to understand their reluctance to subscribe to a magazine they enjoyed because they did not want their names to appear on its subscription list. It was up to me to figure out what appropriate behavior was in each situation and act accordingly. It was also up to me to figure out how to "fix" things for my parents – to make it safe for them, and thus for me. This, I believe, was the beginning of my workaholism.

I found that by "behaving normally" I could affect my family situation in beneficial ways. As long as I held my tongue and "acted normal" I could make things seem normal and safe. If I looked busy and productive, I would not add to my parents' burdens and the household could function more smoothly. I developed a repertoire of "normally busy" activities. It was not necessary to be productive, merely to appear "normally busy" and thus not in need of supervision or assistance.

This coping tool of using "normal busyness" to bring about the appearance of emotional stability became a resource for me in other times of stress. I developed a tool kit of strategies for managing in a tumultuous household. I developed a habit of keeping secrets. I alertly observed, remembered, and inferred the meaning of situations as they occurred, and then did not share what I observed or inferred. I became hyper-vigilant, constantly scanning my environment for information and anticipating possible threats or problems. I began to lie to present the appearance of order and appropriateness, even when I plainly knew otherwise. I developed a secret life in which all of my motives were clear and all of my actions were clearly consistent with my motives. I came to believe in the reality of my secret life, no matter how much it conflicted with external reality. I lived in a dream world insulated by my various survival strategies. In short, I learned how to use work to protect myself from feelings and experiences that I wished to avoid and that I was powerless to prevent.

The impulse to protect myself from painful feelings and experiences was normal, healthy, and wise. What was not normal, healthy, or wise were my choices of strategies in order to protect myself. The strategies I developed carried a high price. I found myself generalizing from the specific instances where protection of some kind was called for, to a policy of protecting myself all the time. At this point, I became a workaholic.

As a beginner workaholic, I needed to be at work all the time. I needed to place myself in a work situation, surrounded by my tools and confronted visually with the materials of my work. I was not an imaginative workaholic. In school, I needed to be in the library surrounded by my papers; as a truck driver, I needed to be on the road; at work, I needed to be in the warehouse with a full inventory, or else on the street, in the market, or on the phone. I needed the combination of fatigue and adrenaline that comes from prolonged overwork. I needed the satisfying oblivion that comes from an exclusive focus on work-related tasks. I enjoyed the privileges of prolonged, visible overwork. I was angry, insensitive, rude, preoccupied, and erratic. I lived on high-powered coffee, and I rode the emotional roller coaster that comes with caffeine abuse. I isolated myself and became proud of my isolation, experiencing it as the consequence of my ability and willingness to outwork my coworkers. I wore my fatigue as a badge of honor. I took my work home with me, treating friends and family the same way I treated coworkers. I took work with me on vacations, or did not take vacations at all. I disdained birthday and Christmas presents because there was nothing I needed or wanted besides work. I grew angry and depressed on Sunday afternoons.

As far as I was concerned, all of my problems stemmed from the chronic disorganization at work and the failure of my friends and family to correctly understand and value my work agenda. My values and my behavior were not the issue. After all, I reasoned, I was able to squeeze my friends and family and their requirements into my busy schedule. I attended mandatory family occasions and met the necessary obligations for presents and cards. I was available if my friends wished to contact me.

Eventually, I got what I wanted. My wife retreated into polite silence. She kept my young son from "bothering" me when I was home. My parents and friends became distant and I began to achieve some success at organizing my work so that it took up all of my waking time and energy. I got up early and was busy all day until I went home and collapsed into bed. My anger and frustration conveniently insulated me from any awareness of how I was feeling. The absence of any real intimacy between my wife and me, and the habit of relying on our six-year-old son to "fix" the quarrels we regularly fell into were not part of my awareness. The fact that I was spending 70 or 80 unproductive hours at work every week was not an issue, either. I was busy all the time I was awake – and that was all that mattered. We had a house to live in and the bills were paid; I had met my obligations to support my family and that was the end of it, as far as I was concerned.

This kind of frozen, loveless frenzy continued for several years. I lived in isolation, fear, resentment, fatigue, and anger in a house of strangers who wondered what had become of me. Out of my sight, the people closest to me, the people I loved the most and depended on the most, began to drift away from me. I was too busy to notice. I remember the day it came to an end. My wife and I were standing by the front door of our house, and she very calmly said to me that, if "we" did not get some help really soon, she was leaving.

We started seeing a counselor, and very quickly the counselor suggested that I might be a workaholic. I simply said, "Yes." I did not even have to think about it. It was just obvious. The counselor suggested W.A. and I went. That was it.

It was hard to squeeze in time for the meetings. I rushed from work straight to the meetings and did not usually have time for dinner. The meetings started at 7:30 PM and I started working at about 4 AM, so by the time I got to the meetings, I was exhausted and angry about having to rush to this new obligation at the end of my day. For the first few meetings, I sat on a couch dozing, trying to listen to the speakers while I wondered what kind of cult I had wandered into. Characteristically, I gathered up all the literature on display and read it all as fast as I could. I had the program figured out after only a couple of meetings. The only reason I kept on going to those meetings was that I had promised the counselor I would. I did not like them, I did not like the people, and I did not experience any great revelation. I was a workaholic and my family was falling apart, and here I was at this meeting full of people just like me.

Gradually, I began to appreciate the presence of other people who shared my addiction to work. I began to appreciate their willingness to talk about their experiences with work addiction honestly and candidly. I began to work the Steps, use the Tools, and see my life begin to change. I was so impatient and so unfamiliar with the process of recovery that I exaggerated the importance of every little change and imagined that every small improvement in my life was the final and most significant change. I had no clue about how much my life could and would change. I joined a group that was studying the Steps intensively, and really began to take a close look at my life.

As I began to work the Steps and commit to attending meetings, I found myself developing a relationship with a Higher Power I called "the Cosmic Forces of the Universe" and later called "the Cosmic Gremlins" or "the Gods of Laughter." I began to pray and to learn how to turn my life over to the Gods of Laughter. As the extent of my powerlessness became apparent to me, I became willing to take a close look at exactly how my character defects, my lack of honesty, and my impatience had affected my relationships with coworkers, customers, and vendors. I became willing to make amends to them.

I began to make amends and to experience firsthand some of the results of the pain I had caused by my workaholic behavior. Left to my own resources, I never would have been willing to confront these situations and witness the anger, hurt, recriminations, and frustration that my workaholism had brought about. Approaching people with the awareness that I was powerless over these situations, as well as the rest of my life, and that the Gods of Laughter had a plan for me, made it possible for me to make my amends with gratitude and humility, instead of fear and shame.

My relationships with my family – my parents, my wife, and my son – gradually began to change. I began to become willing to approach them with a sense of trust in the will of the Gods of Laughter. My impatience with them diminished and I began to respond more truthfully to them. In retrospect, I can see that my new willingness to be present and witness the feelings and behavior of my loved ones was a gift from the Gods of Laughter. At the time, however, I thought it was the result of my having begun to manage my time better. I had, in fact, begun to manage my time better and I was working fewer hours, but it was a long time before I was genuinely grateful to the Gods of Laughter for this gift. My workaholism led me to believe that it was me, my will, and my cleverness that had allowed me to become such a skillful manager of my time.

It has taken me many years and I am nowhere near done, but I recognize the Promises of the Program for what they are. They are being fulfilled every day among those who work the Program. Not all at once. Not once and for all. Over and over, a little bit at a time, one day at a time. I still live on the earth with everybody else and my life has all of the challenges that living on the planet brings with it, but I know I am subject to the will of the Gods of Laughter, and I am grateful and humble. I am more willing than ever before to live truly in the present and to acknowledge things as they are. I am more willing to live at peace inside my own skin and do just the work that is given to me each day. For this I am grateful.

The Gods of Laughter

It has been my experience that recovery from workaholism is not possible without a robust relationship with a Higher Power. Maintaining a continual awareness of a Power greater than me has proven essential to my recovery from the grandiosity that goes with addiction. This awareness has also led to the humility that is a cornerstone of recovery.

As I began to work my way into an awareness of the presence of a Higher Power in my life (for example, by acknowledging the frequent occurrence of uncanny coincidences), I had to admit that something like a Higher Power did show up in my life from time to time. I began to admit to parking karma and traveling weather karma, for examples. But the more I began to reflect on the order of my experience, the more I began to notice that not all of the instances of Higher Power intervention in my life looked exactly beneficial to me from my point of view. Sometimes, things did not work out the way I had in mind or even for my advantage. Sometimes, it seemed to me that my own personal Higher Power was determined to make me the goat of my schemes. At the same time, paradoxically, I was learning to acknowledge, accept, and even trust my Higher Power.

Looking back, I realize that I was beginning to be able to distinguish between those things that I was supposed to do and those things I was not supposed to do (because my Higher Power was going to do them instead of me). Every time I found a new one, it made me laugh. "There I am again, playing god," I would say. Not being very smart, I had to start with some pretty basic things like daytime and nighttime and how many hours there were in a day. Being a workaholic, it was a new experience for me to accept limits on the infinite expandability and compressibility of time.

There were really two issues. First, I had to learn that having a Higher Power did not mean that I was the hero of the story and everything would always work out the way I wanted it to. Second, I had to change my perspective on what I was supposed to be doing, from setting my own agenda to seeking the will of my Higher Power. As I began to recognize the presence of my Higher Power's will in my life, I began to laugh. It was not that I would always do my Higher Power's will, and it was not that things would work out for me even if I did, but it was clear that my sanity lied in the direction of seeking my Higher Power's will and then doing my best to carry it out.

As an addict, I was committed to controlling the flow of the events of my life in order to protect myself from experiences I intended to avoid. All of my actions were directed toward managing the affairs of that unruly obstacle that was my life. I was the manager of my life, not its inhabitant. From the place I occupied outside of the world, I strove fruitlessly to order everything to my satisfaction. Acknowledging a Higher Power was the beginning of a process of rejoining the planet, and rejoining my own life. It meant recognizing that I was part of the world; in the work situation, it meant I was another member of the workplace crew, not an indispensable, heroically legendary figure beyond time and place. It meant seeking my place as one more member of the natural world, no more, but no less.

However, seeking my place in the natural world has proven to be a subtler project than I first imagined. The natural world, the concrete site of my everyday work, turned out to consist of a continuously evolving set of variously relevant contingencies, not all of which I recognized or understood. Mastering them, setting them in order, and then determining my place among them once and for all, proved to be illusions I was predisposed to prefer. I eventually realized that the temptation to consider that my place in the natural world was settled was merely an invitation to begin all over again. It turned out that the seeking was what I was looking for. I began to strive for a perpetual state of seeking. As I began to spend more time seeking and less time pretending to find, I began to notice a peculiar kind of harmony. When I became willing to acknowledge the continuously evolving flow of my experience, and to accept the contingency of my place in the natural world and of my Higher Power's will for me, I felt a kind of harmony. I began to laugh. Laughter became a kind of acknowledgment of the presence in my life of a Power greater than me, of a plan for my life – the Gods of Laughter.

Tales of the Cosmos: Encounters with the Cosmic Gremlins

A relationship with a Higher Power has given me my life back. Only someone more foolish than me would not value this relationship. Nevertheless. Ah, the fabled "nevertheless." The nevertheless that leads to sanity, that deflates pomposity, that prevents grandiosity. There is no good reason to take the whole thing so seriously. My experience suggests that my relationship with my Higher Power is important, but not serious. In fact, some of the gifts of my relationship with my Higher Power have been the recovery of whimsy, lifesaving frivolity, and inconsequential playfulness.

I am a servant of the Cosmic Forces of the Universe (CFUs). This was big news to me. It is not that the CFUs were particularly interested in me or my affairs or even in my awareness of them. The Universe was perfectly capable of going on its own way without any input from me. The CFUs did not especially need my help in managing things, and they did not care whether I knew anything about them or not. Not only that, the CFUs were not especially interested in me, either. They were not about keeping a Cosmic eye on me, my plans, or my destiny. They were not hostile to me; they just did not really concern themselves on that level.

Nevertheless – there is that word again –, there was a point in my recovery when I was quite concerned about the whole Higher Power issue and whether an atheist like me could legitimately have a Higher Power. So, one night I went to a Twelve-Step meeting for food recovery in a log cabin in West Hollywood and listened to a bunch of skinny, beautiful young women talk about how hard it is to work in the film industry as makeup artists, costumers, or other craft workers and maintain any form of sobriety. I clearly did not have anything in common with them and all their talk about Higher Powers. So I was entirely unprepared when, after walking out of the log cabin and into the middle of the street in the cloudy darkness of the night, the Cosmos made itself manifest to me (all right, I might as well say that the clouds parted and a mighty voice spoke to me) and made it clear that, whether I liked it or not, the CFUs were the CFUs, and it was their Universe and not mine, and that was that. They were not mad about it; in fact, they were more than willing to extend a kind of Cosmic welcome to the Universe to me, but they were not about to invite me over for coffee and cookies. It was more in the way of a "since you asked..." kind of experience. So, after I was finished staring at the empty dark sky in astonished awe, carried myself over to the sidewalk, finished shaking, and all the goose bumps went away, I decided that I had a Higher Power.

The Cosmic Gremlins

Just because there are Cosmic Forces in the Universe, and the Gods of Laughter have something in mind for me and I know it, does not mean everything is smooth sailing. It is all well and good to seek the will of my Higher Power and attempt to carry that out. Finding out my Higher Power's will and actually carrying it out turn out to be entirely different matters. My experience is that I fall into my Higher Power's will by accident and only retrospectively realize that I have inadvertently managed to carry it out. On the other hand, sometimes I feel completely certain of my Higher Power's will and realize later that I was wrong. Sometimes I work at carrying out my Higher Power's will and get distracted, misdirected, or find that it is just too hard or that I am just too tired. Other times, everything goes so smoothly that I cannot figure out why it does not go that way all the time. Then, I blame myself for my sloppy recovery, and make a self-judgment that if only I worked harder, then I would find my Higher Power's will more often and carry it out more successfully. Afterward, something reminds me that I am as powerless over my recovery as I am over my disease, and that my sloppy recovery is just what it is – no more, no less.

I am willing to be rid of my disease. I am really, truly willing to be rid of my disease once and for all. Sometimes. Other times I am the willing, enthusiastic addict rushing about and mindlessly overworking. I call the Power greater than me that is responsible for this mess the Cosmic Gremlins. I do not know why my recovery goes so well for a while, and then goes badly. I do not know why things go so badly and then work out, anyway. As I begin to detach from the results of my efforts, and focus instead on the effort of seeking my Higher Power's will, I become aware of the constant interference of the Cosmic Gremlins in my life. It is the Cosmic Gremlins who confuse my awareness of my Higher Power's will with the plotlines of television and movie dramas. It is the Gremlins who hide things in plain sight. I have realized that, in large measure, I was put on the planet for no other purpose than to amuse the Cosmic Gremlins. These Olympian delinquents are perfectly capable of quarreling among themselves and then causing me to enact the results.

If it were simply a matter of being smart and of working hard, recovery would be a relatively straightforward project, and I could look forward to a cure for my disease. The Cosmic Gremlins suggest otherwise. There is no working around them. There is no appeasing or propitiating them. There is only seeking the will of my Higher Power, struggling to carry that out, acknowledging the results, and accepting the results with gratitude. The ebbs and flows of my experience (the ceaseless succession of sensations that are my embodied existence on the planet) are not other than me. In my addiction, I distinguish myself from my experience and judge it. I inspect it to see if it is good enough, as if it is some work project or commodity I can offer to sell or barter. The Gremlins remind me, every day in the midst of every routine motion and chore, that it is they and not me who determine the outcomes of my efforts. What is mine is my embodied presence on the planet. It is my dwelling and my home, and, when I cherish it and do not betray it, I find my recovery.

The Power of Under-scheduling

I used to think I was a very honest person. In W.A., I finally saw how dishonest I have been with myself and others. In particular, I was frequently dishonest about how much time it would take to do something, about how long it would take me to get somewhere, and about my limitations and skills. Of course I could get it done! As soon as you need it!

When I came into W.A., I started keeping track of how much time I spent on various projects at work. Whenever I started a new task or project, I would write down the current time with the project name. In this way I learned a lot about how I spend my time at work.

When I had been in W.A. a few months, my boss gave me a new project: to fact check a long report. She asked me when I could get it done. Normally, I would have guessed, and then started the crazy cycle of working extra hours, stress, and shortchanging other projects to get it done. Instead, I asked if I could get back to her. I decided to start the work and see how much I got done in two hours. I got through a certain number of pages. I then looked at how many pages were in the document, and figured out how many hours I would likely have to spend on the document.

At first, I thought I could spend all of five days a week on this one project. But then I realized I had other responsibilities. In fact, I could not take this project on at all if I did not have something to give up. I turned back to my task log. I had two projects that were ending that week. I could use the time I normally spent on those old projects for this new project. I figured out how many weeks it would take me to finish the new project, based on my average hours per week on the old projects. Then I doubled it, just to be safe and under-schedule.

I told my boss when I could get it done. She told me that was unacceptable, that it had to be done sooner. Again, I was tempted to say, "OK, sure." Instead, I explained how I had figured out the amount of time it would take. If I needed to get it done sooner, we had to take something else off my plate. I suggested that we delay another project assigned to me or give a part of this new project to someone else. None of these suggestions were acceptable to her. She said, "Can't you just streamline it?" Again, I was tempted to say, "Sure." But this time, I said, "What does that mean? Do you want me to check only some of the facts? Only do part of the document? How could I streamline it?"

The reason I could discuss this with her that way was because I had honesty on my side. She could not argue with the facts; I had evidence of how long the project would take and a record of how much time I spent on other projects. For this project to get done sooner, something had to go.

My boss finally said she would get back to me on this. The next day, she called and said that it was OK for me to get it done when I said I could. She was not willing to take any other projects away from me in order to get this one done sooner.

What a miracle it was to have a project where I did not have to lie about my progress, work free overtime to get it done, or skip parts of the work, hoping no one would notice! As it turned out, I got the project done early. My boss was happy. And I had some experience with serenity. Now I know that when I am feeling rushed or stressed about a project, I probably just need to get honest with myself and my boss about how long it will take.

The Benefits of Prioritizing

A few months into my W.A. recovery, I felt a pain in my hand when I clicked the mouse on my computer. I clicked again, and felt the pain again. Before W.A., I would have just kept on clicking until I could not use my hand any more. Maybe I would have taken some aspirin.

I had a number of acquaintances who had repetitive strain injuries, such as carpal tunnel syndrome, which had resulted in serious impairment of their ability to do necessary daily activities, such as dial a telephone. Their injuries had begun with a small pain, but they had continued to work. I already had another disability as a result of my previous compulsive working. I knew I needed to prioritize taking care of this problem. I needed to put off the immediate gratification of completing just one more task.

I called my boss and explained that I needed to find out about alternate mouse technologies, because I did not want this injury to progress. I had to tell a client that my work for them might be delayed. I spent the rest of the day investigating my options. I tried a number of solutions over the next week until I finally found one that worked for me. I also found that I could not work as fast with this new device.

I renegotiated my deadlines with some clients and with my boss. I had to pray frequently throughout each day, asking my Higher Power to help me continue to use this new device. I felt the members of my W.A. were the only people who truly understood what I was going through.

I had to let go of my idea that the faster I worked, the more my Higher Power and others would value me. For me, working more slowly meant I had to turn my entire will and life over to my Higher Power. What if I get fired? What if we lose clients? What if I can never find another job because I cannot work as fast as I used to? Whenever these fears came up, I reaffirmed that I was not willing to risk a permanent disability, just so I could work more or faster. I had to trust that my Higher Power would give me the tools to deal with whatever happened.

More than two years later, I still use this alternative device. I was not fired and we did not lose clients.

I believe that, without W.A., I likely would have continued to work "through the pain" until I was disabled. Instead, every day I am grateful to have the full use of my hand.

The Pleasure of Play

Play is a four-letter word. As an adult, I often experience the feeling of play as uncomfortable. It implies a childlike attitude anathema to appropriate adult behavior, especially if one yearns for a life of success. As a workaholic whose disease displayed symptoms as a young teenager, I became angry and self-righteous at the frolicking behavior of my peers who enjoyed laughter and a good party.

These are but a few symptoms I have shared with my W.A. friends at our meeting. Others in the meeting experienced similar feelings that led to burnout and isolation. So we decided to have a meeting set aside every several weeks to explore the solution of play in our lives as an antidote to our disease.

When I hit bottom eight years ago, I worked more than 40 hours a week, with my weeknights filled with spiritual work in and outside of church. The next year, a friend offered me the opportunity to accompany him and others to a weekend at the beach. The ocean, three hours from my front door, invited me to discover new things about myself: the pleasures of running up and down the shoreline, being chased by waves, and throwing myself into the water. I constructed sand castles, something I to which had not aspired in over 30 years. I accepted the stares and comments of children as they observed my handmade creations. Lying in the sun with the sound of waves crashing upon the shore put me in a succession of naps throughout the afternoon. The cadence of the waves simmered through my body well into the night and into the following morning. Speaking of mornings, I rose prior to the sun's ascending in the east above the ocean. Standing on the beach, I witnessed the voyage of dolphins along the coastline. With their presence ten yards offshore, I accepted their playful energy into my heart.

I carried this experience back to my home, where workaholism runs rampant among government workers and technological gurus. I attended sporting events with an attitude of enjoyment. I enrolled at a local recreation center and played in the pool, where I turned somersaults underwater and participated in a water aerobics class, dancing to hits from the 60s. Approaching these activities, I got out of my head and into my body, feeling my heart's lightness as my response to the world, rather than my intellect's "why?" Yes, I experience slips in this endeavor when I find my days and weeks overloaded. However, I accept this aspect of my recovery, like other aspects, one day at a time.

Play is a four-letter word, and a behavior in which God wants us to experience her pleasure.

Enough

W.A. got started in our metro area and was soon quite robust; there were four active recovery meetings each week (one as large as 20 members), and three more in nearby cities. Perhaps the local Intergroup had already started, as well. At the time, I was fresh into recovery and part of a small group of another fellowship. Another member of this fellowship had attended a recent conference and shared the tapes with me. One of the tapes was on workaholism. It seemed as if I could immediately identify with what the speaker and participants were saying, and I heard mention of those local W.A. meetings in our area.

Like that conference tape on workaholism, our early W.A. meetings seemed mostly about "The Problem." In our community, little workaholic recovery experience had yet been built up, perhaps unlike the first W.A. meeting founded years earlier in New Rochelle, New York. So naturally, New Rochelle would get lots and lots of phone calls with lots and lots of our questions.

Just what the problem might be – our disorder around work and activity – seemed murky at best to most of us. Was it working compulsively and way too much? Was it overdosing on excessive corrosive activity, in general? Was it constant worrying and fear about work performance, careers, and wage earning? Was it compulsive inactivity, underemployment, or a roller coaster of frantic activity and unexplainable unemployment? (Further into recovery, some of us either found an answer or simply lost interest in the search.)

Another big confusion: was active service in W.A. part of recovery, or just another continuation of our compulsivity? We seemed to share a sense of uncertainty, work-related exhaustion, grimness, fear, bewilderment, and more. (Someone mentioned having all the early recovery grace of a dog on the freeway.) Many of us reported keeping our noses earnestly near the grindstone of self-improvement. Certainly we were not a fun-loving bunch.

Some of us thought we could learn a great deal from certain recovered cardiac patients. One member's horrible story was of starting a critical business negotiation, experiencing a heart attack right in the middle of the meeting, staying to finish the lengthy negotiation, and only then finally driving himself to the emergency room. For some W.A. members, there were even greater tragedies: one was murdered (whether it was job-related was unclear), another committed suicide, and still another died of a work-related heart attack.

Our workaholism seemed to keep most of us away from any real closeness with another human being. Many of us shared how we would rush heedlessly along, impatient with anything that slowed us down. There seemed to be almost a compulsion to go on to the end – to get it over with, now. Others shared how, time after time, we had made hopeless attempts to find social confidence in the workplace. Some of us practically demanded to be valued and appreciated, even doted upon, in the workplace. When this did not take place, we often felt a deep sense of not belonging. Our over-dependence and neediness sometimes turned people away from us. For some of us, this led to excuses for under-performing, reasons to leave, or behavior that got us fired.

One W.A member in particular seemed to stand out in a positive way. He was in a partnership with another recovering person. His story about his workaholism was full of pain. He had suffered a near-fatal stroke, yet now he looked and sounded calm and content. When he took me on as a W.A. sponsee, he already had ten years in another program, and that level of recovery and serenity was very attractive. In his home is where we heard my W.A. Fourth Step.

This connection with my W.A. sponsor brought unexpected hope, gratitude, and more of a sense of purpose. It was suggested that it was not a question of how much we worked, when, or why, but how our working affected our lives – what happened when we worked compulsively. In another program, there had been some good advice: "Go to meetings. Do not [do the addictive activity] between meetings. Get into service. Do a Fourth Step. And you will probably never have to [engage in the addiction] again." The support of my W.A. sponsor, freely given, offered similar hope around my work disorder. Because of his influence, I was surprised when I soon found myself making two spontaneous, sincere amends at work.

At some time around this period, I found myself writing out my W.A. story as I understood it at the time. It included a lot of vomiting up of the past and bewilderment about the present, but little actual recovery or strength to share or give away and seemingly little realistic hope for the future. In our local Intergroup there had been animated talk about creating a W.A. *Book of Recovery*, and I was quite stimulated at the splendid prospect of having my own admirable personal history among the very first stories.

That Intergroup effort faded out. Still, I found myself writing my work history. It became quite a revelation: I was always seeking prestigious companies to associate with, maybe to build up my own low self-confidence; I was always drawn to ultra rapidly-growing enterprises that were on the bleeding edge of their competitive field, probably for the excitement, adrenaline rush and splendid chaos; and I was always stumbling into situations requiring a fixer and a prescriber of remedies. Once hired, I over-did and over-exerted to display a mistake-undetectable, praise-evoking work product. I was coolly certain of my indispensability, or anxiously concerned I might not be. Never being a quitter, I did not stop or give up. I took time management classes and stress management seminars. I protected my work to keep it beyond criticism.

In my story I saw that, throughout my work history, I had accepted every single one of the many jobs that were offered to me. This was not a pleasant awareness. Somehow, this might mean that, in reality, I was adrift and directionless in my work life, not purposeful and in command, as I wanted to believe; and that I was heavily into people pleasing, grandiosity, and approval-seeking. My vanity was exposed. I did not have an independent, take-it-or-leave-it attitude, and the prideful balloon was floating above it all. One particularly ugly phrase stood out: "A close, watchful intolerance of other people's incompetence."

I got to see how my other addiction had masked my workaholism, how I had sustained the courage, bluster, and craziness of my compulsive over-working via the medication of that first addiction. I saw how running ten miles a day, graphing my results, and insisting on lowering my times made drudge and work out of what many others found to be release and recreation. I saw how during after-work socializing and with a few relaxants in me, those guarded coworkers who would keep their distance during the workday suddenly found me amusing, engaging, spontaneous, and charming.

I saw how unsupported withdrawal had left me vulnerable to a severe suicidal depression. I had been in the rigid habit of not seeking others' help or not accepting help offered, so I had no clue that the first non-workaholic weeks and months were likely to be periods of great emotional vulnerability. I fled a high level position, feeling wretchedly inadequate and impotent in all ways; I found myself in bed for weeks and weeks, trying to sleep around the clock, while my partner maintained a suicide watch and joined Al-Anon. A psychiatrist's insistence pushed me into Twelve-Step meetings. In my own experience, convalescence from the illness of active workaholism would take a long time.

In early recovery, I found myself feeling so worthless and inadequate that I sought out and took only tiny volunteer positions. I reasoned that, if I was not getting paid, I could not be judged worthless or get fired for not earning my keep.

Repeatedly, during my first few years in recovery, I tried forcing myself back into careers and industries where I had been before my bottom. One prospective job was described as "A rocket ride – and you are hanging onto the outside of the rocket by your fingernails." That sounded just fine with me – apparently, falling back into denial was quite easy and effortless. But the jobs did not last. One contract ended and was not renewed. Three other outfits fired me. Severance pay was nice, but the feeling of shame was not. It seemed to happen more and more often that working for others or with others was impossible, for some mysterious reason. Feeling sorry for myself and ashamed, I still briefly tried three other careers in entry level jobs. None were a fit, so I tried starting a couple of businesses on my own. These failed, too.

Yet, in some ways I was feeling better, or at least different: no late night work; no bringing the briefcase and work papers into the bedroom; giving myself leeway and saying I would arrive somewhere between 10:00 and 10:30, but not 10:17 sharp; still having "working dreams," but not as frightening ones; attending spiritual retreats; not always in the freeway fast lane; saying "no"; meditating; mental health days; pausing; and napping.

The former anxiety attacks, near fainting spells, and terrifying panic attacks had ceased. I had cut back to decaf coffee, learned to walk slower, learned occasionally to look at people directly, and listened when they talked to me. But I could still get pulled into a seemingly critical project or deadline, and then resent all interruptions, especially from family.

Several years into recovery, I was active in three Twelve-Step fellowships, active in service in each, and feeling good about myself when I centered my attention just on these fellowships. (The Twelve-Step principle of regular service rotation can be a spiritual safety net for a recovering workaholic.) More and more, it seemed, I was coming to share the benefits of getting my true feelings sorted out by the simple means of expressing them aloud in meetings.

But the contrast became more and more jarring between the joy of service and fellowship versus the job failures, getting fired and rejected in interviews, and near-zero income and near-zero prospects. The need to make amends to the IRS became paralyzing, while mandatory. Particularly humiliating and despairing was my first day in the two-hour-long line for unemployment benefits. How had I gotten to this point? At least I had remembered just in time not to wear my best business suit that day. (Some people in meetings tell how they would much prefer being in a life-threatening situation than an ego-threatening situation.)

Then, at a Step Study there was yet another reading of a passage I had heard over and over. This time, a member who knew me well repeated it. She had experienced a work bottom similar to mine, yet now she was thriving in her chosen field, enthused about her work, making adequate money, and experiencing dignity, engagement, and peace in her recovery, after many years of floundering. The reading was:

> This all meant, of course, that we were still far off balance. When a job still looked like a mere means of getting money rather than an opportunity for service, when the acquisition of money for financial independence looked more important than a right dependence upon God, we were still the victims of unreasonable fears. And these were fears which would make a serene and useful existence, at any financial level, quite impossible. (*Twelve Steps and Twelve Traditions* 121)

This time, that reading somehow struck home. It must have been important that my friend was doing the reading, especially because she had made it to the other side, was out from under, and was now happy, joyous, and free. This may be the point at which I came to accept my workaholism and its many implications. Active workaholism no longer meant excitement, self-satisfaction, and winning at life, it meant sickness and sorrow. The initial exposure to W.A. years earlier brought the awareness, and the several years following brought the acceptance. Some people say that powerlessness gets us here, while tolerance, patience, and humility can keep us here.

Our lives are unaccountably transformed. A.A. literature addresses progress in recovery and the spiritual awakening that can occur for us. "What he has received is a free gift, and yet usually, at least in some small part, he has made himself ready to receive it" (*Twelve Steps and Twelve Traditions* 107). That seems to sum up the rest of my story these past ten years.

After some more time passed, I found myself in my current service (paying) position, which is with a small, nonprofit bookstore. But in between, I started a business. I delivered newspapers around the metro area for a weekly recovery publication. And a friend knew of a need where he worked, a residential home for newly recovering Latino alcoholics, "Just to help us out, you know, maybe for just a few weeks." It was a clerical position, paying minimum wage plus some meals. This two week taxi job continued for three years.

I took a position at the community recovery center where our W.A. Intergroup now met. The place had another special significance for me. Early in my recovery and as a sour atheist, I had attended weekly guided meditations there, led by a couple in recovery, and eventually found myself connected with my spirit guide and a Higher Power.

Of course, two jobs meant a lesser degree of financial instability and maybe even the prospect of financial recovery, but the many hours of work did hint lightly at a slippery slope for my workaholism. Thankfully, the jobs kept me around many other recovering people. One person I leaned on as my job recovery sponsor had 30 years of continuous sobriety when we met. He had been in and out of prisons and treatment nine times before the tenth try took. He was calm and caring. Every time he saw me, he would brighten and smile, and affectionately call me his "Esteemed Colleague." It was healthy just to be around him and his calm wisdom. His many and persistent tries at a contented recovery were an inspiration.

And then, at home one day I saw a small ad in a little neighborhood newspaper. "Seeking a person with marketing and retail experience, working with volunteers, to manage a new nonprofit bookshop. Proceeds support our local public libraries." I was re-reading the ad, feeling excited and hopeful, when my partner appeared. "Listen to this!" I yelped as I recited the ad. She considers me a tease and a pleasant buffoon, and she thought I was making it all up. So I handed her the ad.

Close by. A ten minute commute. Active in our local community. A kind of a service position, really. Full-time position. Low pay and no medical or other benefits to speak of, but my steadily employed professional partner had full benefits for both of us. And *books*! I loved books. And as it turned out, it was a store I had been frequenting delightedly for the past two years; it had been a lunch break destination for me during two other local jobs I had tried and flunked. As we stared at the ad, I recalled what a career counselor had said during one earlier bout of debilitating unemployment: "Each person is the exact right key for a particular lock somewhere. The task is to find that lock."

I dashed off a letter, sharing my enthusiasm for the store and the position, matching my background to their requirements, while being concerned that I would be seen as way over-qualified, a flake or job-hopper, too old, or something. They interviewed me, they interviewed me again, they hired me, and later they told me they had received 100 resumes. This fall marks my tenth anniversary with the store.

My current position seems like a gift, in a way. And it seems as if the program literature is true, not just hokey and Pollyannaish – we do make ourselves ready in some small ways to receive these gifts.

My present service job with pay does have its temptations toward workaholism. There is always much more to do and do perfectly than available time and energy. Subpar selling for a month or longer can get me questioning my adequacy.

The 50 part-time staffers are all volunteers and can contribute or desist as they choose, so great power and vast ego inflating resources are not readily at my disposal. Many heavy boxes of books await my heroic exertion, or I can deal with them just a few volumes at a time. There is a benign Board of Directors, but they, too, are part-time volunteers with lives away from the store. So there is a negligible audience for approval-seeking, no unreasonable or unappreciatively harsh authority figures to resent, and no career ladder to climb. There are no shareholders to enrich, no stupendous annual goals, and no aggressive expansion plans to fulfill.

I have learned to be a "quitter" and live with myself afterward. It is said in program that being a "quitter" can take courage and make very good sense, if we are quitting something that is not good for us. For me, all of this is a valuable daily reminder of powerlessness, and it is a fun, relaxed enterprise.

Some staffers and some customers are in recovery themselves, so there are on-the-job occasions for in-the-moment sharing of things for which we are grateful, as well as our painful difficulties (such as a parental death, a mentally ill adult child, or the puzzle of money for retirement). Another sense of service comes from the fact that, for many customers and many staffers, the bookshop is a haven during a stressful workday.

As I look at what I have written to this point, it feels like this is becoming too long. There is just not enough time to shorten it! Enough.

My participation in program and my gradual recovery have extended over many years. More and more, it feels true that we act ourselves into right living rather than think ourselves into right acting. It really does work, the Promises can come true, and there is to be found a contented freedom and release from compulsive working and excessive activity.

How to Make Decisions: A Tug of War with a Surprise Third Step Ending

Making *any* decision had always been difficult for me, even when I was a child. But making the *major* decision to retire was as hard for workaholic me as sobering up is for an alcoholic. Then I learned, it is never too late to seek God's caring will.

When my company announced an incentive to retire early, my first reaction shocked me: "I would love to!" I immediately scolded myself, discounting my feelings, and reasoned, "Nonsense. You are only 52. What would people think? Your father worked till 69, found part-time work at 74, and worked till he died. Do not throw away your high paying job, just because you have come to hate it." (I was exhausted from overwork and had been hunting for a new position for months.)

The incentive required retirement before July 1989 to obtain medical benefits; after July, new rules mandated working until age 55 for such benefits. Reason conscientiously insisted, "Hang on for three more years, or the whole world will think you are lazy." Feelings timidly objected: "Do not feel guilty. Please talk it over with someone objective who likes you, before missing this opportunity."

So I told my doctor and was surprised when he said, "Go for it! You have fought insomnia, burnout, and countless stress related illnesses for years." But Reason righteously preached, "You cannot afford it."

Weeks later, my attorney said, "Sounds good. You have enough savings. And you need time to empty your late mother's home, where she lived for 52 years. Your idea to rent it and do part-time freelance editing is excellent."

Why did I not feel reassured? The inner decision-making tug of war wakened me every night: Reason fighting with Feelings. "You have an obligation to continue. Who else could please those perfectionist customers as well as you? How would you stand the loneliness – no office to escape to?" But Feelings persisted, "Two experts think you work too hard and need a change."

Discouraged, I consulted my career counselor. She helped me prepare a "retirement budget." She had me list retirement's advantages and disadvantages. I wrote the pros as cons. Only I could decide, but she obviously believed that downshifting was OK. She knew people who were happily living a simpler lifestyle after a midcareer change. Her common sense made retiring seem respectable. And she pointed out that I could always find another job. But I still hesitated. Time was running short.

Desperate, I thought about visiting my work addiction therapist. But I already knew what she would patiently repeat: "Go with how you feel." Each night, Reason battered Feelings. I was so weary. I missed Mother, who had died of cancer only a few months before. I wished I could talk to her. Wondering if grief was fueling my indecision, I visited a grief support group, where I discovered an inspiring book on transitions that actually recommended "lying fallow" as opposed to producing constantly – a whole new idea to me.

I also regularly attended several Twelve-Step meetings modeled on A.A. I slowly realized that my workaholism had me stuck on Step Three, "Made a decision to turn our will and our lives over to the care of God *as we understood God*." How simple. Here was the answer about how to decide what to do.

After six months of indecision, I prayed, "God, I am turning my life over to You." My fears left. The tug of war ended. I had my first peaceful sleep in months. The next day, I signed the retirement papers, meeting the deadline with enough time to give a month's notice. Was my boss ever surprised! Even before I left the job, life began blossoming, with unexpected people helping me understand God's will for me and feel His caring.

For example, on Mother's Day weekend, Feelings kept nudging me to quit my housework and visit the garden store, which I would normally avoid on a crowded holiday. In case it might be God's will, I drove there. The parking lot traffic jam made me cross. A police officer motioned for me to park near an unfamiliar door. I almost walked into M., loaded down with tomato plants, coming out that door. (Before establishing his own firm, he was my company's public relations director.) When he heard about my upcoming retirement, he said "Great! Work part-time for me." We shook hands on it. The roof gutter began dripping water on our heads, so he left, and I bought my impatiens. Later, the career counselor laughed heartily: "That was no coincidence. The water was God baptizing your future freelancing career."

At work, several coworkers confided that they envied me. There was no sign of the anticipated ridicule. A heartwarming 80 people came to my farewell party, where I gave away "going out of business" cards printed with the Serenity Prayer.

Once I began paying attention to God's will and trusting in His care, help came from unlikely sources. Soon after retiring, for example, I was thrilled to win a supermarket gift certificate equal to nearly half my monthly pension check. It was perhaps today's version of "manna from heaven."

Each time I tried to inventory the objects in Mother's home, I began crying after only an hour and had to stop. Then, while sitting at her little old desk, I discovered her membership book in the women's club at the university where my father had taught. Feelings whispered, "Call their thrift shop." I recognized God's nudge in the whisper, phoned, and learned that the professors' wives had raised $11,000 the year before by selling used household goods. They could use anything I gave them. I quit crying at Mother's house, because I was now helping raise scholarship funds. Both parents would have been delighted. That autumn, the thrift shop filled two vans with useful things from Mother's home. It felt good to plan for the future, no longer weeping over breaking up a home full of memories.

Even my first customer was a gift from God. I had decided to rent the house before I began freelancing. But one wintry day, while I was hunting for kitchen vinyl floor covering, the sales clerk begged me to do some special editing. Her former husband was in prison and had discovered a talent for writing while taking courses behind bars. They had been praying for guidance. Was he good enough to pursue writing as a career? She paid me to critique his writing samples, do the library research he needed, and prepare a report to help him decide whether to pursue his dream.

I began attending a professional freelancers' support group. A speaker from a publisher who visited the group eventually began using my freelance services. Another woman in the group gave me an excellent customer when she moved away. When I got around to contacting M., he no longer had work suited to my skills, but I already had other customers. His early encouragement had served its purpose, and the turndown did not devastate my faith.

My worry about loneliness after retirement was unfounded, too. I had survived more than 60 unfulfilling dating relationships, most of which were sabotaged by my workaholism, and had bitterly resigned myself to spinsterhood after a former boyfriend had broken my heart. God used my friend E. to urge me to join the group for divorced and separated people at a church. The group welcomed me, where the support, reading, sharing, and exercises in letting go helped me understand, accept, talk about, and overcome the grief I had unsuccessfully hidden and ignored for a decade. I symbolically poured out my festering, angry heartache by dumping a treasured sand art bowl from my ex-boyfriend. The tiny colored grains spilled into a box where I recycled soil for potting plants. Then I went to bed and had a good cry, which left me limp, sleepy, and feeling peaceful. When I woke, I was healed. That healing serenity showed up vividly on "before" and "after" psychological questionnaire graphs from the group. My trust of people skyrocketed from ten percent to 65 percent. This course and the Twelve-Step groups taught me new, healthier ways of relating to people.

Trust built my confidence and self-esteem. Now that I felt like a whole person, I began dating, enjoying it for the first time, and getting to know a variety of men. Then my Higher Power brought J. into my life. For our first date, we chose to walk around a pretty lake in a lovely park. We walked many hours in many more parks during the sunshiny autumn, talking and sharing deep-felt dreams.

J. and I were married a year later. It still seems like an impossible dream come true that someone 54 and retired would get married for the first time, becoming an instant stepmother, mother-in-law, and grandma. But then, I am getting used to God's plans being much better than mine. One day at a time, I continue listening to my feelings to discover God's will through His still small voice. Only now, I listen more confidently. Even Reason admits that it is the best way to make decisions.

My first draft of this story ended here. However, the story does not end with "happily ever after." There is an unusual sequel, and the ending has changed drastically. Less than a year into the marriage, J. left me. Another tug of war began in my soul. I started questioning God's will as soon as J. told me that he was moving out. However, something happened on moving day that not only warmed my heart, but also re-centered my faith. Shortly after we met, he had tried to give me a beautiful silver cross, but I felt I did not know him well enough to accept such an expensive gift at the time. I reminded him of that the day before he moved out, and he sadly told me he had lost the cross, but that he would have loved for me to have it. I was deeply disappointed.

Late in the afternoon the next day, about an hour before he drove away, we were in the basement with the movers and a friend of mine, exhausted. To simplify the packing yet to be done, I offered to see that a charity receive any unwanted leftovers, and I asked J. to check the remaining debris, broken boxes, and miscellaneous trash in one area of the basement. He wandered over, bent down to pick up a dirty old broken plastic dishpan, and turned toward me in surprise. He lifted out of it a small cloth jeweler's pouch. He opened the blue pouch and handed me the missing cross.

My heart filled with warmth and serenity. I realized instinctively that my decision to marry him had not been wrong after all. I was so grateful for this unexpected sign from God that His will was indeed at work, even in this painful parting, and that I was in His care, despite the ending of my marriage. This beautiful incident is too full of symbolic meaning and hope to be mere coincidence. The painful tug of war in my soul ended because Step Three and my Higher Power are intact and remain so to this day.

It's About the Body

Around the age of five, I started saying that I wanted to be a doctor when I grew up. Considering that no one in my family had finished high school, the year was 1950, the schools in my small town were among the poorest in the country, and I was a girl, my plan seemed pretty far-fetched. But not entirely.

My mother used to tell the story that I was so strong-willed as a child that she decided when I was two years old to "let me raise myself." For a long time I liked feeling that I was running the show. And it really scared me.

When I started school, I excelled, but sensed that being ahead of the class came at a price. I remember standing in front of the class each week in second grade, staring at my feet, trying not to catch the eyes of the other children, as I ate the cookies the teacher gave me (and sometimes another student or two) for getting all the spelling words right. I spent much of my childhood alone.

Despite the isolation, or perhaps because of it, I felt compelled to achieve. Besides giving me an identity as "The Brain," making straight A's helped me feel acceptable. The awards and accolades also drew attention away from what was going on in the family – the addictions, affairs, unwanted pregnancies, and subtle or not-so-subtle abuse. A lot seemed to be riding on my success.

In high school, I fueled myself with extra food – the more sugary, salty, or greasy, the better. I did not do well at sports, so I rarely played. When I gained weight, which at times I did, I dieted as compulsively as I had eaten. I drank can after can of diet cola. I chose extracurricular activities that would look good on my college application. I finished first in my high school class and was accepted to college.

The higher I climbed, the higher the stakes became. I felt as though I was bluffing my way along and did not really belong in any of the places I was striving so hard to get. I continued to turn to substances for "fortification." I used caffeine and sugar to keep me going in order to study – in fact, 27 cups of coffee one night. I must not have been able to get any amphetamines that particular night, or I would not have needed all that coffee. I graduated from college with honors.

I went on to medical school and did get the M.D. degree. My father once had aspirations of his own of becoming a doctor. For a long time, I resented his having "foisted" his dream onto me. I now consider that I adopted his dream as my own. There was a point, however, when the dream became a nightmare.

Parts of my medical training were traumatic: not just the grueling hours, but also the sights of people sick and injured, sometimes in violent ways. I mostly felt numb to the effects of what I witnessed. For a very long time, I was able to ignore the sensations of tiredness or revulsion and ignore my own physical and emotional pain. In a sense, I needed to be "out of my body." To slow down and feel was too painful, too frightening, or both. When I got into recovery years later, I found out that I did not exactly know how to tell I was thirsty. I had focused my concern on other people's bodies and needs, but had very little awareness of my own.

When I was growing up, nobody in my family seemed to know what to do with strong feelings, especially grief when someone died. My mentors in medical school did not seem to know, either. A sense of failure was the common response to loss. Feelings of vulnerability, confusion, neediness, sadness, and even anger could be sidestepped, at least temporarily, if we stayed in constant work mode. Being compulsive has its rewards in my profession.

My personal brand of workaholism manifested, not only as compulsive activity, but also as mental obsession – relentless, faultfinding, nitpicking, worry, and negativity directed at myself. Oddly, these thoughts seemed to serve as a form of protection – perhaps from failure, rejection, or abandonment. The obsessions gave me an illusion of control. If I were to blame for events and outcomes, I must still be in charge.

In the face of strong emotions, mine or anyone else's, I went "into my head," into the future (planning), or into the past (regretting and replaying past events). There was an almost constant awareness that, if I made a significant mistake, someone could die. Guilt and regret felt familiar and safer than profound sadness, or even joy or happiness, which, of course, could be taken away. It astounds me that I preferred to hang out in my head as much as I did, despite what went on there! The truth is, I am powerless over obsessive thoughts.

I hid behind my white coat. There was a person inside there, but I had a hard time finding her. I could be warm and approachable at times, but friends knew that I disappeared for months on end. Closeness felt suffocating. In order to avoid conflict, I avoided people whenever I could. My schedule barely left room to breathe, but contemplating change made me uneasy. To "let up" felt like failure. I could justify a vacation if it was connected with a medical conference. Leaving work at the end of a day was difficult. I would stand at my desk moving papers from one stack to another, unable to get anything accomplished, but unable to call it a day. There was always more to do.

I sometimes felt burdened by having a physical body. It was one more thing to take care of. When I got sick, I went in to work, anyway. Slowing down seemed risky, or even overwhelming – as though I would die or cease to exist if I stopped. It was almost as though I was risking annihilation. Since my identity was my work, in a manner of speaking, this was a valid fear.

Although I was in the habit of ignoring my body, I could feel anxiety and the sensation of my heart slamming around in my chest every time I raced to the emergency room in response to a call. I raced other places as well – pretty much everywhere I went. I performed tasks hurriedly and often resentfully. Despite all the activity and how revved up I felt inside, I also felt sort of deadened and numb. Many of my actions were reflexive and unconscious.

For me, workaholism brings together grandiosity and low self-esteem – particularly the latter. I believed that my patients deserved someone smarter and better than I, but I also wanted to be in charge of everything myself. Because of my insecurity, I tried very hard to never make anybody angry or upset – a difficult task when surrounded by people who are scared and in pain. Despite all the effort I made, no amount of knowledge or obsessive attention to detail, and no amount of people pleasing allowed me to manage my life or the forces of nature. Everything around me seemed to be, and was, out of my control. I felt alone. I did not know to ask for help. My constant doing lead me to a state of disillusionment and despair. I was miserable. No matter what I accomplished, it was never enough. Despite the fact that I had chosen my profession, I felt resentful and put upon.

My physical health suffered. I got stomach pains and headaches. I developed signs of an ulcer. I vomited blood.

I felt bombarded by all types of requests, including social invitations. My relationships suffered. The man I lived with during my training, and eventually married, had attitudes toward work that were similar to mine. He encouraged me in my career, but the child we had together did not understand our chaotic schedules and long absences. My job, even more than my husband's, required shifts at the hospital that kept me away more than 36 hours at a stretch. Despite my own absences, I became resentful of my husband's unavailability and reacted by withdrawing from him. As a consequence, I felt even more abandoned. Whatever time and energy I had left over from work, I gave as best as I could to my son. I was so exhausted from trying to be "on top of everything" that it is a miracle I could relate at all.

I recall a day I left my son home alone for many hours when he was really too young to tend to himself. I believed that he would be OK, but leaving him to go to work was not rational. It was a compulsion. I did not think, "What is important here?" I just went. Work for me was an addiction – something I did compulsively and could not stop doing without help.

In my early thirties, I had gone into therapy, hoping to learn how to have more successful relationships. I remember one day sitting in my psychiatrist's waiting room, still rushing inside from fighting heavy traffic to get from my office to his. Just as he came to call me in for my appointment, I noticed my nose was bleeding and the center of my upturned palm was filling with blood. That morning I had repeated a familiar ritual – inhaling line after line of cocaine, ignoring the burning sensation inside my nose. I had finished my supply just as the sky was starting to lighten. I had been at it all night.

For many days in a row during my morning commute, I had the recurrent thought of swerving my car full-speed into the concrete embankment along the side of the road. I could not imagine a life other than the one I had worked so hard to create since the age of five. The way I managed to find time for myself was to steal it. Using cocaine gave me the illusion of more time.

Eventually, during my all-nighters, I began to have heart palpitations. One night when I tried to count my pulse and could not, because I could not count that fast, I admitted to myself, that the cocaine could (and possibly would) kill me. I said aloud to whomever or whatever was listening: "Dear God, if you get me through this night, I will never touch this stuff again."

Thankfully, when I got to this stage of desperation, I had people in my life who were already in recovery. They gave me literature to read and offered to go with me to meetings. It was after I got clean from the substance addictions that I realized I was also using work as a drug to medicate or mask feelings, to alter my mood, and to escape aspects of reality I did not know how to face any other way. The fact was, the way I was treating myself was still abusive and insane.

Nowadays, I believe that my compulsive behaviors had a purpose. They helped me survive. They protected a core part of me that did risk annihilation in childhood. At times, I felt overwhelmed, but had nowhere to turn. I learned to use substances and compulsive behaviors as a way to bind my anxiety and to try to replace what was missing.

Once I started getting help for my food and drug addictions and began to wake up to how I was feeling, I could no longer work the hours I was working with the same frenetic drive. I needed to make a change, but I felt ambivalent. I had a distorted view of my role, both at home and at work, which was something just short of omniscience and omnipotence. Carrying what felt like the weight of the world on my shoulders was exhausting. I did not fully understand the concept of surrender, or "turning it over." Even in recovery, I was still trying to get straight A's.

Being genuinely present with my husband or son (or parents!) required skills I did not possess. Practicing medicine felt easier. Despite my shortcomings, I was respected by my colleagues. My patients and their families loved me and I loved them, but I had grown to hate my job and dreaded going to work.

Did I have such a fragile ego that it needed shoring up 18, 20, or 24 hours a day? I knew that I needed to make a change, but I was stuck. I wanted a clear sign about what to do. Anything, up to and including a burning bush, would be OK by me.

One of my best friends, who is a member of W.A. and A.A., had told me about a time she got help making a career decision by meditating on her choices. I had tried to meditate in the past, when I was still working addictively. I felt as though I would jump out of my skin. The restlessness and jumpiness gradually shifted a little over time. One night, I went to an Eleventh Step meditation meeting in my area, determined to get an answer to my question about whether or not to leave my job and leave medicine. During the meditation, when I felt somewhat relaxed, I asked: "Should I stay in medicine?"

Truthfully, as I asked the question, I thought I knew the answer already. I assumed that whomever or whatever answers such questions was going to direct me to stay put because medicine was obviously the most "useful" and worthwhile option I had at the time. (My version of the ruler of the universe back then had a very strong work ethic.) The answer to my question came in auditory form. I literally heard the words: "God is great. God is good. You are lovable. You are loved." The voice was not the usual voice in my head. It was not a black and white, "You should do this" kind of answer. The voice sounded kind.

At times, when I tell the meditation story I omit the sentences with the word "God." For me, the word has associations to fanaticism from which I want to separate myself. Over time I have pieced together a concept of Higher Power. I feel a connection with something larger, smarter, stronger, and more dependable, compassionate, and forgiving than myself. The connection with this something helps quell my anxiety, allowing me to live more freely and enjoy my life.

For a very long time, I tried like hell to be perfect. Nowadays, I would rather be honest and real. I feel more secure and far less overwhelmed when feelings arise. When I have someone or something to turn to, I feel less burdened and less alone. In order to stay sober and to refrain from harmful compulsions, I have had to reach out to both give and receive help. In the process, I get to be an ordinary human with ordinary wants and needs. I get to have a life.

I fuel myself differently these days. I get sustenance and pleasure from art and music, dancing, walking the hills near my house, and especially from my relationships. I have friendships beyond my wildest dreams. I have a job I like that has social relevance.

At night when I wake up, I can meditate to calm myself. It is relaxing to just breathe. I take pleasure in my body and being in true human connection. Slowing down and leaving things out have made more space for me to feel and notice what is going on inside me and around me. Being more conscious in the present moment makes me feel more alive.

I think of recovery as having given me my life back. Sometimes, I feel exuberant and childlike. Strangers on the street comment on my smile. Where I once felt assaulted and bombarded by people, I now seek company and revel in the connection. In a sense, one of my first conscious experiences of spiritual connection, being "one among many," came from reading a newspaper article about W.A. and realizing that I qualified for the program. I was not alone. I definitely belonged.

Practicing the principle of anonymity has been good for me. I offer my skills and experience in the form of service, but instead of hoping to impress, please, or appease someone, I participate because of how pleasant it feels to be useful. My identity is no longer synonymous with my profession. During the times when I feel sad or afraid, I am still glad to be alive. I am grateful. A lot of the time I know that I am acceptable. I am lovable. I am loved.

I have been able to reduce my work schedule and even take a sabbatical. I will not pretend that, once I began to deal with my workaholism, everything was rosy. The year that I took my sabbatical, I felt raw and exposed. Some nights I woke up terrified. I was experiencing feelings that I had kept at bay for years. Luckily, by then I had built a support system. A friend frequently reminds me, "Life is not for sissies." Neither is recovery. In contradistinction to the hero slaying the dragon singlehandedly, recovery takes community. I might be able to pretend that I succeeded in my career by single-minded determination and force of will, but I know that I do not recover from negative obsessions and destructive compulsions alone.

Since coming into recovery, I have experienced physical and spiritual awakenings. Perhaps they are the same thing. My sponsor said recently, "It's all about the body." I think I know what she means. I feel my connection to myself and to a Higher Power as a physical experience in my body, for instance, as a sense of excitement and pleasure when I wake up in the morning. I feel my emotional connections to other people as physical sensations, as well. Listening to someone tell the absolute truth can cause a tingle or bring tears to my eyes. The contrast from earlier times is remarkable, since for so much of my life I was alienated from my body.

Several years into recovery, I started taking classes in mindfulness meditation and yoga. One day, a meditation teacher mentioned that she no longer resisted washing dishes. As she washed them, especially the bowls, she imagined bathing the belly of the baby Buddha. Some days I try her method. When I start to tell myself, "I do not have time for this," I remember that I can "let go" and come back to my breath.

This morning, standing in the golden autumn sunlight at my kitchen sink, I slowly washed several bowls and utensils, glad to be conscious, glad to be able to perceive my hands in the water and my feet on the floor, grateful for the Twelve Steps of Workaholics Anonymous, and grateful to have nowhere that I have to rush to all day.

The condensed version of my story is: I used compulsive overworking as a drug. I could not stop, despite negative consequences in every aspect of my life. No human power (not mine nor that of any other individual acting alone) could have relieved my compulsion. I found relief in community, in connection to myself and other workaholics, and in a connection with a transcendent Power that I experience in the fellowship and in relationship to other members of the group.

Keeping Busy for Life

My father was a general practitioner, a doctor who practiced the traditional way – total availability to his patients. He received calls at home and had a telephone at the side of his bed, as well as a hook for it on the dining room table. There were no answering services or on call schedules in those days. He and I did not interact much. When he came home in the evenings, he read Astounding Stories magazines in his car until Mom called him to eat. In the evenings, he read Saturday Evening Post stories to her as she knitted or darned socks. On the weekends, he worked in the yard, where I sometimes helped by trimming vines and hedges, burning the trimmings, mixing cement, building stone walls and barbecues, laying walks of old brick, or other yard projects. Sometimes he would be in his woodshop turning table legs on an old lathe or sharpening tools on a foot operated grinding wheel. I learned from watching him, and he answered my questions but did not offer much conversation. I was busy with friends, too, all of whom lived within bicycling distance in our small town.

My mother ran the home and the family. She was always busy with home chores or community involvement. If I wanted to talk to her, she told me to find something to do. If I appeared unoccupied, she or my older sisters would say, "Don't just stand there. *Do* something!" If I complained about something, Mom told me to find something to do and I would feel better. In those days, we did not know how to notice our feelings, much less describe them.

And so I learned early to follow the rules and keep busy. The things I learned early lasted the rest of my life.

In college, I joined singing groups and had a job waiting on tables in the campus coffee shop and later in a girls' dorm. I was on the rally committee and had a Model A flivver with no front fenders, which I painted red. I completed four years of college in three years by choosing to take the tough lab courses in the summer instead of vacationing. Later, in medical school, I enjoyed being a subject of class experiments.

In medical school I learned even more about doing without feelings. I learned, "Do not get emotionally involved with your patients," which at some level I interpreted as, "Do not have feelings." I learned to see the patient's disorder (the part of a patient I was concerned with) objectively (as an object, a problem to be solved) and to treat him scientifically (like an experiment). I accepted the illusion of objectivity. And, of course, many times every day, doctors do "experiment" with the many options for "treatment."

My wife and I were married a week after I completed medical school and one week before my internship started. For me, the internship was the next step in my professional career. For my bride, who fixed meals, saved, and re-warmed them, who absorbed my anger over difficulties, and who heard my anxieties when the stakes were high, it was suddenly a totally new life. During that year, I had an episode of gastrointestinal bleeding for which no physical cause was ever found and no nonphysical cause was ever considered. In retrospect, I believe it was due to stress.

The military draft stopped soon after World War II ended, except for the "doctor draft," and after my internship I went into the Navy. After a year at sea and a year ashore I was released from the Navy. During three more years of medical and surgical residencies, I was found to have an inflammation of one eye, for which no cause was ever found. The eye doctor prescribed cortisone eye drops and, although the inflammation got better, a cataract formed in that eye and had to be surgically removed. Then, glaucoma developed in the same eye, resulting in two operations and years of additional eye drops, plus frequent visits to the eye doctor to hold the eye pressure down.

After my residencies were completed, I entered a two-man practice with an established physician. The office was between inner city Oakland and its near suburbs. I took calls from the city telephone exchange at night and covered the practice when the other doctor was away, including delivering babies at any hour. My wife says I was sitting on the edge of my chair whenever I was at home for a meal, anticipating the ring of the telephone. During these years, I developed weakness in one vocal cord and one leg at the same time. The throat specialist referred me to a neurologist, who thought it might be Multiple Sclerosis (MS), or maybe "a virus." I also saw an orthopedist, who thought it was polio, although I had had all of the appropriate immunizations. Both symptoms gradually disappeared. No cause was ever found. No non-physical cause was ever considered. I believe it was stress.

The prospect of a partnership fell apart and I left that practice to work in the medical division of a state hospital. I ran a medical clinic for the hospital community and took a share of night call on the medical wards. When acquaintances in town asked me to run for the school board, I assumed I could do that, too. I found myself campaigning on my own, neither asking for, nor receiving, either financial or volunteer support. I came in second. Thankfully it was no higher, for, on reflection, politics was not my gift, and I had run to please others.

After four years, the state hospital bureaucracy got to me and I looked for a private group. My next 25 years were spent in the family practice department of a large multispecialty clinic. Early in those years, I had an episode of numbness on one side of my face. The neurologist called it neuropathy of no specific cause. I believe that it could have been related to stress.

One professor had warned us, "Medicine is a jealous mistress." My experience suggested that medicine is a siren calling to physicians to devote their entire time and energies to their profession. I often thought it was ideally suited for single people. I realize now that I had lost the distinction between my life and my profession. I was a human doing, not a human being.

At the clinic, I dived into a busy practice. I dictated my notes carefully and learned to keep my feelings out of them, for legal protection. I followed my rule of "doing my share." I volunteered for clinic committee work over breakfast, for county medical society committee work on my afternoons off, and for speaking engagements to corporate employees for the American Cancer Society during my lunch break, which was two hours long at that time.

The patients I saw each day were really interesting people with many stories to tell of the excitement and pathos of their lives. I lived off the feelings of those patients. I loved retelling the gist of these stories to my family at home and did not notice they were not listening. Years later, they were able to tell me they would rather have heard what was going on in my inner world and what I was feeling. I could not have told them. I did not know.

I found that I did not have time to give adequate time to my patients and dictate a complete note without delaying the next patient's visit, so I made brief written notes and completed the dictation after office hours. In order to be home for dinner I would sometimes go back to the office after dinner to finish dictating. My family saw me mostly coming or going. Even when I was home, I was busy moving about the house doing small chores. I did not notice that our children rarely invited their friends inside our home. Only many years later, after I had begun my own recovery and my children thought it was safe to talk to me, did they tell me that in their teens they had wanted to leave home.

I did not know then that I had an addiction to work and was choosing the comfort of the office over the challenge of participating in conversations, games, or other pastimes with my family – a choice for which I would pay dearly as the years rolled on.

One of our sons was an avid skier, and the family went skiing on occasional winter and spring weekends. One Sunday afternoon, after two full days of skiing, I squeezed in one last run before going home. Part way down I noticed my fatigue, pulled off, and stopped, still a little wobbly. I fell sideways, my skis sticking in the spring snow ("Sierra Cement"). I tore a knee ligament, requiring an operation and a full leg cast. Once out of the hospital, I used forearm crutches and kept on working every day.

For years, our summer vacations were taken at the Boy Scout camp where our boys went, which had a family camp for wives and younger siblings. I was the camp doctor during our week in the mountains, and the environment was so refreshing, it never occurred to me that I was working. My wife went along with this for a few years beyond the time our boys had graduated and were off to college. She finally brought to my notice that I did not need to be doing this any longer. Since being awakened, I have enjoyed real vacations!

When portable dictating machines became available, I got one, in order to use every available second to do dictation while walking down the hall between patients. This made my voice warble, so I used the portable recorder while seated at my desk. After months of using this heavy early model, I developed painful tendonitis in the right shoulder. I quit doing committee work on my day off so I could do the leftover dictation then, and I got a lighter dictating machine.

Due to administrative pressure to see more patients, I chose to shorten my lunch period to one hour. There was still time to eat a hearty meal at the clinic's lunchroom, although I could no longer give the Cancer Society talks. When I could not finish all the dictation before supper, I went in early the next morning and finished up before office hours started, sometimes shaving as I drove to work. As my practice got busier, I stopped going to the lunchroom at all, shortened the lunch break to half an hour, and took a bag lunch so I could stay at my desk and read my mail, answer telephone calls, and catch up on dictation while I ate. I no longer participated in clinic committees because they interfered with my morning catch up time.

Sometimes my dictation would back up to the weekend, and I would go in on my Saturday morning off or stay as long as necessary on Saturday afternoon to get the dictation completely finished. If something was planned for the family, or if, during the summer, I had a charter sail on the bay scheduled for Saturday with friends, I would go in at 3 AM Sunday morning to finish dictating before breakfast.

Eventually, the dictation was almost never finished. Monday morning was no longer a fresh start, because there was work hanging over from the previous week. During appointments, I could not interrupt patients to suit the clock, nor did I stop instructions until they were understood, and usually I was behind schedule. I was often tired in the afternoons. I was found to have a mild case of sleep apnea, yet I assumed there was not enough time for a nap.

In the last years of my practice, my son was having difficulty expressing his feelings with his future bride. He sought help and became aware of Twelve-Step programs, most importantly Al-Anon and W.A. I took a whole new look at my relationships with my family, my practice, and myself. I became aware that I was addicted to relationships and to work, for starters. I began a long process of becoming aware of my own feelings, and this felt good. I began to notice how I felt during office interactions.

It occurred to me, but it had never been a serious consideration, that I could see fewer patients. However, I had a relationship addiction to the clinic. It was a supportive practice environment of high quality, and I chose to go along with the requests of the board to see more patients, rather than risk being called a slacker. I was getting close to retirement and chose to keep my earnings as high as possible during my last years to earn the highest possible pension, not having gotten appropriate advice for building a retirement fund until late in my practice years.

I began to ask myself, "How do I feel?" and "What do I need?" and to follow my intuition when I was with patients. I gave patients time to cry, and, on occasion, was led to give them hugs, with their permission. My receptionist learned to allow extra time for some people, and I let her know I liked that. I was feeling good – more like a physician!

One weekend, while vacationing with relatives, I slipped while entering a hot tub and tore my right shoulder muscles. This required surgery, and for six weeks after the operation my right arm was bound to a bolster on my chest. This was the longest time I had ever stopped working and being busy, and I got my first good look at the way I was slowly killing myself, one illness or injury at a time. I let what I saw sink in, and the thought came that it was time to retire. Although I was 62 and had planned to salt away earnings until age 65, I decided to chance it. My wife was pleased. My department head was surprised, but already had a new physician coming who was able to take over my practice. I was able to say goodbye to some of my patients, and I wrote a letter to all of them. I finished all my remaining dictation and cleaned out my office. The final humbling act, turning in my key, was optional. I struggled with the loss of control that would follow if I did. Finally, I really knew it was time to let go of this symbol of special status, authority, and power, and turned it in.

The next Monday morning the same cloud of expectation of unfinished paperwork was still hanging over me, and I could hardly believe there was no more paperwork to do! It was another two days before I could greet the morning with real assurance of my new freedom. It was several months before the tension I had carried from suppressing my resentment about the constant pressure gradually faded away. I still have a quick response to the first ring of the telephone. Now I have the option to let it ring.

The addiction to work followed me into retirement. The activity is different – more physical and less demanding. I still tend to keep doing whatever I am doing without remembering to take mealtimes and breaks. If someone asks me to help set up chairs or carry heavy boxes, I feel comfortable, relaxed, and in the familiar place of being invited to "do something." Now, though, I no longer need to get busy to remove myself from uncomfortable social situations. Practicing the Twelve Steps has shown me options that have made my life vastly more free and fun. My relationships with my wife and children are being renewed and refreshed. And I accept as a bonus gift of this recovery that the sleep apnea has disappeared, I have been able to stop the treatment for glaucoma, and the nerve weaknesses of the early practice years have never returned.

A computer is now a part of my life, and, for a time, the busyness multiplied. I learned that, as long as I run the computer and do not let it run me, it is a wonderful help in many ways. Gradually, I have developed limits and set boundaries with the help of practicing the Twelve Steps, making the time to attend W.A. meetings, and being in regular touch with a sponsor who does not let me ignore or minimize my feelings.

When I feel tired now, I can stop and rest or take a nap. I know there is enough time for what really needs to be done. If an opportunity arises that would keep me from interacting with people or would distract me from the things I need to do for myself, such as rest or read, I can choose to say "no" graciously, without an explanation, and still feel alright about myself. I make full stops at stop signs. I go up stairs one at a time.

A Race with the Clock

"I could work circles around you." I allowed these critical words of my mother to mold me into a "driven" workaholic. There never has been a moment to be wasted, and I just did not work fast enough! After living with these attitudes for 59 years, I became exhausted, burned out, overweight, sick, and unable to relax in my own home.

Time was my key issue. My favorite workaholic behavior was to get so totally involved in a project, so completely focused on accomplishment, that I shut out all the other elements of life. I did not use the bathroom. I did not drink any liquids. My butt would be so numb I would have trouble standing, and I did not have a clue as to what time it was. I simply did not want to be responsible about time. The "charge" of accomplishment was so great that I did not "care" what time it was. There was a lack of reality with time. I looked at the clock; it was 2:10. I went away and did two hours of work. When I checked the time again, I expected the clock to say 2:20; instead it was 4:10. I felt shocked! How could it be that late? I had to rush to my next appointment. I felt flummoxed by time. But when my sponsor wanted me to write down how long each task took, I found that I really wanted to be vague about time. I liked denial.

In W.A., I learned that this is a victim's stance. One of our group members gave me a tape of a song about dwelling on accomplishment and how you must love the precious person you are, just because you exist! She even typed out the lyrics! I was so touched by the love that exists in W.A. This woman is my daughter's age. She actually spent her time on me. In an article on under-scheduling in the Summer 2004 issue of the W.A. newsletter, the writer discussed how recording how much time is spent on various projects gave her the power to stand up to her boss' insistence that a new task be done quickly. W.A. is teaching me how to live.

When I was a child, the worst thing I could do was to waste my father's time. There was so much shame attached to bothering my parents. My fear of wasting time was so great that, for our 25th wedding anniversary, I filled a whole suitcase with projects and flew it with us to Hawaii. My husband said, "You can't waste a second, can you?" I had the attitude, "Jesus is coming! Look busy!" There is a saying in our W.A. group that, if you say the A.A. "Big Book's" Third Step prayer every day, you will stop controlling. I was at a gathering where Twelve-Step items were being sold and I found a tin canister shaped like an antique mantle clock. It had the label, "God Can." Now I say the Third Step prayer, write my action plan, and turn over my day by putting it all in the God Can.

"The intensity sought through our compulsive busyness and constant worry" (The W.A. Tools of Recovery, Prayer and Meditation) is the exact description of my former rushing in order to be on time, in which I have been so lost in space that I did not leave on time and had to rush. When I was a child, my parents left the house rushing, yelling, and screaming, blaming each other or one of the children for being late. I continued this behavior when my daughter was little, always ignoring the clock, and then rushing her, saying, "Hurry up! We will be late!" I never left enough time to get ready to leave, so when she wanted to stop and look at a rock, just like any other little kid, I did not have time to let her. She grew up, so I did not have anyone else to blame, and I was still late!

After all those years of rushing, when I finally made it into the car, I often felt the urge to cry. This meant my adrenaline had dropped because I had used up too much energy rushing. "I will be late for my own funeral – the hearse will have a flat tire," was a joke I used to make. I had a button that said, "I am not late – I am early for the next time!" And then there was the post-it, "Always late but worth the wait." I knew it was wrong to be late, but I (my ego) was too busy to stop my task early enough to be prompt. W.A. opened my eyes to this "rushing," "panic" behavior. "The Problem" of W.A. states, "It is both a substance (adrenaline) and a process addiction (over-doing) addiction." If there is not enough time to finish a job, I got to panic, giving myself an adrenaline rush. It is no joke now. I am sick, and part of my illness is that after 59 years of rushing, my adrenal glands are worn out. I am so happy to have learned the "substance/process" principle. Awareness is the key to change.

One thing is for sure. Since I surrounded myself with tasks (otherwise known as clutter), there was always something for me to do. I was amazed when people said they were bored. I was overwhelmed all the time. I thought I should do everything myself (superwoman), and I had an immature sense of time. I could always use a couple more hours in the day than 24. Once, in the Sunday comics the parents were having a garage sale. They changed the word "garage" to "mirage." I like that better, it is so much less shaming than clutter. At our meeting, we read the W.A. Principles and Tools every week. I have found prioritizing, pacing, and under-scheduling to be a great help.

I despised things I thought were a waste of time. Standing in line at the grocery or post office was sheer torture. We had a speaker once, who said he grocery shopped at midnight because there were no lines and plenty of parking. I totally related. But then, he said, "Grocery shopping at midnight is nuts." Another good reason to go to meetings: we learn from everyone. Commuting was another "waste of time." I found myself eating meals in the car. (In our W.A. meeting there is no multitasking allowed. People really complained about this rule.) I listened to tapes in the car too. And as I careened down from the Caldecott Tunnel, I brushed my teeth with my trusty electric toothbrush. Not only was this a very dangerous activity for driving, *there was spit all over my windshield*! Other W.A. members have told me they kept a toothbrush in the car, too.

By going to meetings, I learned I am not alone. After nearly 20 years in another Twelve-Step program, I do not speed. Once a woman said that speeding is very egocentric, since it means I do not have to follow the rules. I turned the character defect of speeding over in Step Seven, and now when I hear the voice of God say, "Look at your speedometer," I pay attention and slow down. I subscribe to the fabulous W.A. newsletter, *Living in Balance*, which comes four times a year, chock full of W.A. member experiences. In the work world, we are encouraged to call the above behavior "multitasking," but in W.A., we often call it "time-stuffing." Many, but not all, of my credits from one Twelve-Step program were transferable to W.A. As always, humility is key to learning new behaviors.

I never had time to cultivate friendships. I simply had too much to do. After coming to W.A., I learned about *isolation* and how it is one of the ways we can avoid intimacy. (Isolation is the dark room where I develop my negatives.) This is where a sponsor is so useful. I have had two W.A. sponsors. The first one let me call her only once a week and we just had a general chat. The second sponsor and I emailed each other our action plans. When I write my action plan, I take a section labeled "For Ourselves" to mean something for my body, like hand cream. In "For Our Relationships," I state what I will do with my husband or daughter that day to create intimacy. I commit to being with my husband or daughter one day a week. In "For Our Activities," I always try to commit to a 15-minute play activity. I need play in my life because I am responsible for making my life fun. A newcomer at our meeting said, "In Europe they know how to live and in the U.S.

they know how to work." This comment was, for me, an "Expect God at Kmart" experience; we just never know where our next lesson will come from. A cancer doctor once said, "Play is mandatory." In my meditation, I tell myself, "It is safe to play today."

Of course, I over-scheduled. I did not leave myself time to eat lunch or (heaven forbid) time enough to drive if there was traffic congestion. My calendar was so busy, I did not have time to finish projects or clean up. Recently, I was facing a "big chunk of truth about myself" concerning weight loss. I need time to shop, wash, chop, cook and chew vegetables. I need time for exercise, time for meetings and support, and time to plan and write down my food and call it in. W.A. has opened my eyes to the fact that, if I want to lose weight, I will have to give up some of my "precious time."

Prayer and meditation are so important to me. I already mentioned that I say the Third Step prayer every day. I also say a prayer, "Make me patient, gentle, and wise with myself, so I can be patient, gentle, and wise with others." I say affirmations: "You are so smart, you are such a good girl, you work hard enough, you work fast enough, and you get enough done. God loves you, even if you are just sucking air. I love you, even if you are just sucking air." Repeating these affirmations every day has helped me overcome my old childhood criticisms. I am more patient, gentle and wise with myself than ever before. I feel a sense of ease and comfort in just being. I pray, "Help me see beyond what seems to be with people." This has given me so much insight into my relationships. Then, I pray, "Help me see beyond what seems to be with time." This has sometimes kept me from being late and has provided me with insights, such as, "leave time for traveling," or "include time for lunch."

Recovery from "Time Debting"

Before recovery, symptoms of work addiction often included living a compressed life, rushing to beat the clock, and always having too much to do. What does the outside of my life look like now, after six and a half years of workaholism recovery, informed by my recovery from "time debting"? I work part-time from home, telecommuting at a "paying job" while cultivating and exploring new interests. Ironically, W.A. helped me learn about how to sanely cooperate with divine will in coordinating time, energy, and resources, that I now have a job doing that for entire work teams!

In my latest position, as I transitioned to part-time work, I did not adequately engage the W.A. tools of under-scheduling, pacing, and substituting. I had the perception of a sudden surplus of time. The 20 hours I had been working and the ten hours of commuting were freed up: 30 more hours per week! I quickly (unconsciously) filled up my days, mostly with odd jobs and short-term service commitments. Nonprofit and under-resourced organizations that feed my disease's characteristic illusion of indispensability are a great workaholic's stash, if there ever were one!

My sponsor has guided me to have a "72-hour hold" guideline when I am considering adding anything to my schedule greater than a one-time, two-hour commitment. During those three days I check with my sponsor, friends in program, and my Higher Power and Inner Wisdom. When I was in time vagueness around my job transition, and sloppily thought, "Oh, I have lots of time," I was not rigorous with the "72-hour hold" principle and I got into trouble. Then I became aware of what had happened; I could tell my life was too full when I had that "squeezed" feeling with my time.

In the past two months, I reengaged a moratorium on adding any new commitments. This moratorium has often been useful in unmanageable situations. It is a more strenuous form of the "72-hour hold." I simultaneously explored reducing the number of hours I have committed to doing volunteer or paid work. In order to do this, I created a commitment log to gain awareness of all of the time and energy commitments (both formal and informal) I actually had, and about which I had been in vagueness. Thank goodness, the new commitments that I had over-added were in the days/weeks range of commitment, instead of the years/decades range of obligation.

My situation reminded me of when I first came into the program. In early recovery, I became willing to use the tools of substitution, under-scheduling, prayer, and meditation to ground my time and energy in a surrender experience – the "turning it over" that people speak about in Step Three. I applied these tools to my time and energy, as well as paper chaos, to seek relief from the progressive and fatal nature of the disease of work addiction. Focusing my recovery on time debting, I have learned to think of being behind or being late as a form of debting. That is, I have "overspent" my time or energy, and now I am beholden to the past, either through backlog, or by being indentured to activity commitments in the future that exceed my capacity – "time, activity, and commitment overspending," if you will. Backlog includes two aspects that harm me physically, emotionally, mentally, and or spiritually. First, activity debt: unfinished activities or commitments; and second, self-debt: inadequate time for sleep, exercise, relationships, creativity, medical attention, or self-care.

Record maintenance is a tool that has helped me increase awareness about where my time and energy is spent. I have kept records of my time spending. First and foremost, I have kept daily records for over six years of how many hours I have worked at my jobs. This includes being specific down to the minute, including taking breaks and meals, and recording when I leave work. Without keeping records of my time spent at work, how would I be able to know if I had been abstinent and in alignment with my bottom lines?

There are concomitant parts to this practice – how to count hours when I lunch with coworkers without compulsively clocking or ignoring if I am really in a work discussion; how to count travel time for work trips or events; how to accommodate work-related conferences, when the hours add up in a short space of time; and how to not obsess and worry about work while not at work. For this last issue, I often visualize my Higher Power leading me out of the office door at the end of my work day, waving goodbye, and promising to take care of everything until I return.

I have often kept records of my hours of sleep, where unmanageability or "sleep debting" can trigger toxic adrenaline cycling. I review my time logs five days a week with my sponsor. I have become aware of the triggers of my disease and willing to have Higher Power guide me in a different way of being, including avoiding triggers altogether. It is now rare for me to go to volunteer or booster meetings where there are lots of tasks and people looking for other people to take them on. Do not even ask me all the times my disease has sidestepped the 72-hour hold by taking on a lot of little – less than two-hour – service commitments that still added up to trouble!

In addition to work and sleep logging, I have sometimes tracked breaks, resting, yoga, walks, exercise, fun, wellness, and self-care time. Especially at the beginning, my recordkeeping focused on the areas in which I am experiencing Step One unmanageability. To really surrender myself, I have kept records of all of my time in categories.

Recordkeeping is an especially helpful tool if I am considering adding something new to my schedule. When I am praying about a substitution plan, my time logs help me get concrete and specific about how I am currently spending my time. An example of the reality of recordkeeping is: an activity has lasted for five weeks so far and has taken 3.2 hours the first week and two hours a week since then.

What I learn again and again from time recordkeeping is that my addict's internal story of how I am spending my time (e.g., "That project is eating up all my time" – aside from thinking like a victim) is often inaccurate. It is usually a lie, and recordkeeping leads me to rigorous honesty (e.g., "Oh, in fact, that project is only actually taking 1.5 hours per month."). Then my addict may think, "Oh, that is easy, it will take no time at all." In workaholism and time debting recovery, I should hear a "yellow alert" go off whenever I hear those words, but it does not always happen. My fantastical thinking and actual reality might have too much distance between them. The disease is cunning, baffling, and powerful.

When I am recordkeeping, I become the scribe for my Higher Power. My emotional attachments, filters, and baggage loosen up and often fall away, and I can live in reality. I am reminded of what a program friend suggests to me: "Do not use your mind for anything important today." Another friend (simulating a voice over a bullhorn): "Put the work, obligation, worry, and avoidance, down and take three steps back!" What my mind thinks and what is objectively true are not coincident.

All of this information, awareness, and honesty about time helps me work with my sponsor and Higher Power to formulate a time spending plan. Through guidance and learning what is "enough," I am able to proactively co-create a daily plan for my time and energy. This planning has worked differently at different times: anything from a daily check-in with my sponsor about the 24 hours ahead, to mapping out service, volunteer, work, and recovery commitments on a weekly and monthly basis (and even annually for vacations and big fun). Planning ensures space for nurturing, fun, creativity, relationships, and down time.

Here is a simplified version of the categories I use to track my time. Below is the first column of a spreadsheet that includes a column for each day of the week. Sometimes I have tracked time throughout the day, and other times I have used this resource as a form of a Tenth Step inventory at day's end. Some of the guidelines I use for time other than work are: track time to the nearest 15 minutes (so I do not become compulsive about recordkeeping), and count sleep from the night before (which helps me see how abundant rest and sleep sets me up for the day). In all categories, I include time spent traveling to or from an activity as part of the "time cost" of that activity.

1 - Spirituality
    a. Prayer, meditation, sponsor
    b. Spiritual reading, program literature
    c. Service, sponsees, phone
    d. Step work (including daily Tenth Step)
    e. Meetings
    f. Creating, writing, journaling, art
    g. Recordkeeping (hours, financial, yoga)
    h. Out in nature
    i. Other, general spirituality

2 - Restoration
    a. Shelter, body, rest
    b. Sleep
    c. Cleaning
    d. Rest, nap, elevate, breaks
    e. Yoga, move, walk, bike
    f. House

2.5 - Inflow
    a. Work
    b. Transportation to and from work
    c. Other

3 - Divine nourishment
    a. Food shopping (including transportation)
    b. Food prep
    c. Breakfast
    d. Lunch
    e. Dinner

4 - Transportation
    a. Getting gasoline, maintenance, repairs

5 - Self-care
    a. Bathing, shampooing
    b. Feelings
    c. Quiet time

6 - Clothes

7 - Medical and wellness
   a. Doctor, chiropractor, massage

8 - Entertainment
   a. Going out with friends
   b. Movies
   c. Books, reading, library
   d. Processing
   e. Intimacy

9 - Beloveds/Gifts
   a. Cards, email, letters, gifts

10 - Education

11 - Vacation

12 - Personal Business
   a. Opening and sorting mail, getting office supplies, etc.

13 - Dependent Care
   a. Time with family
   b. Walking the dog
   c. Time with pets
   d. Cleaning out the litter box

14 - Savings
   a. Extra energy, naps etc.
   b. Lollygagging
   c. Senseless fun
   d. Restorative yoga

15 - Currency and "debt repayment"
   a. Clearing up backlog
   b. Amends
   c. Clearing up paper chaos

16 - Other

Total Hours (should equal 24)

Over time, with the help of Higher Power, my sponsor, and program friends, I can detect trends and patterns. Overspending time on service or work – Category 1 – while under-spending time on entertainment – Category 8 – is a workaholic classic. While planning ahead for a given week, I have added up my projected commitments and sometimes my plan has exceeded the actual number of hours in a week by 25 to 40 hours! No more "innocent" strategies: "Well, I will just stay up a little later or get up a little earlier to finish that." Making a time spending plan and doing time recordkeeping allow me to have an objective view.

My time spending plan has come in handy when something new comes up: from a gardening project to a service position; moving from full-time to part-time work; and from taking on a writing endeavor to deepening in my experience of the balance of time for creativity, spontaneity, and fun. A time spending plan helps me get out of vagueness so that I can, with my Higher Power's help, develop a plan of action. It is a map for matching my time and energy to my values. In time debting recovery, financial solvency is parallel to time currency. Maintaining records and formulating a spending plan for wellness lead me day by day to honesty and serenity. My keywords are gentleness, spaciousness, and surrender.

A Vision of Recovery from Workaholism

When I am able to live my life without the frenzy of excessive work, I am recovering from workaholism. When I am able to live without substituting the obligations of work for the inevitable joys and pains of life, I am recovering from workaholism. When I am able to take responsibility for my behavior without attributing it to the demands of work or other obligations, I am recovering from workaholism. When I am able to face difficult situations without resentment or fear, I am recovering from workaholism. When I can remember the past without recrimination and guilt, I am recovering from workaholism.

When joy replaces fear and faith replaces desperation, I am recovering from workaholism. When I am at peace in my own skin and fully alive in the present, I am recovering from workaholism. When pride in my own achievements replaces boundless competition, I am recovering from workaholism. When humble membership in community replaces loneliness, I am recovering from workaholism. When faith in the abiding presence of a Power greater than I replaces the arrogant independence of self-will, I am recovering from workaholism.

When I rejoin the human race as one among many, living each day according to the will of my Higher Power, I am recovering from workaholism.

SUPPLEMENTAL RESOURCES

Living With a Workaholic:
For Friends and Family

This chapter is for people with a workaholic in their lives. Perhaps you are just now becoming aware of workaholism and some of its consequences: a newcomer to addiction and recovery. We want to share with you the experience of other family members and friends of workaholics, both before recovery and during early recovery. The effects of workaholism can be just as devastating for family and friends as for work addicts themselves. We hope you will find reassurance and support for yourself, whether the workaholic in your life is in recovery, or not.

The experiences shared in this article are those of recovering partners or spouses of work addicts, and other family members who have lived with a workaholic, such as a parent. Recovering persons living with a workaholic often refer to themselves as "co-workaholics."

Before Recovery

The lives of many recovering co-workaholics in early recovery got worse before they got better. They often used to think their recovery had failed because they had not experienced how life without the active addiction could be a good thing. While getting past early recovery was almost always a crushing experience, it has been well worthwhile. The capacity to seek help and engage with support from outside the family was the most crucial step making possible long-term healing and growth.

Workaholism is often described as a disorder of several dimensions – physical, psychological, social, emotional, and spiritual. There is often an ongoing or recurring loss of control over excessive working and compulsive activity. Despite the adverse consequences, workaholics have a preoccupation with and obsessive investment in work and activity, along with distortions in thinking, particularly what is called "denial."

What do people mean by denial? They may be referring to a central contradiction of workaholism: denying the reality of the addiction while explaining it away at the same time. This often necessitates dishonesty and secrets. Denial means not being able to understand or see things that are too threatening. It is an unconscious self-deception.

Work addicts may experience an ever-increasing need for intense activity and a corresponding increase in the denial of that need. As workaholism worsens, changes occur in their behavior and thinking. Work avoiders and work anorexics may be affected as much as compulsive over-doers. For some workaholics, their sense of importance, powerfulness, and grandiosity – like intoxication – impaired their judgment. For others, anxiety and fear built up around their ability to perform. Work addicts often held two core ideas to explain their view of themselves and the world: "I am not a workaholic," and "I can control my work world."

Co-workaholics say their own behavior and thinking were also affected by the disorder. They joined the denial and contorted logic of the workaholic in order to gain reassurance and an illusion of control about the sturdiness of their relationship. They became preoccupied with the work addict and obsessed with the workaholic's wellbeing. One co-workaholic said:

> Sometimes, I would feel guilty and unworthy when my partner complained that I was not pushing myself as much as he did. I thought his over-involvement with work was all my fault, and that his chronic avoidance of me meant there had to be something terribly wrong with me that I could not seem to figure it out.

Some co-workaholics felt ashamed and began to close out the world, isolating their partner or family further. Recovering co-workaholics variously report they felt anxious, emotionally numb, insecure, powerless, and plagued by a low self-image and a sense of hopelessness. Isolation made it even harder to ask for help and support when they "hit bottom." Their capacity for genuineness and honesty was gone.

Depression and chronic under-functioning often became the norm. Relatives and friends who did not support the compulsive busyness or the rationalizations of the work addict were avoided or abandoned. The remedy for their distress was to try harder to control the workaholic, leading to mutual accusations and further disillusionment and despair. "I tried to fight it. I really tried. But it just seemed to make things worse."

For work addicts, hostility towards change can be very high. One workaholic in recovery said, "I could not figure it out. I was rewarded by the world at large, but despised by my own family." Work filled the void and deepened it; but while they were still overworking, the idea of resigning their perpetual busyness without a substitute was unthinkable. One recovering workaholic said, "There was no way I was going to admit defeat. To do so was to become vulnerable, and I knew for certain that vulnerability always triggered attack."

Why do partners and other family members go along with all of this? Some say their intense need for attachment and their fears of abandonment and being alone dominated everything else. "We were in shared denial."

The Beginnings of Recovery

The beginnings of recovery can occur when one partner or family member "hits bottom." Either the denial, resistance and defiance cannot be maintained any longer, or something else breaks down and a family member reaches outside the family for help. The pain of the addiction or co-addiction outweighs the considerable pain of recovery. One partner said:

> Unfortunately, I was not aware of my partner's workaholism until after he hit bottom, which came in the form of his suicidal depression. I tried to control things and make them better – to 'fix it.' When my stomach was in knots, I would go for a walk outside the house. What helped during those horrible days was going to Al-Anon and to educational programs about addiction.

By the time the work addict halts her or his overworking, the co-workaholic and the rest of the family have been severely impaired. "I did manage to bury my emotional needs, but I was not able to bury my resentments." On the way to withdrawal from workaholism, things can get very bad, with increasing turmoil before the self-deceptions and other defenses ultimately cave in.

For co-workaholics, denial can often lift like a haze, slowly dissolving as they became ready to discern reality more clearly. One recovering co-workaholic said of her family:

> It was something none of us were willing or able to talk about. We were trying desperately not to have the

relationship we were having. Our rock bottom was delayed because we were all resigned to keeping everything together and patching over problems – to make nice. We wanted to have good manners and be a socially acceptable family.

The emotional acceptance of the end of the battle is what recovering people refer to as "surrender." Some recovering persons also refer to this as an admission of defeat or "ego deflation." Surrender was accompanied by a profound acceptance of loss of control. One co-workaholic said, "One day I realized I had no power or hold over the workaholic in my life. I finally saw I could not keep him in line, and that I had to give up my efforts at damage control."

At the same time, workaholics may report that the beginning of withdrawal from workaholism was very hard because reality was so different from their expectations. For many co-workaholics, it was difficult, awkward, and even shameful to accept the problem or look for a helping hand. "We both felt trapped and isolated. It was difficult to accept the fact that I could not do it alone." The introduction to recovery – becoming abstinent – was often full of disillusionment and disenchantment for all. This was especially the case if there was no one in the family invested in recovery. Abstinence may then be what recovering people call a "white-knuckle" holding pattern. "We were in 'remission' rather than in 'recovery.' It was very hard to view workaholism as something that was harmful to my partner and to our partnership instead of a well-rewarded activity."

New abstinence is an intense, critical point. "Our family's recognition of workaholism was supposed to make everything better and put an end to upsets and fights. Instead, it seemed to leave a gaping hole, a great terrifying emptiness." Many recovering co-workaholics and workaholics in early recovery needed to sustain their fledgling recoveries from workaholism, which they did not know how to do. "I focused on just one day at a time, or even smaller increments, to get through. We needed to learn how to hold on."

In some recovering partnerships, both partners report that early on they felt only hopelessness. They had tried every measure they could think of in order to save their relationship, but nothing had worked for them. They accepted that they were powerless to fix their irresolvable issues.

Some had tried therapy before recovery. "I was there because I was unhappy with him, and he was there because I was unhappy with him. It did not work." In this relationship, both partners became willing, or were trying to become willing, to accept mutual responsibility for the destructive patterns in their relationship; both saw themselves as "identified patients," in the sense that they recognized that each of them needed help individually; and both accepted "loss of control" and were willing to accept outside help.

> When he went into recovery, I was shocked. The therapist treating him told me to go to Al-Anon. None of it seemed to make sense. I kept going to work myself, while he was in bed all day for weeks and weeks. I started learning to take better care of myself, and learning to go places by myself. I was becoming less dependent on my partner and more dependent on myself. I was becoming less codependent.

These two partners committed themselves to recovery – which was not the same as committing to each other. "We did not know it at the time, but that was not possible until much later."

Co-workaholics may need to learn to live with ongoing confusion and unpredictability as part of the strain of early recovery. Sudden outbursts may be all too common. "If I became very anxious, it helped me to remove myself, both physically and emotionally, from my partner." They needed to accept not knowing much about anything, which was often so upsetting and unsettling that they sometimes turned to short-term "fixes" and unhealthy behaviors that were harmful to recovery. "As a co-workaholic, here are things that I tried that did not work: blaming, fighting, threatening to leave, ignoring, doing my own thing, working harder myself, and overeating to smother my feelings."

Some recovering partners have found a couple's therapist who could guide them to put their attention and emphasis on themselves as individuals and not to try to "fix" their damaged partnership. Yet, because these partners were fearful of an unpredictable future, or did not have a clue as to how they might be restored to intimacy and commitment together, they were frightened that such a switch in their attention and energy would lead to the end of their partnership. "Holding fast to one another in the midst of all this flux – that was one of our most critical tasks."

Some couples new to recovery do grow apart and end up separating. Other times, in early recovery an unwillingness or an inability to accept a natural ambiguity and confusion led to the end of the relationship, where one partner felt trapped and compelled to choose between recovery or the partnership.

When one partner enters recovery and the other does not, the relationship may be plagued with a divisiveness between the old norm (active addiction or co-addiction) and the new norm (recovery). In that scenario, there are two versions of reality. One version is that there is no addiction and co-addiction in the partnership. The other version is that there is addiction and co-addiction in the partnership. This conflict creates an atmosphere of constant stress while the partners live in two separate worlds. This kind of rupture or disparity can go on indefinitely. Some couples find ways to stay together despite the ongoing heavy strain, while others end their relationship.

Some couples get to W.A. after considerable recovery from other addictions and co-addictions. One such co-workaholic said of herself and her partner:

> We took an inventory of our lives together in a couples' Twelve-Step program. One of the problems we agreed on: we were both too depleted to be present for our relationship, friends, or family. We wrote a spiritual contract that included going to a W.A. meeting together once a week. At the time, I did not think it was a bottom – only that a friend had gotten relief in W.A. and I wanted my partner to get help. It was only after attending the meetings that I began to see the workaholic patterns of my own.

For many recovering co-workaholics in early recovery, reaching outside the family for support and making continued use of that support for a lengthy period of time was the single most important element in sustaining their process of recovery. "We had to accept that change is equal to action, and action is equal to accepting change." Co-workaholics may seek outside help through therapy, religion, and Twelve-Step programs.

One partner attended an addiction education and support group. She learned:

> One of the premises mentioned was that the whole family is affected. If one person is to recover, the family needs to

recover, too. The addict and the codependent both need education and support about their roles in the dysfunction or disease. Recovery changes the dynamic of the couple. When one person is recovering, the other must change also, if they are to stay together and be happy together.

Nonetheless, co-workaholics often report their initial resistance to outside help, including their resistance to Twelve-Step programs for co-addicts. "At my first several meetings, I was just a guest rather than an active member."

People often report a rude awakening from their wishful thinking that abstinence and recovery were supposed to mean no more problems:

We figured that we would be done and cured, probably within six months, or 12 at the most. In hindsight, it is clear that my recovery had barely started at one year and that our partnership was just taking baby steps. I had been frustrated that I was not 'making him better.' We both felt we were 'running late' in recovery.

Many family members in early recovery may have a difficult time interacting. They may have no idea how to approach each other, and fear making mistakes that could lead to feeling out of control or lead to relapse. Co-workaholics report they could not tackle problems, disagreements, or feelings head on without ending up polarized in a battle over who was right and who was wrong – in essence, shaming each other and fighting over who was to blame. "I see now that I could not get to my own issues because I was able to hide behind his flagrant ones." An early focus on individual growth and responsibility can prepare them to come back later as allies and deal with differences or conflicts without getting totally out of control or engaging in conflict avoidance.

Progress in the Here and Now

A co-workaholic's focus on their own individual growth and responsibility can sometimes be at odds with the needs of the children in the family. When they reach outside the family for help for themselves – therapy, religion, and Twelve-Step programs – co-workaholics may have less time, energy, and focus for their children. It may be difficult and painful to pay heed to their self-reclamation needs while straining to meet the best interests of their children.

For some co-workaholics, even with resistance and impasses, they gradually understood they could not rely on their partner or the partnership itself to fill a hole or heal them. That is a task for the individual. "We alone can do it, but we cannot do it alone." We are learning to put ourselves first.

Co-workaholics who have reported that their self-worth was vested in their workaholic partner – caretaking or controlling the workaholic – also indicate that early recovery was a time of deep sorrow, pain, and resistance to building their own separate individuality and recovery program. They said they wanted to sidestep the workaholism (to overlook it or ignore it) in order to focus instead on bettering communication and other facets of family life.

A partner said:

> Regarding my own recovery, now I focus mostly on myself. I spend much less energy on my partner's issues. The problem in both of us seems much deeper and more cunning than before recovery. I am aware of unconscious adrenaline-seeking behavior that can be stirred up even with things we agree to do as a couple on the weekend. I am aware of the problems of my mind that can turn future worry into catastrophes. For a while, my own financial insecurities played into those of my partner, and fueled an illusion that money was the reason we needed to work so much.

Another co-workaholic said:

> I went to my individual Twelve-Step program and it was three years before I gave up the idea that I could get my partner to stop. It was four years before she surrendered to her compulsive overworking. It was hard to look at myself and impossible to do it alone.

Still another co-workaholic said, "I had a lot of fear that our relationship would not survive all the changes in recovery."

For some co-workaholics, the recovering addict's recovery program was regarded as an unwelcome guest, a gatecrasher, and a trespasser. Those outside the Twelve-Step program may say they resent the recovering addict for going to meetings, going out for coffee, or talking on the phone. What about their partnership? It is horrendously difficult to accept that the newly recovering person has plenty of energy and time for Twelve-Step friends, but no time for their relationship.

Actions that have helped recovering co-workaholics with their initial recuperation from the effects and consequences of work addiction are: attending their own meetings, connecting with other recovering co-workaholics between meetings, and switching their efforts onto their own recovery. At meetings, co-workaholics hear how other people's experiences and problems are similar to their own, helping them feel less alone, isolated, and adrift. "If others have been there and survived, there is hope." As the self-deception and other self-protective measures lessened, co-workaholics and workaholics in Twelve-Step programs set out to "work the Steps." This includes looking at one's own beliefs and behaviors and beginning a process of recognizing and accepting reality before recovery, as well as in the here and now. "I started learning how to be less critical of myself. I saw some of my own tendencies towards busyness, and in recovery I limited the number of projects I was willing to undertake. Now I recognize when I am starting to get overwhelmed and I try to mitigate it."

Recovering people commonly say that early recovery meant grief and defeat as much as optimism, and uncertainty and doubts as much as a return to any comfortable routines there might have been before hitting bottom.

> In early recovery, it is important to realize you may be living together, but you are not really much of a partnership. You are polarized about practically everything. You have routines together, pay bills together, even sleep in the same room together, but there is no real sense of deep connection or bright future together, at least for the time being. Somehow you have to figure out how to stay connected while you are disconnected.

Partners in which both members began their individual recovery process have said that they did not end up getting back to the lives they had before recovery. This was a brand new experience.

Partners recovering from the consequences of workaholism and with significant progress in recovery often point out that it was not within their capabilities to have an intimate and committed relationship together without first laying solid, stable individual groundwork. In early recovery, they said:

> It was not that we did not communicate well together – we did not communicate at all. There just was not any connection. I had faith that our shift together would happen in time. He had to emphasize and concentrate on his recovery. I was not kidding myself that all our problems had gone away. I figured we would get to the other stuff later on. But I did not feel frantic or rushed. There was progress in the here and now.

These partners said that their shared recognition of workaholism and the vocabulary of recovery served to hold them together until they could direct their energies back toward themselves as a couple. One co-workaholic suggests, "Believe your partner if he or she states, 'I am a workaholic.'" Another said, "Even though each person has to put his or her primary program first in order to maintain health, the partnership needs to be strengthened and nurtured too." Some couples turned to therapy in order to satisfy their needs to express angry feelings while protecting themselves from the dangers of uncontrolled argument.

When both partners arrange their partnership around W.A. and other Twelve-Step programs, the family gains from the outside buttressing of mutual new attitudes about workaholism and actions in recovery. "Meetings gave me support and encouragement, and, of course, a place to share my pain. I came away each time with hope, peace, love, and growth." Early on, however, the future can look pretty bleak:

> It was scary for us in the beginning because we did not know any couples who were both in recovery. Our society is organized around production and consumption, not connection and relatedness. After a long time in program, we have seen numerous couples separate or get divorced – or simply give up and accept the status quo – because they were unable or unwilling to accept mutual responsibility for the disorder or health of their partnership.

It is common to many recovering co-workaholics that they want to finally have their persistent troubles "done and over with." "We told ourselves we should have gotten past all this by now." Some problems indeed are often better, but they are not fixed. "In early recovery, it was invaluable to hear that other couples had experienced the same kinds of problems we were now having, and to be able to see the positive changes they had made. 'Progress, Not Perfection' was one of the slogans."

Another partner said:

> After some time in recovery, I have adjusted to a lower standard of living. My paychecks from my part-time job are no longer just the extra, but about half of our combined income. It took years to become accustomed to not having my partner in corporate America. I now appreciate more what we do have together, and I appreciate that we really have to work as partners to have a good standard of living.

The Evolving Adventure

A few co-workaholics say their lives improved almost at once in early recovery and that things just kept improving from there. While true for some, most others report that recovery was a gradual, evolving adventure, where change and progress became evident only in hindsight. They say it was not recapturing something they had in the past yet had lost; instead, it meant wide ranging adjustments and unforeseen transformations which only slowly evolved into a new sense of assurance and wellness. Later in ongoing recovery, they were better able to work on their partnership and the rest of their family, once the partners were solid in their individual recoveries.

Some recovering couples were well into recovery before the work addict was able to "show up" emotionally for the relationship. "He is not as driven as he used to be, and he is somewhat more available to me. But he still resents getting interrupted in the middle of a project." Some co-workaholics were astonished to find out that they themselves had not been emotionally available or open to an intimate, committed relationship. Looking back, they realized the unavailability and distance of their actively workaholic partner had felt familiar and comfortable to them. Movements toward greater closeness and connectedness in later recovery often felt unfamiliar and uncomfortable, but were worth the effort.

Some partners who were several years into recovery could see in their partnership many healthy developments that were simply not conceivable during the first year.

We work as partners more to plan large expenditures. We have more time together. We plan our calendars together. I can more clearly communicate my needs, and he more willingly alters his behavior to meet them. We enjoy our days off together. We have learned to be more flexible with our schedules. On our days off we may have ten things to do – but we are both willing to see how things go and to stop pushing to get everything done. We put rest as a top priority.

Trust, warmth, and mutual responsibility were restored only gradually – in fits and starts – evolving slowly and occasionally with slips back into the old, painful patterns. For some couples, the period of difficult adjustment and repair lasted more than ten years. But eventually, they say, they have become a healthy family with a stable relationship, shared values and goals, more affection and love, and solid individual recoveries as distinct selves.

Finally, even with several years of recovery, many co-workaholics remain active in their program of recovery. Their ongoing involvement in outside support – Twelve-Step programs, therapy, religion – helps them keep the focus on themselves as individuals while avoiding isolation or falling back into old, destructive patterns. They socialize and share with other recovering couples who are working to change themselves in order to stay together. They say that they have not "graduated" from healthy reliance and dependency on their support system. "We alone can do it, but we cannot do it alone."

A partner said:

Things are different. I left a very workaholic job and work part-time now. My partner has more responsibility, but takes vacations and comes home early many nights. We get regular exercise, we help each other prioritize and make a realistic action plan, and we are happier and have energy for each other and our family and friends. Our agreed plan of action is to keep those commitments to our spiritual contract, which nine years later still includes a weekly meeting of W.A.

They have learned from their own experience that recovery is certainly possible and definitely worth it.

To Employers and Helping Professionals

I am writing to you as an employer and a helping professional and as a workaholic. You no doubt are reading this book because someone recommended it to you or because you care about a workaholic.

Before I came into recovery I would not have noticed the characteristics of a workaholic. I probably thought they were exceptional workers, since they were willing to stay up all night and work double shifts. Multitasking, staying late, working weekends and vacations, accepting that things were always in crisis: we all thrived on it. We bragged about the drinking and drugs we needed to calm down and to get going each day. We were proud of the hard work and sacrifices. We worked for driven organizations; we were all a team. Peak performance was expected and tight deadlines were unfailingly met. "Workaholism" was a foreign word. What is funny is, at the time, I worked for a health care organization.

Books have been written about the organization or society as an addict. Workaholism is found in many organizations, including some you might least suspect, such as schools, clergy, and nonprofits, as well as ones you would suspect, such as law firms, technology companies, and Fortune 500 corporations. Hard work, independence, and money are admired cultural values, so is pulling yourself up by the bootstraps. Workaholics come from all areas of life, including single mothers, laborers with two jobs, self-employed workers as well as "type A" corporate managers. The research also points to several patterns of workaholism, from the stereotype of the driven employee consistently working 60- to 80-hour weeks to the more surprising portraits of work anorexics and binge-and-crash adrenaline junkies who thrive on and are unconsciously committed to never completely finishing projects or to only relinquishing a task with maximal drama.

I wish now I had known more then. Some good people's lives could have been helped. I have seen heart attacks and strokes occur at work as a result of workaholism. I have known a number of workaholics who were hospitalized for depression or who actually committed suicide. There were many serious accidents and divorces. Nearly every employer and helping professional feels a moral responsibility for the wellbeing of their employees. But we were and still are in denial as professionals and as a society. Workaholism is not identified as a problem, but the consequences of it are. Until a workaholic is facing serious health risks or has made a huge mistake due to fatigue and stress, we stay part of "the harder you work the more you get" club.

We are rewarded for practicing our disease. We were powerless to stop ourselves. It was not until I got in recovery myself that I could see the insanity in others.

To my surprise, there is a world of recovery out there. I know now about the hope and help of W.A. meetings. The tools and literature were once like a foreign language to me. I would have told my fellow sufferers how the meetings were helping me stop the self-destructive cycle. Workaholics have to find balance in a workaholic world. We need the regular help of a program of recovery in order to keep our sanity. The best thing to do is to help others get into the program of W.A. If you have a staff member or patient with an issue, tell us if you think our problems may be due to workaholism. If so, we are hurting the organization as well as ourselves. You may want to look at excessive overtime as part of the pattern of the disease. Ask if we are ready to have a normal life. You could give us a copy of this book, *The Workaholics Anonymous Book of Recovery*. If we are having a workaholic slip, ask how the meetings are going, what Step we are on, and do we have a current sponsor? People in recovery appreciate interest in our program, since it has a meaningful influence in our lives.

Workaholics in recovery make great employees. We are hardworking, loyal, and creative. The driven, stressed, and inflexible aspects of us are lifted as we seek recovery. As you read this book, some of the ideas may seem strange to you. But they have worked for us. If you believe your organization has a workaholic climate, a whole change can take place toward health and sanity if more employees get into recovery. This could be a new beginning for all.

The History of W.A.

As with A.A., there was a time when W.A. did not yet exist and had to be created. In the early 1980s, a number of people began to recognize that their work behavior was pathological – impacting their lives much how a substance does when it overtakes the will of the addict. Individuals in search of a solution found each other in the workplace, at home, and on the playing field. Those that were willing to be first in service formed groups modeled after those of other Twelve-Step programs. In April 1983, one of the first formal efforts to create a fellowship around workaholism began in New York when a corporate financial planner and a schoolteacher met. They formed a group in an effort to stop working compulsively and to help others who suffered from the disease. In their earliest meetings, spouses participated as well. These pioneers hoped to reclaim the strength that they had previously experienced through the A.A. and Al-Anon fellowships. In retrospect, the related family and friends were perhaps better suited to a Work-Anon group – albeit they did not form a separate organization for their recovery at that point. W.A. literature was initially drafted meeting-by-meeting or adapted from other Twelve-Step programs. Many of the early writings were authored by V.M. – one of the leaders who gave life and structure to the first W.A. groups.

Within the next several years, others (without knowledge of the New York effort) also started to label work addiction as an illness and to hold meetings in their communities. Several recovery groups were established in Southern California. Eventually, the workaholics from Los Angeles and San Diego merged with those in New York to collaborate on the creation of new literature and to carry the Twelve Steps to those still struggling with the addiction. Meetings also started up in several other areas in the Northeastern and Southwestern United States. Magazine and newspaper articles helped to announce their existence. In the late 1980s, a number of groups developed in the San Francisco Bay Area when a nurse – previously acquainted with A.A. – noticed that her compulsive, intense work behavior was impacting her health and relationships even more severely than alcohol had. She sought help at the Dry Dock, San Francisco's A.A. recovery center. In 1987, she established W.A. as a California nonprofit corporation to represent that first official Intergroup.

Requests for information came in from other countries as meetings began around the world. Despite all being based on the Twelve Steps, however, groups often had different definitions of the problem as well as unique ideas for the Tools and other literature. As more workaholics discovered each other's existence – and their striking similarities – many pushed for the sharing of concepts, including the development of a standard meeting format and an approach for responding to public inquiries about workaholism. On March 31, 1990 – after an exchange of letters among several of the first W.A. groups – four workaholics and two of their spouses met in the basement of St. John's Presbyterian Church in West Los Angeles. Representing the fellowships of New York, Los Angeles, and San Diego, they titled their meeting the "Workaholics Anonymous First World Service Conference." At this initial gathering, they shared the history, progress, and hopes for the future of their respective groups as well as identified a number of common problems they had encountered. Issues included dealing with referrals from concerned spouses, dealing with referrals from medical doctors and psychologists, dealing with inquiries from those with no Step experience, developing a meeting format for very small groups, substituting telephone support where meeting attendance was impractical, and confronting the cultural fact that workaholism was not yet accepted as a widespread and serious disease. The workaholic conference attendees assumed the responsibilities of the new international organization and mutually pledged to hold their offices until elections could be held at the next convention. During such period, the newly formed Workaholics Anonymous World Service Organization (W.A.W.S.O.) sought permission from A.A. to adapt the Preamble, Twelve Steps, and Twelve Traditions; began to develop new Articles of Incorporation and Bylaws; assembled a starter kit for new meetings, including a suggested meeting format and other core readings; began compiling a list of relevant literature and gathering stories of recovery; developed a roster of all the known W.A. meetings worldwide; and communicated with each W.A. group.

On November 7, 1992, enthusiasm was high as about 30 participants gathered to represent many of the 63 existing W.A. groups – including those from Canada, Germany, and Japan – at the Second World Service Conference at Summit Medical Center in Oakland, California. The attendees ultimately placed all W.A.W.S.O. authority in the hands of five co-chairpersons: (1) for the registration of groups, (2) for answering mail and telephone inquiries, (3) for outreach, (4) for managing the treasury, and (5) for facilitating communication among the co-chairs and committees. Committees were then established to reexamine and officially file the Bylaws, develop a list of suggested literature, publish a newsletter, circulate announcements, and raise funds. The early nonprofit incorporation of W.A. in Northern California continued to provide Intergroup services for those ten meetings until a decrease in attendance led to insufficient donations for the continued support of such efforts. Later in the 1990s, that original corporation was disbanded and the small residual treasury was donated to the new international organization.

A few years later, the growing consensus that W.A. establish an Internet presence and start using email encouraged efforts to further structure service within the fellowship. A W.A. member from Boston created an unofficial webpage, including some W.A. literature and providing a reply address. This attracted interest as newcomers used it to look for meetings and gather information. It eventually became too much for one person to maintain. The W.A.W.S.O. Board ultimately embraced electronic media, and – with the help of members of the Boston meeting and others – a URL was attained and the website launched at www.workaholics-anonymous.org.

Since 2002, W.A. has benefitted from the service of a full Board of Trustees. This volume was first published in 2005, followed thereafter by the workbook. The fellowship has since grown by leaps and bounds, and it now includes a number of telephone and online meetings. Service to others fuels the organization's evolution as well as helps to maintain individual recovery. W.A. is comprised of the efforts of all members – the collective result of many small acts of service done one at a time – proving that a Higher Power can guide recovering workaholics to serve in a balanced way. Many W.A. members have been relieved of the perfectionism and procrastination that often characterized past attempts at helping others. Every member is welcome and encouraged to surrender grandiosity and provide service in whatever capacity that individual recovery allows, however humble it may be to start. Such service enables W.A. members to practice setting abstinence boundaries in a safe environment and to insure that the organization continues to exist for current members and for all others who wish to recover in the future.

The W.A.W.S.O. may be contacted at:

Workaholics Anonymous World Service Organization
P.O. Box 289
Menlo Park, CA 94026 USA
Telephone: (510) 273-9253
Email: wso@workaholics-anonymous.org
Website: www.workaholics-anonymous.org

Meeting lists, W.A. literature, and registration materials for the annual conference are available on the website. There are also links to update group information, to subscribe to W.A. electronic publications, to request sponsorship, and to offer service to the fellowship – including contributions pursuant to Tradition Seven. For those interested in finding local support in an area without an existing meeting, there are also the options to sign up as a meeting catalyst in order to be notified if others state an interest in starting a meeting nearby and to request a meeting starter kit that includes materials for starting a new meeting and attracting new W.A. members for mutual benefit.

Suggested Format for W.A. Meetings

[Please adapt for your own group purposes.]

[Pass out the suggested readings: the Characteristics of Workaholism, How Recovery Happens, the Twelve Steps, the Twelve Traditions, the Tools of Recovery, and the Promises.]

Introduction

"Welcome to the _____ meeting of Workaholics Anonymous. My name is _____ *[first name]*, and I am a workaholic and the leader for this meeting. Will all those who wish to please join me in a moment of silence, to do with as you wish, followed by the Serenity Prayer?"

[Pause.]

"God grant me serenity to accept the things I cannot change, courage to change the things I can, and wisdom to know the difference."

"Workaholics Anonymous is a fellowship of individuals who share their experience, strength, and hope with each other that they may solve their common problem and help others to recover from workaholism. The only requirement for membership is a desire to stop working compulsively. There are no dues or fees for W.A. membership; we are self-supporting through our own contributions. W.A. is not allied with any sect, denomination, politics, organization, or institution; does not wish to engage in any controversy; neither endorses nor opposes any causes. Our primary purpose is to stop working compulsively and to carry the message of recovery to workaholics who still suffer."

"Now is the time we introduce ourselves by our first name only. Please let us know if you are here for the first time or visiting from outside this area so that we may welcome you. Again, my name is _____, and I am a workaholic."

[Allow other members to introduce themselves, acknowledging each one in turn.]

"I will pass around a list for names and phone numbers. Anyone who puts contact information on the list is indicating a willingness to communicate about the program with other W.A. members between meetings."

[Pass the list.]

"Are there any W.A.-related announcements?"

[Make announcements and allow other members to make announcements as needed.]

"Can someone please read _____ [suggested reading]?"

[Allow another member to read, then repeat the question for each additional reading: 1. the Characteristics of Workaholism, 2. How Recovery Happens, 3. the Twelve Steps, 4. the Twelve Traditions or "Tradition of the Month," and/or 5. the Tools of Recovery]

Speaker/Topic

"The format of this meeting is _____."

[If it is a speaker meeting, introduce him/her. For a Step or topic meeting, announce the purpose and then request a volunteer to read any relevant literature.]

Group Sharing

"We ask that you avoid cross-talk. Avoiding cross-talk means that when we speak, we address the meeting as a whole. We speak in the first person and do not give advice. As stated in the W.A. Preamble, '[o]ur primary purpose is to stop working compulsively and to carry the message of recovery to workaholics who still suffer.' As such, we also ask that you be conscious of the majority by making an effort to keep your comments solution-based and focused on our topic wherever possible. Please do not share again until everyone who wishes to has had an opportunity to share. We keep the Twelfth Tradition of anonymity in mind, placing principles before personalities."

[Request that someone volunteer to time the shares if the group desires. Instruct the volunteer on the preferred length of shares and method used to signal sharing members.]

"The meeting is now open for sharing. Again, the topic is _____."

[About 15 minutes prior to closing, if appropriate and desired by the group, ask if there are any newcomers who wish to share.]

Closing

"Our meeting is now completed. If you did not get an opportunity to share, please stay after the meeting and talk with someone."

"By our Seventh Tradition, we are self-supporting – declining outside contributions. I will pass the basket. If this is your first meeting, please do not feel pressured to contribute. The money we collect goes to pay for rent and literature as well as to support our outreach to other workaholics."

[Pass the basket.]

"Can someone please read the Promises?"

[Allow another member to read the Promises.]

"In order to preserve each member's anonymity, we ask that all you see here – and all you hear here – stay here. The opinions expressed are personal ones. Please take what you like and leave the rest."

[Thank those who read during the meeting. Repeat welcome to newcomers and congratulate anyone celebrating a W.A. birthday or abstinence anniversary.]

"In closing, we are thankful to have this opportunity to grow in respect for ourselves and to learn a healthy attitude toward our work. No matter how deep-rooted and desperate our workaholism, no matter how hopeless our problems seem – we start from where we are. By living the program one day at a time, we begin to experience the freedom and happiness it offers. As we grow closer to a Higher Power, we find we have become transformed. We have what we always sought – love and peace of mind. What seemed impossible is now a reality. If we continue to take action on our program, step by step, we find life becoming richer and more joyful."

"Let's end our meeting with the _____ prayer." [*Serenity, Third Step, Seventh Step, Eleventh Step, or other prayer selected by the group.*]

[*Pray.*]

Meeting Stories

Meeting Success Strategies

Our local W.A. group is doing a number of beneficial things that we thought we might share with the fellowship. For example, at the beginning of each meeting, the leader asks if anyone has any successes that they would like to briefly share so that we might support members making progress towards abstinence from compulsive working. Such statements range from "I left work on time everyday last week" to "I got to bed early last night." After each member speaks, the rest of the group claps and cheers. We started doing this because another Twelve-Step group meets downstairs from us – and we could hear them celebrating every week. We wanted someone to get excited for us! Where else will someone jump up and down for you just for arriving at a meeting on time? Also, while we do not have set topics for particular weeks, we usually use one of two formats. When a newcomer is present, we go around and each person tells a little of his or her story: what it was like, what happened, and what it is like now. In the absence of any beginners, the leader picks a piece of literature to read. We then go around the room, each person reading a paragraph or two and sharing on that portion. This approach seems to help those of us with shorter attention spans to stay focused better than trying to listen to one longer reading prior to open sharing.

Meeting Highlights

The Tuesday night meeting in our city has been going strong for about five years. In the three years since I joined W.A., its attendance has grown from two to four people each week to about four to eight regular members. We have made tremendous strides in our individual recoveries and unity as a group through planning and putting on two "W.A. Days" – for members of other fellowships in our region – as well as by helping to put on a W.A. World Service Conference. We have designated key holders to make sure that the room is open, but we do not preselect leaders because we are such a small group. Instead, we rely on an attendee to volunteer to give that service as it reduces commitment pressure and allows members to contribute more or less according to their energy levels.

Our regular meeting has a rotating weekly format: each month we have a speaker, Step reading, games night, and "grab bag" topic discussion. Our inclusion of a games night was inspired by another W.A. group's inclusion of play in their format and the experience of recovery through play at the first W.A. Day. We tried a number of different meeting structures, ultimately settling on brief shares followed by 30 minutes of noncompetitive play. The game that has worked best for us is charades. We have learned to laugh more – which builds our sense of community. I leave the meeting wanting more of this goodness, and I have added more recreation to my life since we started this practice. Our inclusion of a "grab bag" topic discussion is also unique. At this meeting, every member writes down a question/topic and places it into a basket. We then pull them out and read them one at a time, allowing volunteers to share for two minutes on each question/topic. This format leads to interesting and focused discussions on topics we might not otherwise have addressed as a group.

Area Meetings Throw A Retreat

Made possible by the combined efforts of members of two W.A. meetings in our area, and also attended by members of two other local groups, a regional retreat provided a great advance for the recovery of everyone involved. Several people arrived early and went to the busy retail and restaurant district near the meeting place (a W.A. member's home) for a deli lunch in the fresh air. Attendees then all gathered, signed in with telephone numbers and email addresses, received nametags, and sat down for a round of brief introductions and shares. It was suggested that everyone leave a ($10) donation for W.A.W.S.O. in the basket provided. An announcement was made that, even with the election completed, three of the active posts on the Board were yet open and that every person present was encouraged to consider whether she or he might step up for such service. The gathering officially opened with a W.A. meeting, with different members reading the Preamble, Characteristics of Workaholism, and Twelve Steps. We passed the Tools of Recovery around for everyone to share in reading. One member from a local meeting was the speaker, and then we proceeded to open sharing. We timed each person for three minutes so that everyone got an opportunity to participate. After, we read the Promises and closed the meeting. We reconvened after a half hour break, sitting down for a few introductory comments about meditating and then a period of silent meditation. Then we had a second W.A. meeting followed by more free time.

We returned again to try something called laughing meditation. A regular part of many people's lives in India, it is often done in clubs or large groups. Physicians and psychologists have found it beneficial for mental and physical health. After a short explanation, we all sat there and laughed for ten minutes. At the end, we were breathless and happy. In the course of the afternoon, one member volunteered to be the new Facilitator and another to be the Treasurer of the W.A.W.S.O. With everyone's minds then turning to food, menus were laid out for a number of neighborhood takeout restaurants. We made our choices, put cash in separate envelopes, and telephoned in the orders. It was an evening of fine dining. Afterwards, we shared in the cleanup and then chose to play charades. Everyone had a great time until we finally dragged ourselves away and headed home. The retreat had offered us all a day of inspiration, fellowship, fun, and recovery.

Abstinence in W.A.: Top Lines & Bottom Lines

Abstinence

The Workaholics Anonymous Tool "Top and Bottom Lines" defines abstinence in the following way:

> For many workaholics, abstinence means far more than relief from compulsive working and activity on a physical level. It also means an attitude that comes as a result of surrendering to something greater than the self. We do not merely avoid work, mistaking a lack of activity for recovery. We aspire to freedom from compulsive thinking and worrying. Each of us is free to determine our own way of being abstinent according to personal needs and preferences.

Unlike substance addictions where abstinence is clearly defined as the absolute cessation of use of problem mood-changers, work addiction is a process addiction that can take many different forms. We cannot simply label one or more behaviors unacceptable across the board as even the most common manifestations of the disease may present in ways that are more blatant or subtle depending upon individual circumstances. Further, we have found that it is often the motives, attitudes, and energy that we bring to a particular situation that render our behavior compulsive rather than the nature of the activity itself. How then do we know when we are abstinent versus when we have lapsed into active addiction? Each workaholic must define personalized boundaries and goals for their own recovery. These guidelines then serve as a helpful tool to measure our progress as we work the steps.

Bottom Lines

Bottom lines define the point where we cross over from abstinence to work addiction.

The triggers and behaviors that signal active workaholism are different from person to person. The first task in developing our own list of bottom lines is to reflect upon Step One – our powerlessness over the addiction and the chaos it has caused in our lives. We sit quietly and write a list of the unmanageable behaviors that we take or have taken in the past when lost in our disease. It is helpful to then share this exercise with a sponsor or other W.A. member for feedback and support.

The next step is to prioritize the list, picking one or two items from which to define our initial bottom line abstinence. Here are some examples of bottom lines that workaholics have surrendered to:

- I do not work (or do chores or service) more than 6 days per week.
- I do not work more than 45 hours per week.
- I do not start – and will stop – working when I feel hungry, angry, lonely, or tired (H.A.L.T.).
- I do not bring work to the table during meals.
- I do not allow work to encroach upon the time I commit to be with my family.
- I do not rush or drive unsafely, even if I am late.
- I do not blame others for my stress.
- I do not schedule a new commitment without first discussing it with another W.A. member.
- I do not take on a new commitment without giving up an old commitment. (Or, more specifically, I do not take on anything greater than a nonrecurring 2-hour commitment without first putting it on a "72-hour hold" – during which time I pray, speak with my sponsor, and create a plan to substitute out something else of equivalent time and energy.)

Bottom lines can also be written in the affirmative to capture baseline behavior that we learn is critical to sustaining our sanity and serenity:

- I sleep at least 7 hours per night.
- I pray and meditate daily.
- I attend a meeting at least once per week.
- I read literature for at least ten minutes per day.
- I connect with my sponsor at least once per month to go over Step work.
- I make outreach calls to at least five other W.A. members per week.

As the principle of gentleness suggests, we are kind to ourselves and patient in our efforts – knowing that our new way of living requires much practice. Bottom lines signal when our behavior has strayed from healthy to potentially harmful, however, we do not use lapses as excuses to beat ourselves up; rather, we view them as welcome reminders of our human imperfections and the need to continue practicing the steps and using the tools one day at a time. As workaholics, it is important that we not "work" the program with the same blind zeal that brought us to our knees in the first place. We start simply, knowing that we can always add more bottom lines as our awareness grows.

As we create a concept of abstinence with the help of our Higher Power and program friend(s), we strive to set bottom lines that are realistic for us to maintain at the present time. If we then find that we are consistently unable to honor one of these commitments, we adjust it to better reflect what we can do – knowing that we will continue to make progress with Higher Power's help. Bottom lines should be hallmarks of our success rather than setups for failure. Our bottom lines will change over time as we grow spiritually and more becomes possible. We have found that recovery is habit-forming as well: the more we have, the more we will want.

Top Lines

Top line behaviors represent our goals and visions.

Top lines are aspirational, giving us a sense of direction and ongoing purpose in the individual recovery process. For example, a workaholic with a bottom line of "I do not work more than 6 days per week" might have a top line of "I will take off 2 days per week." Our success with bottom lines gives us hope that we will, in time, achieve our top lines.

Eventually, our top lines become bottom lines, and we develop new top lines like "I will take off 3 days per week." Here are some examples of top lines:

- I will not work more than 9 hours per day or more than 40 hours per week.
- I will take off 2 days in a row per week.
- I will enjoy a day with no to-do list at least once per week.
- I will sleep at least 8 hours per night.
- I will spend a day doing something fun with my children at least once per week.
- I will take an annual vacation that has nothing to do with work of any kind.
- I will eat my meals sitting down in a relaxed manner.
- I will always put my health before my work.

Conclusion

While we workaholics find we have much in common with each other, our precise disease triggers and the behaviors that constitute active addiction may differ. Bottom lines are the markers of abstinence. Top lines are the signposts on our paths toward recovery and freedom from worry. Both are important because they show us where we came from as well as where we hope to be heading. While our bottom lines help free us from pain, our top lines promise joy and fulfillment.

Bottom lines and top lines allow us to create structure within our program of recovery that is tailored to our individual patterns. We follow the direction of our evolving bottom and top lines with the help of a Higher Power, a sponsor or co-sponsor, a supportive W.A. fellowship, and our own desire for sanity and serenity.

Turning Work into Play

Attitudes

As workaholics, we have used work and activity to deny our being and escape our feelings. Overdoing may have been our only means of gaining approval, finding a sense of identity, and justifying our existence. Any loose commitment to play, as compared to the seemingly all-important obligation to work, may have seemed somewhat frivolous. We may have felt so guilty enjoying ourselves that we made recreational activities into a series of profitable or otherwise useful projects so that we could feel productive. Or, perhaps we were raised with the idea that work is respectable drudgery (the daily grind, the rat race) and that play should be allowed only as a reward for immense effort.

In either case, we have difficulty assigning intrinsic value to play for its own sake. Work is what we feel we must do for money and a sense of self worth. In fact, the more painful it is, the more we prove to ourselves that we have earned our keep. Play is seen as self-indulgent procrastination. The idea of being paid for something effortless or fun may sound ridiculous.

If we are self-employed, we probably have the idea that we cannot charge much if we love what we do. We might suppose that we are justified only by our suffering; however, buyers do not valuate our struggles when making decisions. Consumers simply want to know that a product or service is going to meet their needs. In fact, when something is created or otherwise rendered in a blissful state, that feeling often shines through and attracts a market on that primary basis.

Some of us have realized that spending a majority of our time fixated on the achievement of status and material wealth –while simultaneously sacrificing opportunities for pleasure – is absurd. We have since come to understand that our attitudes toward work and play can be the same. No matter what we do, we can approach the activity with presence, openness, and lightheartedness rather than focusing on outcomes for our peace of mind.

Rewards

Some of us find ourselves working in the wrong fields – failing to capitalize on our interests and natural talents. Or, we may be pursuing our passions but in a workaholic setting or manner. In all cases, we came to W.A. because, whether we realized it or not, we were working out of our egos rather than our hearts. We worked to be stimulated and distracted; to be validated, respected, and loved; and to take pride in how much we could push ourselves to do. Sometimes we subconsciously worked to sabotage ourselves because proving we were failures made us feel comfortable and in control.

Sometimes upon striving we received extrinsic rewards: a partnership, a second house, or just a bigger paycheck. We may have begun the work because we liked it – but once we connected what we did with accolades and awards – those markers of success gradually became more important than what we had to do to get them.

Whatever our situations, we had destructive attitudes towards work. We set impossible deadlines and forced projects before their time. We refused to take breaks, working through pain and exhaustion, and then we wondered why we resisted what we once looked forward to doing. We sometimes found ourselves unable to work at all – paralyzed by perfectionism and taking refuge in other compulsive behavior.

Recovery

In W.A., we know that a Higher Power is our employer. Through the Twelve Steps, we turn our life over to the care of something greater than ourselves. We ask for guidance on what to do, when, and how. We realize that our bodies and our minds have limits; that we must nurture them with rest, a healthy diet, and exercise. We learn that any activity, no matter how pleasurable, can become tedious if overdone. We understand that tired work is wasted work because we often have to redo it.

Enjoyment of the process becomes our criterion. Often we can use our will to continue working but without enthusiasm. Instead of concentrating on output, we can ask ourselves if we can keep going without sacrificing a positive attitude. We will find that the answer is often no. Once we grasp the idea that we deserve to savor what we do, we will no longer have to ask. We will not have to wait until our eyes droop and our neck aches. We will know long before that to turn off the computer, put down the phone, or close the book: to stay in the present and truly experience our feelings. What we are doing is growing a healthy self, one that savors life right now instead fantasizing over future rewards. Once we get in touch with ourselves, we become clearer about what really matters.

Workplace Changes

This clarity changes how we see our environment. Suddenly, we notice others in the workplace who do the same tasks – but with peace and serenity. We realize that we do not have to overdo or try to become indispensable to keep our jobs. We are treated differently as we begin to establish boundaries and no longer allow others to reinforce our addiction. Even if we are responsible for setting the pace, we are often amazed at how the level of creativity and cooperation increases as our expectations become more realistic.

Or, we may realize that we must leave. If we are not using our talents, work may now feel even more alienating and meaningless. We may find that our values have changed and that we are no longer willing to act in unethical or self-abusive ways. We may work for a cause we believe in but in a way that contradicts recovery principles. We now believe that in order to be of the greatest benefit to society, we must set healthy examples by choosing healthy workplaces and modeling sane behaviors.

Instead of flogging ourselves and forcing a project before its time, we work refreshed, at the moment of ripeness, and everything falls into place. We begin to shift our focus from achieving results to behaving in accordance with our moral code in every situation. In this way, we have a new standard for success. Work, like play, has become its own reward.

Outside the Workplace

Whether we have made peace with our situations, found the healthier positions that were looking for us, or created saner environment ourselves, these shifts have also affected the rest of our lives. Because we are satisfied, we no longer feel compulsively driven to accomplish things in general or to reward ourselves for enduring unsatisfactory work. Our health improves when we believe we are always entitled to excellent self-care.

Contentment becomes a natural part of living. Ironically, we achieve more and we do it more easily. We do not need to acquire more or do more in order to feel that we are enough. The feeling of inner emptiness and the craving for ego inflation disappears. A sense of self worth is no longer achieved through work alone.

Our relationships change. We attract people who have firm boundaries – those who like themselves, are independent, and are not controlling. We no longer need to be needed or to earn friendship through caregiving. When we do service, it is after we are truly grateful and happy with our own lives. What we provide is of a higher quality because it is given freely and without resentment.

Affirmations for Workaholics

1. The slower I go, the faster I grow.
2. The more I play, the more my Higher Power works.
3. I have time to spare and time to share. Time is my friend.
4. When I take time, I make time. I refuse to rush.
5. My life is full yet under-scheduled.
6. I am more effective when I am more selective.
7. Because my overdoing is my undoing, my top priority is my being.
8. Before I do anything, I first do nothing.
9. I do everything easily and effortlessly.
10. I am a human being, not a human doing. I seek to enjoy rather than endure.
11. The less I struggle, the more open I am to inspiration.
12. My Higher Power wants me to realize my vision of joyful work and a balanced life – and gives me whatever I need to achieve it at the right time.
13. I draw to myself everything I need for a joyful, balanced life.
14. I am entitled to my right work. I deserve the enjoyment, recognition, and health that it brings.
15. I live by divine appointment – with broad margins.
16. I receive full assistance and cooperation from all persons necessary for realizing my goals. I attract only loving people.
17. Doing my right work strengthens all my relationships and brings me closer to those I love.
18. I am safe when I choose to take risks.
19. I am still in the midst of activity, and I am vibrantly alive in repose. I take emergencies leisurely.
20. Even when offered something great, I say no if I need rest. Rest is the best thing I can give myself.
21. My body is my friend and my temple. I bless and thank it daily, obeying its signals.
22. Emotions are information. I honor their important messages.
23. I love myself no matter what. I am perfect just the way I am. I am enough. I have enough. I do enough.
24. I do not try to grow. I accept myself as I am, and I grow automatically.
25. People bring me important messages when I listen mindfully.
26. My highs come from my Higher Power.
27. I work to live rather than live to work.
28. There is no place I have to go and nothing I have to do.

29. I cannot help anyone if I cannot help myself.
30. I expect and welcome surprises.

Our Favorite Slogans

1. Work Smarter, Not Harder.
2. Just For Today.
3. One Day At A Time.
4. First Things First.
5. Easy Does It.
6. Easy Does It, But Do It.
7. Let Go And Let God.
8. Let Go And Flow.
9. Live And Let Live.
10. Keep It Simple.
11. Listen To Learn.
12. Don't Quit Five Minutes Before The Miracle.
13. If It's Not Broke, Don't Fix It.
14. The Three A's: Awareness, Acceptance, Action.
15. The Three C's: Didn't Cause It, Can't Control It, Can't Cure It.
16. Good Enough Is Still Good.
17. Sometimes, The Best Plan Is No Plan.
18. If It's Worth Doing, It's Worth Doing So-So.
19. It Feels So Good To Finish.
20. Progress, Not Perfection.
21. Life Begins After 5:00PM.
22. Know When To Quit.
23. Avoid H.A.L.T.: Hungry, Angry, Lonely, Tired.
24. Think.
25. Act, Don't React.
26. Give Yourself A Break.
27. Finish What You Start.
28. Put It On Your "Not To Do" List.
29. This Too Shall Pass.
30. How Important Is It?
31. We Came. We Came To. We Came To Believe.
32. Utilize, Don't Analyze.
33. Where There's Life, There's Hope.
34. But For The Grace Of God.
35. You Can't Run Your Life On Empty.
36. There Is Enough Time, Money, and Love.
37. Everything Can Wait But Love.
38. You Aren't Livin' If You're Driven.

39. Don't Succumb To Production Seduction.
40. Be Here Now.

Recovery Reminders

1. Think timelessness: savor the sip rather than gulp.
2. Slow is beautiful and powerful. Move glacially.
3. Success is the quality of the journey. The means determine the end, and the body keeps the score.
4. A goal is an excuse for the fun of a race.
5. Work is the highest form of play.
6. Spontaneity and surprise are the spice of life.
7. Gratitude relies upon small and frequent pleasures.
8. Importance not urgency; values not goals; quality not quantity.
9. Recovery-related: rest, relaxation, recreation, and renewal.
10. Critical mind/sick mind; positive mind/healthy mind; still mind/divine mind.
11. Space out activities to avoid becoming spaced out.
12. Simplifying is not subtracting: it is adding time and space.
13. Strive more for availability than ability.
14. Try underwhelming yourself.
15. Regarding creativity: do not think consciously. "Drift, wait, and obey." –Rudyard Kipling

The Work-Binge Sales Pitch

The Book or TV Show
Mind: There are only two more pages until the end of the chapter. The show is almost over. I must finish.
Body: It is late, my eyes are tired, and I cannot concentrate.
Action: Put a bookmark in the book or turn off the TV – and go to bed.

Exercise
Mind: I have not yet done my daily exercise.
Body: It is late, I am sneezing violently, and my eyes are tearing.
Action: Take some vitamins, drink hot tea, enjoy a warm bath – and go to bed.

The Social Commitment
Mind: I promised that I would go, and they are expecting me.
Body: It is very early, I have a splitting headache, and I only got three hours of sleep.

Action: Cancel the date, do something to soothe the pain, and go back to bed.

The Work Deadline
Mind: I have a responsibility to get this done. Everyone is counting on me, and the company will suffer unless I finish on time. This project is urgent. If I let down my boss, I could lose my job. I will be perceived as slow, inefficient, and irresponsible.
Body: I am exhausted. It can wait. Nothing is more important than my wellbeing.
Action: Go home and rest. Apologize if warranted and try to negotiate a more realistic timeline.

Coworker Approval
Mind: She said that if you want something done, give it to a busy person. He said, "You are so capable. How do you do it all?" I can fit in that extra project they handed me.
Body: I cannot help as I am already on overload. This is not my responsibility or department.
Action: Smile, hand back the work, and politely let them know that they will need to ask someone else.

Random Stress and General Perfectionism
Mind: No one can do it the way I want it done but me.
Body: I am only human, and sometimes I need support. All I can do is my best. This task is not as important as it seems right now.
Action: Pray, meditate, and play. Ask for help as needed.

Where the Time Goes

There is never time to...	**But we make time to...**
put things away	search for them
do things right the first time	correct mistakes
drive safely	suffer accidents
be patient and polite	apologize for rudeness
ask a question	regret assumptions
read the car manual	have repairs done
heed body signals	be sick
listen	request a repeat
make extra keys	wait for a locksmith
read the instructions	replace a ruined appliance
prioritize work	stay late

monitor the fuel gauge	run out of gas
rest or relax	breakdown or burnout
ask for directions	get lost
make a checklist	run home for a forgotten item
cool our temper	have a heart attack
meditate or pray	worry
have a dental check up	get a tooth extracted
create and follow a budget	deal with debts
mend a small tear	buy a new garment
process feelings as they occur	see a therapist
choose friends wisely	end painful relationships
select healthy food	endure malnutrition
wait for guidance	untangle chaos

Working Compulsively vs. Joyfully

If we could see ourselves when lost in our compulsion – furrowed brows, clenched jaws, tense shoulders, and perhaps sitting on the edge of our chairs – we would immediately recognize our behavior as unhealthy. Having a clear idea of what we are choosing to move away from can help to signal us when it is time to lean harder on our W.A. program. Knowing what our goals and visions of recovery are can help to let us know that we have arrived and that it is time to celebrate our success.

Working Compulsively vs.	Working Joyfully
Very long hours	Setting boundaries
Impossible standards	Reasonable goals
Insatiable appetite for results	Contentment with progress
Tight scheduling	Space allotted for unexpected
Adding more work	Substituting as needed
Constant rushing and tardiness	Realistic, leisurely timing
Nonstop activity	Periods of rest
Driven and adrenalized	Going with flow, slower pacing
Sense of urgency	Relaxed attitude
Perceived need to complete work	Delaying tasks without worry
Focusing on the time-sensitive	Prioritizing what is important
Reacting to pressure	Following inner guidance
Fragmented attention	Focused intention
Inefficient and making mistakes	Effective on the first attempt
Rigid and tense	Flexible and relaxed
Intolerant of new ideas	Open-minded

Impatient, sense of struggle	Calm, sense of ease
Perfectionistic	Accepts limitations with grace
Loss of humor and creativity	Light, playful perspective
Abrupt with colleagues	Responsive to others
Loss of spontaneity and happiness	Takes pleasure in the moment
Out of touch with self	Aware of energy level and mood
Multitasking	Doing one thing at a time
Mind and body out of sync	Unity of thought and action
Jerky movement	Steady rhythm
Overcomplicating and analyzing	Simplifying and accepting
Blurred perception	Vivid impression
Unaware and mechanical	Mindful
Quantity-oriented	Quality-oriented
Polarized thinking	Entertains various perspectives
Lack of trust in colleagues	Willingness to delegate
Comparing and competing	Cooperating
Sense of victimization	Sense of empowerment
Neglecting self and priorities	Balanced, healthy lifestyle
Worrying and over-planning	Staying present
Needs to perform	Shows up to participate
Manipulating and controlling	Surrendering and experiencing
Independence	Interdependence
Doing	Being

W.A. Tools of Recovery, *Book of Recovery*, First Edition

Listening: We set aside time each day for prayer and meditation. Before accepting any commitments, we ask our Higher Power and W.A. friends for guidance.

Prioritizing: We decide which are the most important things to do first. Sometimes that may mean doing nothing. We strive to stay flexible to events, reorganizing our priorities as needed. We view interruptions and accidents as opportunities for growth.

Substituting: We do not add a new activity without eliminating from our schedule one that demands equivalent time and energy.

Underscheduling: We allow more time than we think we need for a task or trip, allowing a comfortable margin to accommodate the unexpected.

Playing: We schedule time for play, refusing to let ourselves work non-stop. We do not make our play into a work project.

Concentrating: We try to do one thing at a time.

Pacing: We work at a comfortable pace and rest before we get tired. To remind ourselves, we check our level of energy before proceeding to our next activity. We do not get "wound up" in our work, so we don't have to unwind.

Relaxing: We do not yield to pressure from others or attempt to pressure others. We remain alert to the people and situations that trigger feelings of pressure in us. We become aware of our own actions, words, body sensations and feelings that tell us we are responding with pressure. When we feel energy building up, we stop; we reconnect with our Higher Power and others around us.

Accepting: We accept the outcomes of our endeavors, whatever the results, whatever the timing. We know that impatience, rushing and insisting on perfect results only slow down our recovery. We are gentle with our efforts, knowing that our new way of living requires much practice.

Asking: We admit our weaknesses and mistakes. We realize we don't have to do everything ourselves, and we ask our Higher Power and others for help.

Meetings: We attend W.A. meetings to learn how the fellowship works and to share our experience, strength and hope with each other.

Telephoning: We use the telephone to stay in contact with members of the fellowship between meetings. We communicate with our W.A. friends before and after a critical task.

Balancing: We balance our involvement in work with our efforts to develop personal relationships, spiritual growth, creativity and playful attitudes.

Serving: We readily extend help to other workaholics, knowing that assistance to others adds to the quality of our own recovery.

Living in the Now: We realize we are where our Higher Power wants us to be – in the here and now. We try to live each moment with serenity, joy and gratitude.

WORKS CITED

Alcoholics Anonymous. 4th ed. New York: Alcoholics Anonymous World Services, Inc., 2001. Print.

Twelve Steps and Twelve Traditions. New York: Alcoholics Anonymous World Services, Inc., 1953. Print.

Made in the USA
Middletown, DE
08 April 2024

52751224R00137